WHEN ALL THE FRIENDS HAVE GONE

A GUIDE FOR AFTERCARE PROVIDERS

edited by
O. Duane Weeks, Ph.D.
and
Catherine Johnson, M.A.

Death, Value and Meaning Series
Series Editor: John D. Morgan

Baywood Publishing Company, Inc.
AMITYVILLE, NEW YORK

Library of Congress Catalog Number: 99-462163
ISBN: 0-89503-215-5 (cloth)

Library of Congress Cataloging-in-Publication Data

When all the friends have gone : a guide for aftercare providers / edited by O. Duane
Weeks and Catherine Johnson.
    p. cm. - - (Death, value, and meaning series)
  Includes bibliographical references and index.
  ISBN 0-89503-215-5 (cloth)
    1. Death- -Social aspects. 2. Death- -Psychological aspects. 3. Bereavement. 4. Grief. 5.
Helping behavior. 6. Undertakers and understanding. I. Weeks, O. Duane, 1938- II.
Johnson, Catherine, 1945- III. Series.

HQ1073.W54 2000
306.9- -dc21

                                                            99-462163

Foreword

The funeral is over. The flowers have withered. And friends are perplexed. Friends keep asking: "Don't you think it's about time that he/she gets over it?"

It's understandable. They may be deeply concerned about the bereaved. They want them to resolve their grief quickly and completely. They want the survivors to be their "old selves" again.

What they don't understand is that "getting over" the death of a loved one is not like "getting over" a cold or an illness. The bereaved may *never* be their "old selves" again. Part of them may have been buried with their beloved. Their grief does not travel along a straight line and then suddenly fade away and disappear. Resolving the tidal wave that makes them feel they are drowning in a sea of sorrow almost always takes longer than most people anticipate. The horrific experience of death is uncharted territory.

A compass to help along this protracted, painful journey is this remarkable book, *When All the Friends Have Gone: A Guide for Aftercare Providers.* Dr. Duane Weeks and Catherine Johnson have assembled a sparkling array of experts to blaze the trail for those helping the bereaved who may be lost "in the valley of the shadow." With guidance from every possible perspective, nothing is missing from this marvelous collection. Each chapter is thoughtfully researched and lucidly and sensitively written. This groundbreaking guide should be required reading for every aftercare provider.

Back to the question posed at the beginning of this foreword: When does one "get over" it? An old spiritual reveals the answer:

> It's so high you can't get over it.
> It's so low you can't get under it.
> So wide you can't get around it.
> You must go *through* the door.

iii

In other words, one does not "get over" the loss. One goes *through* it.

With this book as your companion, you will be better able to guide the bereaved on their journeys through grief.

> *Rabbi Earl A. Grollman, D.H.L.*
> A pioneer in the field of crisis intervention
> and author of twenty-six books, also
> travels and lectures extensively
> around the world.

Contents

Introduction

The history of aftercare as a formal entity consisting of organized memorial services, support groups, and individual counseling, is quite short and probably dates back only twenty-five or thirty years. However, anecdotal incidents abound about informal aftercare, where earlier generations of funeral directors and their spouses offered a cup of coffee, a telephone conversation, and a sympathetic ear to their bereaved client.

As we begin the twenty-first century, aftercare is found in many guises. It is still the funeral director taking time to have a cup of coffee while listening to the widower's lament. It is found in the hospital chaplain's office, where widowed women and men gather for shared expression of feelings and comfort. Aftercare is evident when hospice workers organize and present a seminar on how the recently bereaved can cope with the holidays. Aftercare can be seen when a group of widows and widowers enjoy dinner and a movie that have been arranged by their aftercare coordinator. Aftercare is provided by a certified counselor who is assisting the bereaved mother of a completed suicide rebuild her shattered life. Aftercare is visible whenever anyone in the community is willing to sit down and help another through the long, burdensome, hurtful mourning process, a process that really is only beginning during the visitation and funeral or the memorial service. Mourning is a necessary but painful experience that continues long after the formal death ceremonies have ended. Aftercare begins when those ceremonies are done, when all the friends have gone.

Since aftercare is no longer limited to funeral home participation but has found its way into hospital and hospice care, synagogues, churches, and schools, it has evolved into an area of great interest to those who work with the bereaved. Because of this interest, there is a great deal that can be shared among caregivers. Aftercare workers fall on a continuum from those who are hoping to develop an aftercare program on the one end, to those who coordinate very sophisticated aftercare efforts on the other. This book is written in an effort to share the views and experiences of people who have learned to respond to some of the questions but do not yet have all the answers. It is meant to serve as a guide and learning tool for the aftercare provider, whatever his or her position, because the time has come to step up our aftercare endeavors to a higher standard of service.

With many disciplines being represented in aftercare, individual aftercare providers with differing educational, spiritual, and work experiences, there are bound to be significantly different perceptions of aftercare and its many facets. It is the editors' hope and expectation that this text will provide a common understanding for ethical and practical issues that arise for many of us in this important endeavor.

The contributed chapters of this book are separated into three sections. The first, "Funeral Home Aftercare," has to do with the efforts expended by mortuary personnel. From developing and starting an aftercare program sponsored by a funeral establishment to a look toward aftercare in the twenty-first century, the first section is a comprehensive approach to important issues of funeral home care following the disposal rites and rituals. The second section, "Aftercare in Other Venues," is concerned with aftercare provided by organizations other than funeral homes. This section includes timely information about aftercare sponsored by and organized in homes, hospitals, schools, and the military. The third section, "General Aftercare Issues," involves considerations applicable to aftercare in any situation. Issues of multicultural aftercare, moral and ethical behavior, and self-care for the aftercare provider are discussed.

As you read about the various ways aftercare has been provided for the bereaved in the last three decades of this millennium, we challenge you to think of creative ways of adapting these programs to fit the needs of your clients, your organization, and your community. As the new century unfolds, formal aftercare is still in its infancy. Build on the work of others. Be innovative. And, most of all, appreciate the experience of helping the bereaved.

SECTION 1

Funeral Home Aftercare

CHAPTER 1

How to Develop a Successful Aftercare Program

Catherine Johnson
O. Duane Weeks

Aftercare is not a new concept, as most experienced funeral directors understand. Aftercare may be perceived and defined differently depending on the circumstances. The bereaved, the social worker, and the funeral director all may have different perspectives. Because the aftercare concept originated in several ways, tracing the specific history is difficult and facts are illusive. It is important, therefore, to clarify what we mean by a funeral home-based aftercare program. Funeral home aftercare may be defined as an organized way to maintain a helpful and caring relationship with clients, offer continuing services to client families beyond the expected body disposition and accompanying rituals, and provide death, loss, and grief education to both clients and the community.

The concept of organized aftercare probably began in the early 1970s with the formation of widow and widower meetings. These meetings were often educational (how to change the oil in the automobile engine, how to manage a checking account, or how to prepare a meal), usually social, and intended to comfort the recently bereaved. *The American Funeral Director* described one of the earliest funeral home aftercare efforts when it detailed such widow/widower meetings in 1974 [1]. The concept of aftercare was formalized further in 1981 when the National Funeral Directors Association created the Pursuit of Excellence program, which was intended not only to recognize good caregiving and educational programs sponsored by funeral homes, but also to encourage a more comprehensive use of aftercare materials.

Today's aftercare can be as simple as the early widow and widower meetings or as complex as offering individual grief counseling. It can be open-ended and continuing or time-limited with specific participants. It can involve many mourners or just one. Whatever aftercare is, it must always be helpful and it must always meet the needs of our clients and our communities.

WHY FUNERAL HOMES?

For many years, those involved in funeral service have been caring for their clients following the funeral ceremonies. Doka maintains that caring lies deep in funeral directors' history [2]. "Historically, funeral directors, over the years, have cared for those whom they have served through phone calls, home visits, and being a friend of the family. Most funeral directors continue offering support in this manner" [2, p. 38].

Funeral homes must be leaders in providing aftercare. It is a natural extension of the care that they provided leading up to and including disposal of the body and death rituals. Because funeral home staff members are seen as helpful, they would have little difficulty maintaining positive relationships with the bereaved. Thus, they are natural choices to provide aftercare services. By doing so, they continue a relationship of trust and strive toward a high quality of bereavement services. If a funeral home does not provide aftercare in its community someone else will, and that person or organization may have little or no training and provide an inadequate program that has a negative effect on those it is intended to help. As Canine says, "If we are intrigued by the idea of using funeral service to redefine death in this country, then we must be sure to complete the life cycle by including the needs of the living following the death" [3, p. 135].

Simply put, for generations funeral directors have established reputations in their communities as caregivers for the dead and bereaved. The tradition continues because providing the best possible services for families and community and doing all that can be done to encourage a healthy emotional adjustment is, after all, the right thing to do. It is old-fashioned, neighborly concern.

DETERMINING NEEDS

Alan is a successful businessman with two teenage children. Both the children and Alan are active in sports and other community activities. Last year Alan's wife, the children's mother, committed

suicide. Alan has indicated the need for counseling, both for himself
and for his children.

Certainly the act of suicide and its consequences on family members call for distinctive aftercare involvement. Issues of guilt, blame,
anger, and regret must be addressed in special ways by the aftercare
provider. Doka asserts that for any sudden death, including suicide,
grieving is complicated, intense, and demands "even more than normally that a survivor struggle to cope both with the loss and its
aftermath" [4, p. 11].

Not all deaths precipitate the traumatic suffering that often follows
suicide, but all deaths may be viewed on a continuum from minimally
to extremely traumatic. Survivors who experience a minimally
traumatic death may be less likely to require immediate and extensive
aftercare intervention in their lives than those who experience an
extremely traumatic death.

Since there are many variables with respect to death and many
variables regarding the survivors, it is to be expected that survivors
will have highly diverse needs for formal aftercare ranging from no
needs at all to extended and involved therapy. It is the responsibility of
the aftercare provider to help determine the needs and the most appropriate responses to them.

John Donne has written that ". . . no man is an island entire of itself.
Every man is a part of the continent, a part of the main, . . . and every
man's death diminishes me" [cited in 5, p. 331]. Indeed, every person's
death does change everyone else, particularly within the social bounds
of a village, neighborhood, or small town. Including the concept of
neighborhood allows us to understand that individual deaths impact
those in cities as well as those in smaller communities. The 1997
suicides of several teenagers in the South Boston neighborhood, for
example, provided the impetus for changing patterns of interaction
between teens and adults, patterns that spread throughout South
Boston and the northeastern United States. Thus, a combined attempt
to address the needs of survivors and apply suicide prevention
measures for other teens in the neighborhood has had wide-ranging
community effects.

The aftercare provider must be attentive to the needs of the community as well as to the needs of the immediate family survivors. How
do we determine needs of the community? What needs are already
being met and by whom? Which are appropriate for you or your company to meet? Who else may provide for the community needs?

The answers to these questions may be determined by surveying
potential aftercare clients, contacting local hospices, hospitals, or other

agencies, discussing proposed aftercare services with community leaders, and networking with colleagues in funeral service.

Some needs may already be adequately addressed by another organization. For example, for several years we had an annual fall presentation to help survivors work through the fall and winter holidays without the person who had died. A local hospital began offering a similar program, so it seemed expedient for us to send our clients to their program and focus our efforts on other projects. Were we possessive of that part of our program? No. Were we able to expend our time and energy to meet different needs? Of course.

There are also aftercare efforts that may not be appropriate for you or your company. Some funeral homes serve clients of particular ethnic or spiritual persuasions. These funeral homes may identify a community need of clients other than their own and encourage another organization to address that need. Working in cooperation with another organization or colleague to provide the best possible aftercare to your community can be a "win-win" situation. If needs are being met professionally and adequately, duplicating services is unnecessary and you can turn your efforts to other needs.

ESTABLISHING GOALS

Once the needs of your community are determined, the next step in creating an aftercare program is to establish goals. Primary goals include providing social support for family members, educating them to normalize the grief process, offering ongoing emotional support for grieving individuals, identifying community resources, and informing the general public about death, grief, and loss.

During this goal-setting stage, it is important to be realistic in your vision. For instance, is it feasible to offer social support and personal grief counseling to your whole community, or, because of limited resources, will you offer these services only to clients who were served by your funeral home at the time of the death? Although public relations is not to be a primary goal of an aftercare program, it may well be a secondary consideration. If so, your program will be very different than if you seek to serve only your own clients, walking with them on their personal journeys through grief.

Regardless of your goals, there are many choices to be made in the design and implementation of your program. For example, if social support is a goal, how will that support be provided—by informal phone calls, organized potluck dinners, or formal bereavement support groups? Thus, the next aspect to consider is designing an aftercare program and determining which of the following four identified levels of aftercare you would like to develop (see Table 1).

These categories are established to differentiate between levels of care rather than as specific boundaries across which a caregiver dare not wander. There are varied approaches and alternatives available to caregivers, and it is a combination of our individual identities, interests, and commitments that determine which aftercare concepts will be offered.

Casual Level

Just as teachers care about the welfare of their students and physicians care about the health of their patients, funeral directors care for the well-being of their bereaved clients. The tendency to console clients long after the funerary rites have concluded is a natural trait and certainly is not a recent phenomenon. Generations of funeral directors and their spouses have provided coffee, along with a great deal of compassion and unlimited listening, to soothe emotional distress. This informal level of service does not require an accredited and

Table 1. Designing the Program

Program Level	Staff	Activities	Cost
Casual (informal)	No extra staff	Visiting, chance meetings, sharing booklists, brochures	Minimal
Fundamental (formal)	Extra staff but no extensive training	Telephone calls, newsletters, socials, dinners, travel	Moderate
Standard (formal)	Extra staff with specific training in bereavement issues	Support group sponsorship/ facilitation, lending library, special holiday programs, community education, cards on special days	Substantial
Premier (formal)	Extra staff: master's degree or higher with concentration on counseling and grief/loss issues	Individual counseling, children's programs, in-service training, community advisory boards, spokesperson for media	Substantial to unlimited

licensed counselor. Rather, informal aftercare is provided by genuinely caring staff members from any area of responsibility within the funeral home who are willing to spend some time to listen, support, and assist.

Examples of specific, helpful aftercare activities at this level include sharing information about local resources, providing pamphlets about grief and loss issues, furnishing lists of appropriate books, helping complete forms of entitlement, and listening while the bereaved tell and retell their story as a part of the grieving process.

Illustrations abound of funeral home personnel who have provided this informal aftercare support. A funeral director meets her recently widowed Kiwanis colleagues at a luncheon meeting and provides information about cemetery requirements for burial markers. A receptionist shopping in a local grocery store encounters a grieving father and suggests helpful books or resources. A bereaved widow phones the funeral director to ask for assistance in filling out insurance forms for a policy that was discovered days after the funeral ceremony. Finally, a funeral director, receptionist, or other staff member encounters a recently bereaved person who needs to talk about the death circumstances because the repetition lessens the horror and the loneliness.

These illustrations of informal bereavement support demonstrate that to be its best, support must be freely given. It must be a continuing contribution of each funeral home staff member and offered without hesitation or conscious effort.

Fundamental Level

The three formal categories differ from the informal category in that the activities contained within this grouping are planned and organized, whereas the informal activities are more spontaneous acts of kindness and helpfulness. However, it is presumed that informal acts are an integral part of the formal—no formal program would be complete without these informal, sincere elements.

One example of the Fundamental Level of aftercare is calling surviving family members several weeks and months following the death. Any funeral home staff member can take a few minutes to call bereaved family members, ask how they are doing, and be willing to listen to their responses. Although the specific time is not necessarily planned, certainly the activity is organized and purposeful. This technique necessitates more than a haphazard approach to telephoning; it requires an ongoing commitment to regularly contact families who have been previously served.

In the same vein, organized visits following the funeral rites may be seen as Fundamental Aftercare efforts. Post-funeral visits may be in person or via telephone, can be brief or lengthy, but their purpose must be to help the bereaved grieve the death that has occurred. If, however, the intent of these visits is to collect payment on the funeral bill, sell a grave marker, or market a prearranged funeral service, then these visits cannot be considered aftercare. Such visits are ethically questionable attempts to increase the funeral home profit margin. Although it is the intent of the visit that basically determines whether or not it is an aftercare experience, the caregiver must be cautious that behavior while visiting does not cross ethical barriers from aftercare into selling.

During these aftercare visits, if a client requests information about prepaid funeral arrangements, marker purchases, or other services not yet provided, it is in the best interest of the client and the funeral home for the aftercare provider to refer the request to another staff member or postpone the discussion until a more appropriate time. It is unprofessional and unethical to combine aftercare visits with sales presentations. Simply put, the aftercare visit must not result in direct financial gain to the aftercare provider.

Another aftercare activity that is of a fundamental nature is the mailing of a newsletter, whether it is generated within the funeral home or commercially produced. Many funeral homes have found computer applications of desktop publishing to be the perfect vehicle for publishing their own newsletter. These desktop publications have the appearance of professional periodicals, yet retain the personal touch that many families appreciate. Several commercial newsletters are offered, usually quarterly, for funeral homes to send to their previous clients. These newsletters are not as personal as local publications, but they contain articles, usually of high quality, and often written by nationally recognized authorities who provide helpful information about grief and bereavement.

Social events, including social hours, dinners, theater excursions, and travel, are other examples of formal, fundamental aftercare. These are events that must be planned, organized, and supervised. They do not, however, require specially trained staff members. They may be the responsibility of a staff member or a volunteer may be invited to assume this responsibility. The use of volunteers is, in fact, another element of fundamental aftercare. Because training in counseling or the social sciences is not a prerequisite for someone providing this category of aftercare, volunteer workers might be a well-suited alternative for those funeral homes whose staff does not have the time to participate in these important efforts. However, care must be used in the use of volunteers. The screening of potential volunteers needs to take into account the individual's motivations, qualifications, and past losses, for the bereavement volunteer must be beyond his/her own immediate grief in order to be objective about the grief of others.

Standard Level

Unlike the first two categories of aftercare programs, the Standard alternative is the first in which professionally educated and trained aftercare personnel must be employed. Because this level of aftercare includes starting and maintaining bereavement support groups, the aftercare staff must also screen potential group members and refer some to more appropriate/helpful resources.

The type of support groups offered may be as varied as the individual needs within the community. Some groups are short-term (once a week for 8 weeks) while others are ongoing (twice a month for as long as the client needs); some are general bereavement groups including people regardless of the relationship lost, while others are specific to the cause of death or to the relationship (young widowed or family members of cancer victims). Yet, one thing these diverse groups have in common is the need for a skilled, well-trained facilitator.

Another service provided in Standard Aftercare programs is the acknowledgment of emotionally difficult days for the bereaved. Support may be provided by a phone call or a personal card on a wedding anniversary, the birthday of a deceased child, the anniversary of the death, or Mother's and Father's Day. One widow who called the funeral home to thank the staff for a card on what would have been her fiftieth wedding anniversary said that it was the only card or acknowledgment she had received and that thoughtfulness made a dreary day a little brighter. A mother whose adult son died received a Mother's Day card from us. She lived two thousand miles away, yet when she was in town two months later, she came into the funeral home to thank us for the card. She said that when she received it she cried the rest of the day. Yet, she maintained that it was the best thing that had happened to her, for she had been too busy until then to take the time to grieve.

Of course any employee or volunteer can make a sympathetic phone call or send a card, but it takes a sensitive and specially trained bereavement worker to determine when calls should be made and to whom, or select the appropriate card for a certain occasion. An inappropriate card, or one sent at an inopportune time, can be harmful to the mental health of the recipient and to the reputation of the business.

Just as the creation and/or selection of cards for special occasions requires an awareness of and sensitivity to bereavement issues, so too does the determination of which books to include on a book list given to families as suggested reading. Not long ago, so few books on grief for lay people existed that all could easily be listed on one page. Now, however, such books proliferate, which requires someone knowledge-able to narrow down the choices so the size of the list is manageable.

Likewise, if you are fortunate to be in a geographic area large enough to offer many bereavement services, it is up to your trained aftercare specialist to be aware of them and to assess their effectiveness. To include all resources on a list to be shared with your client families without regard to the quality of the programs would be irresponsible. You are the grief professional and your clients look to you for knowledgeable opinions and reliable referrals.

Creating and maintaining a lending library is also part of Standard Aftercare. Too often bereaved people cannot access a particular book, even if they have been given a book list. Local libraries may have very limited selection and local bookstores may not have access to pub-lishers that produce some of the most helpful resources. Sometimes the bereaved simply do not have enough energy to put forth any extraordi-nary effort to acquire a book. Establishing a simple check-out system and method of follow-up if books are not returned is not very time consuming and is a helpful service for clients. Some of the more exten-sive funeral home libraries also include videos for adults and children on grief-related topics. The funeral home thus becomes a valuable community resource.

Special programs for the bereaved are also included in the level of Standard Aftercare. Seminars for handling the holidays are well attended in most communities, for as the holiday season approaches many family members become apprehensive about the added stress of holidays that are surrounded with family traditions, as are Thanks-giving, Christmas, Hanukkah, and New Year's. It can be a relief to explore alternatives to handling such issues as the empty chair at the dinner table, how many stockings to hang, or whether to/how to talk to the children about the one who died. For some attendees, it is the first time anyone has given them "permission" to change some family tradi-tions (even if only temporarily), encouraged them to discover many alternatives, or created an environment that acknowledges the impor-tance of self-care.

Other special program topics may include "Surviving Suicide" to offer information and support for family members, or "Rituals for Healing" to explore the value of creating one's own rituals for various turning points in the journey through grief. Like the special cards, such programs should be tailored to meet the needs of your grieving com-munity. Some of these may be annual events, such as "Handling the Holidays," while others may be a one-time offering to meet a specific need, such as a program on multiple losses following a natural disaster.

Community education, too, is an integral part of Standard Aftercare. Writing articles for the newspaper, providing speakers for churches or service organizations, and creating opportunities with other groups or institutions (retirement homes, senior citizen centers) for classes on grief and loss issues are all ways of not only educating the community but also training them to be more supportive helpers and friends for the bereaved. Some funeral homes even have a regular radio program on grief issues.

Another responsibility of a professional coordinator is to determine when and if clients need to be referred to another mental health provider. Although many who have experienced a death will eventually reorganize their lives to a certain comfort level that does not involve the physical presence of the deceased, others will need the help of funeral home staff, particularly the bereavement services coordinator. Still a few others will need further counseling. Their grief may be extreme, perhaps complicated, and they may require special treatment; or their issues may go beyond simple grief and include pre-existing emotional problems. With a high divorce rate, an increase in the number of single parent families, and an upsurge in violence in today's society, many issues inherent in dysfunctional families may predate the grief and require therapy beyond the scope of the funeral home-based grief counselor. For those with such pre-existing conditions, a professional can provide a referral to a more appropriate source of help.

Finally, the Standard Level includes the preparation and presentation of special holiday programs. It is widely recognized that mourning rituals function in several ways—facilitating individual grief, affirming family loss, and even enabling an entire community to heal [6]. Memorial Day is a favored time for funeral homes and cemetery staffs to create special springtime beauty with a meaningful memorial service. According to Catherine Sanders, our society "offers little with which to bridge the empty months and even years after a death. It . . . leaves the bereaved hanging—with no community support and few with whom to share" [7, p. 149]. Memorial Day, already culturally designated as a day to remember the dead, is an appropriate time to address Sanders' concern by offering a special ceremony for grieving families to share with each other and enjoy the support of the community.

Christmas, too, offers a beautiful opportunity to create and share a ritual that "provides the path for needed mourning, healing, and commemoration" [6, p. 209]. The coordination of a Christmas Memorial Service can be time-consuming, but it is also rewarding. Rando points out that "holidays may be a particularly important time to have a ritual of continuity to demonstrate that the deceased continues on as a memorable and special part of the mourner's life" [8, p. 322]. The following comments have been received by our funeral home staff:

> I just wanted to say how much I appreciated the Christmas Memorial Service. I felt a very strong spiritual and emotional bond with others who had lost a loved one. Most importantly to me, however, was a sense of peace I felt knowing that nothing will ever extinguish the flame of our love.

> My husband and I attended the Memorial Service. The wonderful service, program and reception were very meaningful to both of us. . . . The events put on for those of us who grieve the loss of a loved one go far beyond your business obligations and exemplify the extraordinary concern you have for those of us in grief.

> Please extend my special thanks to all the participants of the Christmas Memorial this past Sunday evening. The entire evening was extremely special and I hope all of you realize how much something like this helps those of us who are grieving. We are in desperate need of remembering our loved ones, yet society does not allow our tears! Your service was done so beautifully and it was very uplifting for my damaged soul.

Premier Level

The most comprehensive and sophisticated level for aftercare programs is the fourth one, Premier. It includes all of the elements of the first three levels, yet goes beyond what can be considered Standard. Thus, this program is also well organized and is facilitated by specially trained staff. This advanced level category may include such services as individual grief counseling, in-service training for funeral home staff, or a children's resource center. In fact, some funeral homes have created a separate facility designed solely for bereavement services.

Providing training for other professionals in the community is also part of a Premium Aftercare Program, including obtaining approval of Continuing Education Units (CEUs) from governing bodies. Some funeral homes also offer ongoing bereavement information and support services for juvenile detention centers, churches, foster care systems, and community colleges. In addition, aftercare personnel serve on advisory boards, such as school crisis intervention teams, The Compassionate Friends, and Hospice Foundations.

Further, a professional bereavement person also may be called on to represent the funeral home, indeed the whole field of death, grief, and loss, when a particularly unusual circumstance has drawn the attention of the media. The bereavement professional can provide the media with a clear and acceptable articulation of the complex issues involved.

SELECTION OF MATERIALS

Thoughtful consideration must be given to the selection of materials to be used by your staff, regardless of the level of the program you create or the level of training of your staff members. One choice is to purchase professionally produced items—newsletters, pamphlets, books, videos, children's programs, cards, or support group curricula. There is a wide variety of fine products in the marketplace. However, there are also some outdated, inaccurate, and mediocre resources still in print. Thus, the time saved by purchasing a commercial product may be negated by the time it takes to review and evaluate the many choices available. Although there is no reason to "reinvent the wheel" when it comes to materials for your program, it must also be recognized that there are many "wheels" out there to compare and from which to choose.

Another option is to create your own aftercare materials, which allows more freedom to individualize and may be more cost effective. Inexpensive computer programs from Hallmark or American Greetings, for example, allow you to select from a large array of artwork, either using their messages or creating your own. Likewise, desktop publishing programs assist you in the creation of eye-catching brochures or newsletters. On the other hand, though these may be more personal and cost effective, they may be time-consuming to produce.

A third approach to the selection of materials is to combine purchased, commercial products with your own creations. Buying brochures may meet your need for sharing information on grief, whereas you may wish to achieve a more personal message by creating your own cards for the anniversary of the death.

With regard to the creation or selection of your aftercare materials, John Reynolds sums it up:

> Regardless of your choice, all aftercare literature should be scrutinized carefully before making a decision. The information should be sensitive, well-written, and nicely presented. Remember, whatever you decide is a reflection on your firm, your name, and your reputation [9, pp. 78-79].

More importantly, the well-being of your clients is your primary concern in the selection of your materials.

SELECTING PERSONNEL

Training and personal qualities must be considered when selecting personnel. Of necessity, they are interrelated and must be considered, each dependent upon the other, as part of the whole.

Training

There are well-intentioned women and men who are anxious to work with the bereaved. Because most of these individuals have experienced grief and understand the path of bereavement, they feel they have something to offer others in similar circumstances. Often they do have something to offer, but they may not have the background or objectivity to be a qualified bereavement support person.

In addition, some who have experienced death losses may attempt to enter bereavement work in order to deal with their own unresolved feelings. Beware of using these people to work with your bereaved clients. Often unaware of their own vulnerability, they will be unable to help others in a healthy way.

Bereavement work is "people work." Because bereavement work must somehow harmonize temporary and changing emotions with the permanence of death, it involves high levels of knowledge, empathy, and guidance. It is difficult work that demands much mental discipline from bereavement workers. Specialized skills and information necessary for working with the bereaved are formally learned in the social sciences. There are many valuable courses in psychology and sociology that deal with dying, death, and bereavement.

In addition to structured college courses, less formal training is received from intensive seminar sessions offered by such organizations as the Association for Death Education and Counseling, the National Center for Death Education, King's College, or the Center for Loss and Life Transition. Addresses for these organizations may be found in Chapter 9 by Vicki Lensing, "Aftercare: Past, Present, and Where Do We Go From Here?"

In aftercare, as in other aspects of funeral service education, there is an unresolved issue of minimal educational requirements. Must an aftercare facilitator be licensed as a professional counselor? Can a person with less than a graduate degree successfully perform aftercare duties. It is the responsibility of funeral home owners and managers to determine the aftercare standards for the person developing and guiding their program, regardless of the level of program they choose. It is important to keep in mind that even with an advanced degree, the training for someone in social work is very different than training for counseling or for chaplaincy. That training and philosophy will be a guiding force for an emerging aftercare program.

Personal Qualities

The capacity for empathy and compassion are, without a doubt, paramount personal qualities to look for in all your funeral home personnel, including aftercare staff. Because of the involvement of your aftercare staff with the client over a lengthy period of time when the client is likely to be most vulnerable, it is difficult to maintain an impersonal relationship characterized in other businesses. Worden notes that:

> . . . working with the bereaved may make us aware . . . of our own losses. This is particularly true if the loss is similar to losses that we have sustained in our own lives. If . . . not adequately resolved in the counselor's life, it can be an impediment to a meaningful and helpful intervention [10, p. 108].

Therefore, it is imperative that the aftercare provider has confronted his/her own death anxieties and reconciled past losses. Failure to do so could not only be a disservice to clients, but also make the aftercare specialist vulnerable to burnout.

In order to avoid what Figley calls "compassion fatigue," it is also important that your bereavement specialist is someone who is able to maintain a balance in her/his personal and professional life [11]. It is easy for improperly prepared aftercare workers to care so much for others that they lose perspective of the priorities in their own lives, giving up more and more of themselves to help others. This is a people-helping profession. Yet, it is imperative that we maintain balance in our lives, remembering that we are there to walk WITH our clients on their journeys through grief, not to walk FOR them. We must be confident that others have the strength and ability to do their own grief work. Our job is simply to accompany them, maintaining our own identities and our own lives beyond the job.

Another personal trait to seek in your aftercare employee is the ability to work well with others. Understanding the needs of and cooperating with funeral home personnel is essential to build a strong aftercare program. Aftercare responsibilities do not rest solely on one person. Rather, they are a collective effort, from the person taking the first death call to the funeral director collecting flowers from the graveside to the aftercare person facilitating a support group and sending cards on the anniversary of the death. Like the commitment to quality funeral service in general, commitment to a high quality aftercare program involves "everyone in an organization, not just managers or owners" or aftercare specialists [12].

At the same time that it is important to have someone who works well with others, it is also vital that (s)he is able to work independently. Because aftercare is a very specialized area of work and because many funeral homes do not yet have such staff, some aftercare specialists feel isolated in their job—there may be no peers in their geographic area with whom to share ideas, brainstorm solutions, or get specific feedback. Grief counselors frequently are working in isolation without the advantage of a consult group. This work environment is especially difficult for professionals who are accustomed to the camaraderie and opportunity for feedback experienced working in small groups or teams.

Because the timing of aftercare intervention is very important, aftercare personnel need to be well organized in their approach and their record keeping. Regardless of the system you use, it needs to be one that gives the aftercare staff the maximum amount of information regarding the families they will be contacting with a minimum amount of extra paperwork for already burdened funeral directors and secretaries.

An aftercare professional also needs to value ongoing learning. Recognizing the importance of new studies, research, theories, and methods insures that your clients are being served by someone who is current on grief and loss issues. There is no indication that the pace of new information will diminish and it is important that your staff is knowledgeable regarding the emerging literature.

Likewise, participating in professional organizations is beneficial to the caregiver, to the client, and to your firm. Groups such as the American Psychological Association and the Association for Death Education and Counseling offer sources for professional growth, recognition, and renewal.

PROFESSIONAL SKILLS

Specific skills to seek in your aftercare staff will vary with the level of program you are initiating. However, there are some that we consider basic.

Good Listening Skills

Wolfelt points out that the funeral home staff members may be among the very few who actually listen to grieving family members

[13]. Good listening requires a desire to truly understand, patience to avoid rushing the client, and skill in knowing when to talk and when to be silent, when to paraphrase, and when to question.

Public Speaking Skills

Your aftercare staff will undoubtedly be representing your firm in presentations to various community groups, whether the object is to educate people about grief and loss issues or if it is to inform the public of the various services you provide. You want this person to be representative of the level of professionalism and care provided at your funeral home.

Broad Range of Counseling Skills

Regardless of psychological orientation, your aftercare staff needs to be skilled in attending to the client, being aware of nonverbal communication, responding empathetically, and probing gently [14]. These counseling skills also need to include group facilitation if you are sponsoring grief support groups.

Ability to Normalize the Grief Response

In order to normalize the many aspects of grief and reassure clients that they are not going crazy, the skilled aftercare provider needs information regarding the grief process as well as the ability to convey that information in a reassuring manner.

Assessment and Referral

According to Worden, "a person doing grief counseling may be able to identify the existence of pathology which has been triggered by the loss . . . and, having spotted such difficulty, may find it necessary to make a professional referral" [10, p. 48]. It is not the function of the funeral home to serve as a mental health facility; nor should its staff be treating deeply-rooted, complex psychological problems. Thus, aftercare specialists need to maintain a network of other professionals for referrals.

Adherence to a Professional Code of Ethics

Recognizing the potential impact of grief counseling and death education regarding death-related topics on the client, it is an implicit responsibility of the aftercare professional to adhere strictly to a code of ethics. Such codes have been established by the Association for Death Education and Counseling (ADEC), the American Psychological Association, and other related professional organizations.

QUALITIES OF
SUCCESSFUL AFTERCARE PROGRAMS

In aftercare each provider may have his or her own definition of success. Universally, however, there are three criteria by which aftercare efforts may be evaluated. The first criterion is helpfulness. Does your aftercare program help those who are bereaved? If so, that is a mark of success.

The second criterion is flexibility. Adapting to the changing needs of clients and the community in general is important. For example, your local medical center may have sponsored an afternoon grief support group, but because of budget cutbacks, no longer offers the group. This may be an opportunity for your funeral home to fill a need. Likewise, if you have been sponsoring an adolescent grief support group and your local hospice now includes teens in their children's program, your focus can change to meet other needs. Such adaptability is another mark of success.

Finally, the third criterion is closely linked to the first two: renewal. Is your aftercare provider working with your clients to work through their grief and renew their lives as constructive members of the community? Do your clients grow through your program and move out on their own, or is your aftercare program really an exclusive social club? Are the newly bereaved entering and welcomed into your program? Moreover, is your aftercare staff finding sources of professional renewal within your program? Renewal, then, is the final mark of success for your aftercare program.

We have wrestled with the dilemma of evaluating aftercare efforts. We are confident that these criteria are indisputable. We are unable, however, to suggest a practical method of objectively measuring the degree to which they exist. Certainly, letters of thanks and favorable comments from clients are valuable indicators of a successful aftercare program. These indications, however, are subjective. Are they enough? Do we need more objective measures of success? Or can we be content with an intuitive, gut-level knowledge that our aftercare efforts are the best that can be provided for the bereaved and for our community?

CONCLUSION

Funeral service for the twenty-first century is being challenged from many directions. Writing to funeral service professionals, Sherry Williams notes:

> We must confront the emotions and emptiness of grief but look to you as a source of information, compassion, support and hope. You become the place for us to gather and connect, to remember and honor a relationship [15, p. 10].

In order to meet this continuing challenge, we must be ready to provide quality aftercare programs within the funeral home setting, staffed by competent professionals and geared toward meeting the changing needs of our clientele.

REFERENCES

1. C. O. Kates, Services for the Bereaved: The Evans Program, *American Funeral Director, XCLII*:2, pp. 38-39, February 1974.
2. K. J. Doka, The Pro's and Con's of Aftercare Services, *American Funeral Director,115*:4, April 1992.
3. J. D. Canine, *What Am I Going To Do with Myself When I Die?* Appleton & Lange, Stamford, Connecticut, 1999.
4. K. J. Doka, Sudden Loss: The Experiences of Bereavement, in *Living with Grief After Sudden Loss,* K. Doka (ed.), The Hospice Foundation of America, Washington, D.C., 1996.
5. J. Hayward (ed.), *The Complete Poetry and Selected Prose of John Donne and the Complete Poetry of William Blake,* Modern Library, New York, 1941.
6. E. Imber-Black and J. Roberts, *Rituals for Our Times: Celebrating, Healing, and Changing Our Lives and Relationships,* HarperCollins, New York, 1992.
7. C. M. Sanders, *How to Survive the Loss of a Child: Feeling the Emptiness and Rebuilding Your Life,* Prima Publishing, Rocklin, California, 1992.
8. T. A. Rando, *Treatment of Complicated Mourning,* Research Press, Champaign, Illinois, 1993.
9. J. J. Reynolds, Aftercare Services, *American Funeral Director,* December 1993.
10. J. W. Worden, *Grief Counseling and Grief Therapy: A Handbook for the Mental Health Practitioner,* Springer, New York, 1982.
11. C. R. Figley, *Compassion Fatigue: Coping with Secondary Traumatic Stress in Those Who Treat the Traumatized,* Bruner/Mazel, Inc., New York, 1995.

12. D. Isard, A New Definition for Funeral Service, *American Funeral Director,* October 1993.
13. A. D. Wolfelt, *Interpersonal Skills Training: A Handbook for Funeral Service Staffs,* Accelerated Press, Muncie, Indiana, 1990.
14. G. Egan, *The Skilled Helper: A Systematic Approach to Effective Helping,* Brooks/Cole Publishing Co., Pacific Grove, California, 1990.
15. S. L. Williams, Is Aftercare Really a Part of Funeral Service? *Today in Death Care, 9*:11, 1997.

CHAPTER 2

Defining the Essence of Aftercare

Lyn Miletich

In his book *Out of Solitude,* Henri J. M. Nouwen asks a thought provoking question: "How can we be or become a caring community, a community of people not trying to cover the pain or to avoid it by sophisticated bypasses, but rather share it as the source of healing and new life?" [1, p. 39]. The answer to his question defines the essence of aftercare in funeral service. Indeed, a solid and well-founded aftercare program can provide a container in which this healing and growth after loss can occur.

In this chapter the importance of recognizing and acknowledging the clear boundaries and limitations of an aftercare program will be explored with an emphasis on how the process of definition itself can create an empathetic and soul-full environment within the death care industry.

Aftercare can be defined as a means of helping survivors cope after the loss of a loved one. In today's fast-paced, high-tech, and extremely mobile society, the family and social systems that previously provided emotional and physical support are not present as they were even a generation ago. Career moves resulting in geographic distances from family and friends are not uncommon. Potential breakdown of close physical and emotional intimacy becomes even more pronounced during times of life crises. The often increasing geographic distance as well as the lack of close extended families has created a void that needs to be filled. In response to that unmet need, some funeral homes are now offering "Aftercare" programs for their clients and community members. These programs vary widely from community to community both as a function of community dynamics and of the varied background and experiences of the personnel who are responsible for developing and implementing them.

One author suggests that "aftercare begins with the funeral" [2, p. 41] and meets the residual needs. He defines these residuals as "those needs that did not get met, those needs that surfaced as felt needs, and any needs arising from the grief caused by a continuing love for a person who is no longer present" [2, p. 41]. In order to meet these residual needs, a successful program offers a variety of follow-up services for clients to encourage healthy emotional adjustment and to provide assistance in integrating to the reality of the loss and in rebuilding one's life in a constructive and positive fashion.

The mission, then, of an aftercare program is to provide opportunities for healing after the death of a loved one through a variety of bereavement support services. Theory and research in the field of grief and loss have shown that the bereaved need three things to assist them in their grief process: education, support, and permission to grieve [3]. Meeting these needs as an outgrowth of funeral service makes sense. Where better to do so than in a setting that already has significance for those that have lost their loved ones? Successful aftercare programs will have components that respond to all these needs in the form of literature and educational materials available, assistance with follow-up on paperwork, grief counseling or at least referrals to appropriate community agencies for the same, and bereavement groups which provide a forum for support while at the same time granting the permission to do the necessary grief work after the death of a loved one [4]. Underlying all of these components must be a commitment to survivors so they are encouraged to embrace and move through the various phases of the grief process in a way that integrates the loss of their loved one into the fabric of their lives.

A successful program will also be one that responds to the needs of the clientele in a way that promotes healing and pays attention to the cries of the soul with compassion and understanding. Aftercare services can model compassionate care because its foremost commitment is to serve the families in a way that leaves them feeling enhanced and not exploited or violated in any way. If this foundation of empathetic caring is not built and respected, there is a danger of exploitation, territoriality, and duplication of services within a community that will only engender competition instead of cooperation.

Although sharing the common foundation of creating a healing and compassionate environment, each funeral home is responsible for determining the boundaries and limitations of its own aftercare program. Indeed, it is vital to recognize that inherent in setting up the program is establishing boundaries and being clear about what one can and cannot do based on community resources, time restraints, finances, etc. It is clear that success can be defined based on the community in which the program is situated. What works in one particular environment may not be successful at all in another. It doesn't mean that there is a right and wrong way of approaching aftercare. It is more that it needs to be judged within its particular framework. Programs will obviously differ based on the size of the population, whether they are situated in an urban or rural environment, the client base of the funeral home, what is already available in terms of bereavement services within the community, and the personnel available to administer the program. The bottom line, though, is always whether the scope of any program is conducive to the growth and healing of the individuals whom the funeral home is serving. There is a danger that the purpose of the aftercare program could be misunderstood. It may be perceived that the funeral home is providing bereavement support only for its financial benefit, rather than the emotional well-being of its customers. The question of "Whose needs are being served?" is one that needs constant re-evaluation.

DEFINING PROGRAM BOUNDARIES

Identifying a Clear Vision

Programs must be based on an analysis of community needs and resources. One does not need to be all things for all people. If the particular dimensions of a program include mailings, phone calls, individual and family counseling, support groups, and educational opportunities for the bereaved, that is plenty. Within each of these categories it is then necessary to determine the specific operating details. When does your aftercare program start? Is it important for the aftercare provider to meet every family as they walk through the door, or is your operation too large for that consideration? How will the position of aftercare provider be structured? Is there flexibility so that, if needed, s/he is available in certain situations to meet the presenting need at the time?

For example, if your aftercare provider is on staff and on site in the funeral home, he or she may be available to meet with families, upon request, during the time of arrangements or viewing. Early introduction has the advantage of making future follow-up much more personal. It also provides an opportunity for family members to ask questions they may have about the bereavement support program and receive grief-related literature. The aftercare provider may also be called upon to discuss clients' concerns regarding participation by certain family members, such as children, in viewing and attendance at the funeral/memorial service.

Having a clear vision makes it easier to evaluate not only the program, but also the ways that the aftercare provider is being called on to serve.

Keeping Aftercare Services and Pre-Need Sales Separate

The position of aftercare must be a separate entity and not incorporated into the pre-need sales division. Otherwise, bereavement follow-up services could be misconstrued as just a way to increase revenue for the funeral home. Problems about potential conflict of interest could arise and the motives of the aftercare provider questioned. The Association for Death Education and Counseling provides a Code of Ethics that supports this allegation. It clearly states that "Members do not use their professional relationships to further their personal, political, religious, or business interests" [5, p. 29]. By avoiding dual relationships, the integrity of the aftercare provider is maintained and the welfare of the client is promoted with respect and clarity. The position, then, needs to be non-revenue producing and the aftercare provider preferably would report directly to the president or on-site manager of the company.

Maintaining a Non-Territorial Approach

Cooperation as opposed to competition is key in serving families who will avail themselves of the bereavement services provided. There is often more bereavement work to go around than there are hours in a day. The opportunity for increased referral and interaction among aftercare providers within the same geographic locale or vicinity is maximized when particular services are not duplicated. This is especially true if the various bereavement services providers (e.g., hospice organizations, grief and loss divisions of health or social service agencies, local funeral homes, etc.) network and meet regularly for the purpose of keeping one another informed about their particular offerings.

Hiring a Professional

Aftercare providers enter the field from a variety of personal and professional backgrounds. There are some vital criteria to consider in hiring. It is crucial that the person have a master's degree in a counseling related field with additional training and/or certification in grief counseling and death education and appropriate experience for the responsibilities of the job. Aftercare providers need to be good diagnosticians and be able to clearly assess the needs of the individual and/or family seeking support in order to provide or refer to the most appropriate bereavement follow-up services around. They need to be clear about the goals and boundaries of the program and be able to follow them. For example, if the guidelines of the aftercare services are clearly short-term referral counseling, as opposed to long-term mental health therapy, then the need for short-term care should be respected both for the welfare of the client and the mental health preservation of the aftercare provider. In today's society it is also critical for aftercare providers to be supported by malpractice insurance, whether it be under the auspices of the funeral home or privately funded.

Aftercare providers also represent the values and mission of their organizations. Can they be role models within not only the company, but also in the larger community? Are they clear about their own personal boundaries when working with clients and other internal and external customers? How have they dealt with loss in their own lives? Are they capable of embodying hope and empathy?

> Everyone alive has suffered. It is the wisdom gained from our wounds and from our own experiences of suffering that makes us able to heal. Becoming expert has turned out to be less important than remembering and trusting the wholeness in myself and everyone else [6, p. 217].

These qualities are just as important as professional degrees and certification.

Giving Clients Options

Customers need to be informed regarding the variety of bereavement follow-up services that are available through the funeral home. However, it is also important that these be presented in a way that they can gracefully refuse. For example, clients initially may not accept telephone follow-up calls or referrals to support services either within the funeral home or the community. As awareness of their need for support becomes more apparent with the passage of time, they may be open to services previously declined. Maintaining respect for the clients' decisions and personal boundaries is a way of honoring them and their needs at any particular time throughout their grief process.

Expanding the Role of the Aftercare Provider

A unique consideration of the position of aftercare provider is to broaden the responsibilities of the job to also include offering support and training to the entire staff. The aftercare provider could be available for the funeral home/cemetery personnel for discussion of personal and professional concerns within a confidential setting. Responsibilities might also involve offering staff training in areas of grief and loss, stress management, etc. Expanding the position to include staff responsibilities would probably make more sense and have greater effectiveness within a larger organization due to the increased staff size. It makes the position and the services available much more visible as well as increases staff awareness and cooperation in referring to the aftercare program and the bereavement specialist.

ESTABLISHING BOUNDARIES OF PROGRAM COMPONENTS

Setting Boundaries within Each Facet of the Program

Defining the limitations within each component of the aftercare program is important because it provides clarity and structure. This enables the aftercare provider to assess where the clients' needs can best be addressed within the spectrum of care. It is also a statement to the client that this is a well-thought-out program designed to promote healing within a safe and supportive environment.

Following are some questions to consider when establishing guidelines for each facet of the support services: Whom in the community do we serve? Are the bereavement services offered through the funeral home limited to customers or are portions of the program available for participation by the greater community? What are the determinates for the individual/family counseling? How will that determination be made? What is the maximum length of time where follow-up is provided? What else is available in the community? How and when will referrals to community resources be made? Will the bereavement support groups be open or closed? If the groups are open, then what guidelines, if any, are to be established?

It is my belief that having open support groups does not necessarily mean "anyone can show up at any time." That does not serve the purpose of creating an empathetic environment for clients. Potential members need to be pre-screened for their readiness and appropriateness for group support and interaction.[1]

Nouwen's concept of a caring community, which becomes an environment for healing through the sharing of pain rather than its avoidance, is most evident when the crisis of exposure is minimized so optimum movement and acceptance of the grief process is facilitated. Providing structure creates a "safe container" for the healing and integration of grief and its often transformational experiences to occur.

MAINTAINING BOUNDARIES

Assess the Program on a Regular Basis

It is important to listen to responses from the larger community including that from the referral sources as well as the clients. Solicited and unsolicited feedback can provide information as to how well the community is being served and what is working or not working. As important as it may be to look at the numbers being served, do not judge solely on that basis. So much of any work that involves great depth and interaction in peoples' lives at a time of crisis is a qualitative more often than a quantitative response. Consider where the referrals are coming from: Is it word of mouth from other satisfied consumers and/or other agencies in the community? How visible and well known is it that aftercare services are provided? What is happening within each facet of the program? A recent bereavement support group participant described his experience as being in "a place where the process of 'confession' to one another brings healing to one and all." If that quality of experience is occurring, then care for the soul is being evidenced within a nurturing environment.

Establish and Maintain Ethical Standards

The company needs to commit and support the program and the aftercare provider. This occurs by establishing and maintaining appro-

---

[1] Following are guidelines for consideration: recent loss, within the last year to eighteen months; adults only; no major multiple losses within a short period of time and no active alcohol or drug dependencies. Clients with severe depression or other forms or mental debilitation are not appropriate. Interested participants should call the facilitator first.

priate standards of confidentiality, by showing respect and sensitivity to each person being served and by providing the necessary support staff. It is crucial that the physical space provided for bereavement groups and grief counseling be warm, inviting, and one which suggests an environment of trust and safety.

Pay Attention

The voice of the soul which cries out for compassion needs to be listened to and met with the compassionate care that it seeks. Thomas Moore reminds us that "care of the soul begins with observance of how the soul manifests itself and how it operates. When people observe the ways in which the soul is manifesting itself, they are enriched rather than impoverished" [7, pp. 5-6]. It is important to enrich the experience of the bereaved rather than exploit them. This is a danger unless the question "whose needs are being met?" is asked and answered honestly. Exploitation happens when the clients' needs for compassionate and professional care are denied through holding on to them beyond the appropriate time for their benefit, duplicating services within a community, and not listening to their requests and feedback.

Another way of paying attention to the cries of the soul is to listen for subtle or expressed desire for the ongoing need for rituals that capture the heart of the grief process. Anniversary dates, the placing of the marker or headstone, religious or social holidays are only a few examples of occasions to ritualize not only a particular passage of time, but acknowledge changes in the individual and family patterns. Although the funeral or memorial service is an important acknowledgment of the death and celebration of life, it is often only the initial step in the healing process.

EXPANDING BOUNDARIES

Remain Fluid

Stay focused with the changing needs and directions in the industry and make shifts as needed. As the death care industry moves from being merchandise-driven to service-driven, so will the changes be experienced in aftercare as well. Shifts are currently being recognized in the increased numbers of cremations, often with less emphasis on traditional memorial or funeral services. However, this does not mean that the need for memorialization is eliminated. Rather, the opposite is often occurring. New ways of providing opportunities for celebrating, acknowledging, and remembering as well as offering ongoing support demand more knowledge, creativity, and direction. It is also important to pay attention to cemeteries and memorial parks that often have lifelong relationships with families. In these changing times, how can aftercare be a viable part of these operations as well? Of course this will differ within geographic regions and communities. Stay aware of trends. They will help guide the future.

Another aspect which requires attention is the cultural diversity within a particular region or locale. Outreach services may also extend to a variety of specific ethnic populations. Is the knowledge base there to accommodate the changing needs? How versatile is the aftercare program for this accommodation?

Keep Relationships and Networks Alive

The bereaved often have needs other than grief issues. Connecting them with other people and agencies is caring for them as whole individuals who are trying to make sense of what has happened in their lives. It is part of creating community which enables this healing and new life.

Be Open to Surprises

Being on the leading edge of anything is a form of pioneering. As much as we can plan and predict, the territory of aftercare is being charted and created through experience and experimentation.

BY-PRODUCTS OF A CLEARLY DEFINED PROGRAM

When the scope of an aftercare program is clearly defined, there will be space for creative and fluid expansion over a period of time. Then it is realistic to expect the following results:

- decrease of confusion;
- easier decisions about when to change the boundaries;
- expansion of public relations opportunities; and
- increased visibility and integration within the funeral home staff as well as the community it serves.

It is not an easy task being the "caretaker of the soul." Empathy and compassion are the underpinnings of any well-defined after-care program. Morrie Schwartz, in his final conversations as he was dying, shared this wisdom born out of his end of life experience: "Be compassionate, and take responsibility for each other. If only we learned those lessons, this would be so much better a place" [8, p. 163]. Learning these lessons means responding with compassion to create a well-defined, empathetic, and soul-full community of healing and new life.

REFERENCES

1. H. J. M. Nouwen, *Out of Solitude,* Ave Maria Press, Notre Dame, Indiana, 1974.
2. S. Lineberry, Is Aftercare a Part of Funeral Service? *The Director,* March 1997.
3. A. Wolfelt, *Understanding Grief: Helping Yourself Heal,* Accelerated Development, Inc., Muncie, Indiana, 1992.
4. O. D. Weeks and C. Johnson, Developing a Successful Aftercare Program, *The Director,* pp. 12-18, December 1995.
5. *1997-98 Directory of Members,* Association for Death Education and Counseling, Hartford, Connecticut, 1998.
6. R. N. Remen, *Kitchen Table Wisdom,* The Berkley Publishing Group, New York, 1996.
7. T. Moore, *Care of the Soul,* HarperCollins, New York, 1992.
8. M. Albom, *Tuesdays with Morrie,* Doubleday, New York, 1997.

CHAPTER 3

Legal Concerns and Strategies in Aftercare Development for the Funeral Professional

Stephen R. Rocco*

I explore the issue of the funeral professional's legal liability in aftercare with some degree of trepidation. As we know, aftercare provides a continuum of specialized care for the bereaved in communities where such resources are often lacking. Our profession also exists in an increasingly litigious society. American law has demonstrated an understandable, but I believe excessive, sensitivity toward families in their lawsuits against funeral homes. This dilemma has created some unease within our profession as funeral directors assess their legal risks in the relatively new world of formal aftercare.

This chapter will identify, and hopefully allay, some of our profession's legal concerns in this area. It will assess our legal relationships and responsibilities to families in the aftercare phase. It will also evaluate our direct and indirect acts as nontherapist helpers who wish to assist the bereaved.

True prediction of the law's evaluation of our duties in aftercare is somewhat speculative. No legal case with national significance exists specifically on a funeral director's liability in this area. This is not surprising given that formal aftercare is more a phenomenon of the

---

*This chapter is written in memory of Stephen Rocco's father, Horace A. Rocco, who died on February 12, 1999. He was the most caring funeral director the author has ever known.

1980s. Recent statistics indicate that 50 percent of funeral homes in this country now provide some form of aftercare [1]. Given this proliferation, my guess is that litigation in one of the multidimensional areas of aftercare will arise in the near future. Some legal cases related to this issue do exist, and these offer specific guidelines for our profession. I feel confident that, with some precautionary steps, the funeral professional can fulfill his/her desire to help others while minimizing any legal exposure.

One legal journal defines funeral service as "the profession of administrating or supervising funerals for profit" [2]. Improper rendition of these services—a failure to meet certain standards of care toward both the decedent and his family—may result in liability as in any business relationship. The funeral profession is uniquely at risk in the damage portion of any litigation, however, as the law increasingly bases any recovery on the feelings of the living for the dead. In assessing liability against a funeral home, one judge commented, "What else were the mourners bargaining for other than peace of mind that their loved one would be buried properly" [3].

Although not stated, care for a family's "peace of mind" is as inherent a part of the funeral contract as is the sale of the casket. Our level of care is being stretched unrealistically wide when one examines the range of duties for which funeral directors have been successfully sued. Significant damage awards for obscure psychic injuries such as fright, humiliation, anger, or sadness have been received by the bereaved in their lawsuits against funeral homes [4].

The legal concerns previously outlined have largely been shaped by lawsuits originating at the time of burial or at-need. The law assesses our legal relationship with families—our duties, acts, omissions—and directly measures them with the skills customarily followed by funeral directors. But what is our legal relationship with families in aftercare? This question may well be dispositive of liability. Will judges determine that our services are entirely gratuitous, or will they focus on the business ramifications of creating "goodwill" in our families through aftercare? As more funeral homes develop such programs in the next decade, family members may well expect that these programs are a normal part of our contractual relationship, with their costs built into the funeral director's overhead.

American law has historically encouraged its citizens to help others through crises. "Good Samaritan" laws exempt from liability volunteers who may negligently come to the aid of others. These laws specifically apply to private citizens in noncommercial transactions. Thus, it would appear that no blanket immunity exists for funeral directors, however altruistic their goals may be for the bereaved or the community at large.

The law further finds that we have a general responsibility for those to whom we would ordinarily owe no care, once we voluntarily undertake certain actions. The law's sentiments may be found in a case discussing a funeral director's duties leading a funeral procession.

> . . . we recognize that a funeral director has no general duty to orchestrate or lead a funeral profession. However, once a director voluntarily undertakes to do so, the director assumes at least a minimal duty to exercise good judgment [5].

It would appear to me that we owe some legal duty to families in the aftercare relationship. The definition of those duties will be determined by both the level of perceived misconduct and the person engaged in the conduct. Let's examine three hypothetical aftercare scenarios in which funeral directors may establish some legal responsibility to the consumers.

CASE 1

A funeral director, identifying himself in some of his own literature as a funeral counselor or grief facilitator, maintains an ongoing relationship with a family member following a funeral. The person frequently returns to the funeral home for "advice" about his loss and other personal problems. The funeral director also provides reading material from his small library to this person. The person sinks into a deeper depression and later attempts suicide. His family commences litigation against this firm alleging 1) that the funeral director is not properly skilled to provide therapy and 2) (s)he had a general duty to refer the person to a mental health expert to prevent the attempted suicide.

Common sense may instruct us that the above case holds little liability risk for the funeral professional. Indeed, courts have addressed and limited the liability of nontherapist counselors both for their direct counseling and for any duty to prevent suicide. Referring to a certain range of helpers as "band aid counselors" one court wrote "extending liability to voluntary, noncommercial and noncustodial (counseling) relationships is contrary to the trend . . . to encourage private assistance efforts" [6].

Where concern does exist is for those counselors who "hold" themselves out as professional therapists. Beyond what the counselor defines as his/her own qualifications to the person, courts are now defining how the relationship appeared to the counselee. One leading case decided in 1988 specifically involved nontherapist pastoral counseling [7]. The pastors had assisted a young man who eventually committed suicide. While ultimately absolved of liability after a contentious nine-year legal battle, the pastors' message to the public about their counseling ministry was carefully assessed by a divided court. The judges examined the pastors' backgrounds, counseling sessions, and publications to the community. In a stinging rebuke of the decision, one judge wrote that the pastors' "duty" was simply to recognize the limits of their own competence.

The message to funeral professionals is to strongly control, both verbally and in print, their role in the aftercare relationship. While virtually no funeral directors would refer to themselves as grief therapists, the law may define how a reasonable person could have perceived our role. Due to the ambiguous nature of the term counselor in our society, some suggest that we describe ourselves as grief facilitators. I believe this description is also unnecessary. My preference is to describe ourselves as "funeral professionals" who simply want to provide ongoing assistance to serviced families and to the general community.

Many funeral directors have received additional grief training to assist families. There may be a natural tendency to utilize this knowledge to help families. Firms may also advertise these skills to carve out a special niche in the soon-to-be competitive world of aftercare. Caution at the individual or managerial level should be exercised when describing our skill level, especially in printed literature. Juries may have to later assess what a "reasonable" consumer would have expected from these messages.

CASE 2

A funeral home hires an aftercare coordinator, a licensed mental health person, to direct its aftercare program. This person provides comprehensive services, including direct counseling to the families served by the funeral home and outreach education to the general community. The funeral home is sued by a family member who alleges that his condition worsened following "treatment" by the therapist/ employee.

This case addresses a funeral home's legal responsibility for the acts of its employees. The aftercare coordinator, who may perform a myriad of functions for a funeral home, is more of a nontraditional hiring. The law is quite clear that employers are generally liable for the careless acts of their employees. Similar to its culpability for a staff embalmer who poorly embalms a decedent, the funeral home will be responsible for its employees' acts occurring within the "scope of their employment." This standard is fairly broad and courts will examine if the funeral home generally benefitted from the employee's acts. In defending this rationale, one court wrote:

> Without such a rule of employer liability, an employer could easily avoid any responsibility for employee wrongdoing . . . simply by issuing orders not to perform any wrongful acts. Thus employers would have less incentive to hire, train, supervise and discipline properly [8, p. 30].

Employers have even been found liable for their employees' acts which are executed in direct violation of company policy. This is illustrated in a 1992 case in which a family was awarded over $200,000 against a crematorium corporation [9]. The employee, described as an agent of the corporation, independently performed religious services for a decedent and scattered his ashes at sea in direct violation of the terms of the contract. The jury imputed the agent's acts and omissions to the crematorium. Ironically, the jury did not hold the employee personally liable for his own acts even though it was free to do so.

The clear message to the funeral profession is to meticulously check the qualifications, backgrounds, and credentials of any employee. Since an aftercare coordinator represents a nontraditional hiring, funeral homes should carefully research what the firm's goals are prior to interviewing any applicants. A written job description should be prepared to gauge the prospective coordinator's ability to adhere to those goals. This written contract may well determine a funeral director's later liability.

The funeral professional should thoroughly research the history of the aftercare coordinator. A mental health person should be licensed and/or registered by the particular state board which regulates that profession (i.e., psychologists, social workers, family therapists, etc.). This board can be contacted about whether any complaints, civil or criminal, exist against that candidate. If a social worker is sought, funeral homes should consider hiring only those that are licensed, independent, and certified (L.I.C.S.W.). This licensing status indicates a high level of social work competence. Funeral professionals should also carefully examine the resumé of the aftercare applicant—does the applicant have particular expertise working with the bereaved? Has (s)he led groups for the bereaved?—if this is a goal of the funeral home. Has the person received specialized grief training at places such as the

Association For Death Education and Counseling (A.D.E.C.) or the National Center for Death Education (N.C.D.E.)?

If the aftercare coordinator is to work for the funeral home on a part-time basis, this status should be carefully discussed. How will the coordinator segregate his own clientele from the funeral home's? What happens if families serviced by the funeral home wish to become private clients of the coordinator? Obviously these therapists should maintain their own malpractice insurance in order to inhibit such lawsuits against the funeral home.

CASE 3

The funeral director occasionally refers families that (s)he has served to a grief therapist in the immediate area. This therapist has also provided some limited aftercare services for the firm, such as educational seminars during the holidays. The therapist is not on the funeral home's payroll and the funeral director has very little control over the therapist's work. A family sues the firm alleging that the therapist was incompetent or guilty of some misconduct. They allege that the funeral director failed in his/her duty to recommend a suitable therapist for their family.

This case leads to a discussion of liability when our relationship to the aftercare worker is limited. The therapist is not an employee of the funeral home. In his job status he resembles the trade embalmer who is controlled only to a narrow degree by the funeral home. The law normally refers to such workers as independent contractors or consultants.

Independent contractors, not the employers, are generally responsible for their own wrongs. Thus, in the strictest sense, the funeral home would be absolved of any liability in the above scenario. The law has shown a proclivity to make exceptions to this rule when 1) the employer does not pay careful attention to the specialized type of work the contractor must perform and 2) the contractor's work poses unusual risks to others. Given the special nature of aftercare referrals, both of these exceptions may post special concern for funeral directors.

In recommending a particular therapist to a family, a funeral professional is essentially confirming that this person possesses a certain skill. The law may well scrutinize funeral directors' decisions even more carefully given the emotional damages which will accompany haphazard referrals to professional caretakers.

Everything that has been mentioned previously regarding background checks on aftercare personnel applies to this discussion. The law has often cited the employer's negligence in not validating the independent contractor's licensing requirements to do a particular job. Funeral directors should verify skills offered by the coordinator. In addition, if the person is a board-certified therapist, his personal history can be reviewed by the appropriate state board of registration. The independent contractor/therapist should carry his own liability-malpractice insurance which should be carefully examined for coverage amounts.

On the subject of liability or malpractice insurance, it is a necessary staple in funeral service today. One legal commentator justified this protection with these words: "They (funeral directors) can console themselves with the thought that they entered such a business voluntarily and every business must pay its way. Risks that are unavoidable should be insured as a normal business expense" [10].

In malpractice litigation, the law compares a funeral director's alleged misconduct with "the skill and knowledge normally possessed by members of that profession in good standing" [11, p. 3]. Aftercare represents a new form of "professional services," services that are evolutionary and changing day to day. Could these services be excluded from any liability coverage? Funeral service is typical of many professional groups today. Lawyers, for example, may engage in investment counseling. Litigation has arisen as to whether legal malpractice insurance covers their perceived investment failures. The language of the insurance policy is often dispositive of liability.

Liability insurance companies generally exclude claims that result from dishonest, fraudulent or criminal acts, or omissions. They have no such hesitation to define just what professional services for a particular group are covered. This particular item—whether our aftercare duties are covered in the language of our insurance policies—should be carefully addressed with our insurance agent.

Many of the precautions previously outlined already exist in funeral homes throughout this country. Funeral service has largely faced the reality that the law holds the funeral professional to extremely high standards. Malpractice insurance, as well as in-house and outside legal education, are standards inherent in the profession today. Aftercare implementation simply requires a similar level of attention.

Aftercare does represent a challenge in that it is outside of the normal knowledge realm of the funeral director. We now may need to know the distinction between an independent versus a certified social worker. Similarly, the structure and components of different bereavement support groups will soon be a part of the everyday vernacular of the funeral director. Aftercare remains a wonderful opportunity to help others, provided that we know our professional limitations and carefully train our aftercare personnel. It represents a new professional reality and our participation simply continues our evolution as true death care professionals.

THINGS TO REMEMBER

- Formal aftercare is a new area of potential liability for funeral directors with few existing legal guidelines in existence.
- Establish clear aftercare goals for the firm and a written job description for anyone hired to coordinate those goals.
- Funeral directors must firmly define their therapeutic role in aftercare relationship with families. The law may assess our role as to how a reasonable consumer would have perceived it.
- Carefully assess whether your aftercare coordinator is an employee or an independent contractor as liability may hinge on this distinction.
- As an aftercare coordinator represents a non-traditional hiring for our profession, research the qualifications, advanced licenses, training, and liability malpractice insurance available for that person.

REFERENCES

1. *Hartfort Courant,* April 19, 1997.
2. 15 Am. Jur. Proof of Facts 3rd. *Funeral Directors,* Lawyers Cooperative Publishing, Rochester, New York, Section 1 P. 58, 1994.
3. J. Tomain, Contract Compensation in Normal Business Transactions, 46 *University of Pittsburgh Law Review* 867 P. at 903, 1992.
4. S. Rocco, Mental Anguish Litigation: Is a Families' Peace of Mind an Inherent Part of the Funeral Contract? *The Director,* April 1997.
5. *Union Park Memorial Chapel v Kathleen Hutt,* 670 So. 2nd 64 at 66, 1996.
6. *Waller Nally v Grace Community Church,* 763 P. 2nd 948 at 960, 1988.
7. *Waller Nally v Grace Community Church,* 763 P. 2nd 948, 1988.
8. R. Wood, Independent Contractor Torts, *Legal Guide to Independent Contractors,* Wiley Law Publications, New York, 1996.
9. *Tyme Saari v Jongordon Corporation,* 5 Cal. App. 797, 1992.
10. D. Whaley, Paying For the Agony, 26 *Suffolk Law Review* 936 at 957, 1992.
11. W. Freeman, Introduction, *Liability in the Business Professions,* Quorum Books, Westport, Connecticut, 1995.

CHAPTER 4

Aftercare Programs and Ethical Awareness: A First Step in Quality Care to the Bereaved*

Robert Bendiksen

There have been so many changes in care of the dying and the bereaved that one can hardly keep abreast of them. During the past quarter century, for instance, there has been a surge of interest in palliative care for the dying and hospice. More recently, this type of organized support has been extended to aftercare services among business professionals in funeral service. And this is not the only change, as not long ago cremation was not valued by funeral directors; that certainly has changed, locally as well as nationally. So too, has the funeral director's concern for what happens to bereaved family members after the cars leave the cemetery and the accounts are settled.

The term "aftercare" rings true for many bereaved individuals and their care providers. The need is there, but just what is the nature of that need for the funeral director's "aftercare" service? What constitutes aftercare and who should be involved? Is training needed and should programs be accredited? Are there certification opportunities? Little has been done to document answers to these and similar questions raised by funeral directors who, as business professionals, have

*The author acknowledges the assistance of sociology colleagues Dr. O. Duane Weeks and Dr. Robert Fulton in the preparation of an earlier version of this chapter which was presented in a workshop on "Ethics and Aftercare" at the Wisconsin Funeral Directors Association annual meeting in Green Bay, Wisconsin on May 11, 1998.

explored various models of aftercare. This chapter addresses several dimensions of aftercare for the bereaved by examining practical assumptions, general principles, core values, and ethical concerns in aftercare practice.

In this overview, one might wonder where the line is between (legitimate) business concerns for profit and a "calling" (ala Max Weber) to do good for the bereaved, during and long after a funeral or memorial service and the disposal of the body. Is it possible, truthfully, to serve both the personal needs of grieving family members and the organizational interests in search of profit? This is not an easy question to answer, as there are few occupations that make it their "business" to exclusively serve grieving individuals and families. Certainly, the clergy are viewed as a similar caring profession whose "calling" includes responding to the needs of bereaved members of their congregations. However, many parish pastors would not object to someone else conducting funeral services in at least some instances when the person who has died is not in their parish.

This is an important time in the history of funeralization in North America, particularly with the emergence of aftercare and other innovative options in funeral practice. Our task in this chapter is to review some of the practical and ethical applications currently found in aftercare settings by reviewing recent articles in several funeral service journals. Problem solving is nothing new to business professionals, such as those in funeral service. As we review some of these practical ideas, we will explain aftercare, showing how it is practiced in a number of settings, and identifying potential practical and ethical problems in providing the best type of aftercare in a particular setting. Practitioners in funeral service may be assisted, as a result, in developing ethically informed plans for putting aftercare theory into practice in their own communities.

LITERATURE REVIEW

According to Duane Weeks of the New England Institute of Funeral Education at Mt. Ida College in Newton Centre, Massachusetts,[1] approximately 50 percent of funeral service organizations report

---

[1] Personal communication. In preparing this chapter, the author asked Dr. Weeks to survey the literature in several funeral service magazines and journals. He sent me about two dozen articles that were very helpful. Half of these articles were reports on a variety of examples of aftercare services and grief support, while the other half were targeted at how aftercare is structured and why aftercare services are being provided in greater numbers than ever before.

having some type of structured aftercare program even though all funeral service involves aftercare in an informal and non-directed way. Certainly, pre-planning counseling, immediate post-death functions, and follow-up contact have the potential for providing "support" in a time of need.

Eloise Cole, a bereavement specialist for the past twelve years at Grimshaw Mortuaries, Phoenix, Arizona, wrote a short piece on "Grief Relief" in which she recommends that people who wish to establish support groups consider: group style to determine best type of group for your clients/purpose; assurance of confidentiality to foster trust among group members; facilitator skills, such as being a good listener, sharer, leader, communicator, and being aware of needs in the group; group methods that include a variety such as music, art, personal mementos, and speakers to encourage participation; and a subject or topic that might be a general discussion of grief or specific topics such as men and grief, childhood bereavement, or perinatal deaths [1].

Ronald Barrett, a psychologist at Loyola Marymount University in Los Angeles, wrote a very interesting article on "Mourning Lessons: Learning to Cope with Loss Can Start at an Early Age" in which he reminds us of the real world of children today, of the world of developmental differences, of the presence of violence, and of the role of the funeral director [2]. He claims that funerals are important rituals in making grief and mourning acceptable expressions of loss. "In addition to addressing the emotional needs of mourners, funerals provide a valuable occasion for death education, and children learn a great deal about their religious and cultural heritage in the context of grief and mourning" [2, p. 63].

The next article in that same issue of *The Director* was by Paul Steinbach who wrote about the important work in aftercare for children in Detroit by the Children's Center of Wayne County, Michigan, specifically their new project "The Sanctuary: Recovery for Children of Homicide." This program received financial backing from the National Funeral Directors' Association in a project to stem the cycle of violence through effective child grief recovery following the violent death of a family member [3]. Perhaps future reports will include evidence of the success or failure of this Detroit program.

This report was followed by an article on "No Silence about Violence" by Sandra Graves of the University of Louisville in Kentucky and of Accord Aftercare Services [4]. The No Silence about Violence program reaches out to middle and high schools across the country, thanks to a variety of sponsors, including a number of funeral directors. She wrote, "Hats off to the funeral directors who see their role as part of a community resource for positive change" [4, p. 34].

Several other articles featured particular individuals and funeral homes. An October 1996 article in *The Forum* spoke of their success in finding a post-funeral "visitor" to follow up with families they had served. This position was filled by LaGrand Nielsen, an eighty-nine-year-old widower. He was described as a person with ". . . personal experience with the loss of a spouse, . . . astute understanding of fairness and ethics, . . . unrelenting quest to squeeze one more moment of life from each day . . ." [5, p. 27].

Barbara LesStrange writes a column called "Focus on Aftercare" for *The American Funeral Director* in which she interviews a variety of individuals who represent creative programs of aftercare in funeral businesses. Don Carson, of Carson Funeral Home in Maquoketa, Iowa, was quoted as claiming that "The funeral home is where aftercare should start. The funeral industry is changing as a whole right now. With the onset of more cremation societies and third-party casket distributors, the funeral homes need, and are identifying, another vehicle of service to offer to their families. That vehicle is aftercare" [cited in 6, p. 95]. Carson's program is essentially one of mailing support literature to families several times during the year following the death in their family.

Boles Funeral Home and Crematory in Southern Pines, North Carolina is owned and operated by Jamie and Melissa Boles, who also own an ambulance service. Jamie Boles identified families with no church affiliation as having fewer bereavement resources in general. Their aftercare program director is Doris McRae, who counsels individuals and sends monthly grief recovery help letters as well as runs grief seminars for a variety of audiences. Boles said that aftercare has enhanced ". . . the significant increase in our pre-need and at-need . . . because of this new program." He also holds a traditional view that ". . . God has given women the natural ability for compassion. I feel a woman can often better empathize with those who are suffering" [cited in 7, p. 104].

A third interview was with Timothy Lockwood of Lockwood Funeral Homes, Inc. in Lake Geneva, Genoa City, and Twin Lakes, Wisconsin in which Lockwood added his support for aftercare. Existing staff provide a creative approach that includes a "Tree of Memory" during the Christmas season. Names of family members are placed on the tree and a service of remembrance is held. Lockwood, in his interview, reminded all of us that ". . . the most difficult situation to handle is having to deal with our own grief" [cited in 8, p. 64]. Funeral directors who live in small towns often are asked to bury people they know as friends. Seasoned professionals must not fail to recognize their own grief in time of loss.

A fourth interview was with Barbara Fullerton who works in the capacity of an aftercare coordinator for Fullerton Funeral Home, Inc., located in Baldwin, Long Island, New York. She is a certified bereavement facilitator and co-facilitates a bereavement group in her community. The Fullerton Funeral Home was one of the first on Long Island to begin a formal aftercare program. Fullerton was asked to speak to students and public groups as a result of her work in aftercare. She has found that ". . . locating support groups for young widows and widowers, and siblings, both child and adult, has been particularly difficult. I think people, men in particular, are sometimes more comfortable sharing their feelings about their loss with a woman . . ." [cited in 9, p. 43].[2]

THE AFTERCARE CONCEPT: A PARADIGM SHIFT

Vicki Lensing claims that aftercare has many meanings. In spite of this definitional confusion, there is a new organization in funeral service that is called The National Association of Bereavement Support Providers in Funeral Service (NABSPFS) [10]. Their mission statement reads, in part: ". . . that death is a part of the life cycle and grief is a normal response to that loss. We are committed to informing, educating, and supporting individuals, organizations, and communities emphasizing and affirming the importance of ritual closure, funeral service and memorialization of those who have died" [10, p. 24].

John Reynolds wrote a most interesting article in which he builds on the insights of Steven Covey, author of "The Seven Habits of Highly Effective People" (Simon & Schuster, 1988). Covey tells the story of a paradigm shift that has taken place during the past few decades in business practices across the spectrum. Reynolds claims that this societal trend (i.e., paradigm shift) has reached funeral service businesses, especially in breaking down the difference between profit and not-for-profit services. ". . . As funeral service continues to evolve, aftercare has become a flash point for reconciliation of the tension between service versus profit . . ." [11, p. 30]. While health care businesses have become

---

[2] The topic of men and grief is explored in depth in the book *Helping Men Cope with Grief,* edited by Dale Lund (Baywood Publishing Co., Inc., in press). The idea of grieving as a process is clearly explained by Thomas Attig in *How We Grieve: Relearning the World* (Oxford University Press, 1996). A broad perspective on death, grief, and bereavement may be found in *Death and Identity* (Third Edition) edited by Robert Fulton and Robert Bendiksen (The Charles Press, 1994) and *Handbook of Bereavement: Theory, Research, and Intervention* edited by Margaret S. Stroebe, Wolfgang Stroebe, and Robert O. Hansson (Cambridge University Press, 1993).

more corporate, many funeral service businesses have become more community service minded.

Interestingly, during the past two decades, health care organizations have been moving from "not-for-profit" strategies to "for-profit" corporations or sub-corporations. Reynolds says the health/mental health care industry has become more commercialized, funeral service has become more community-service oriented." It seems like everyone is "experiencing organizational and identity crises as they are forced to re-examine their relationships to making money" [11, p. 30]. Reynolds takes a systems perspective when he argues that aftercare should not be valued as simply an advertising idea, rather: "From a quality service perspective, aftercare needs to be integrated, not separated, into other aspects of funeral service" [11, p. 32].

The powerful point that John Reynolds makes is that "The funeral profession's paradigm shift may result in the public and other professionals recognizing funeral directors as helping professionals" [11, p. 32]. Thus, a paradigm shift from thinking of funeral service as a business to that of a helping profession might include: conceptualizing pre-need as a type of advanced directive; explanations of funeral options as death education; funeral homes and mortuaries as community resources; newsletters as a way to facilitate access to care for the bereaved; and intentional approaches to management that take systems seriously.

AFTERCARE GUIDELINES

Duane Weeks and Catherine Johnson claim that " 'Aftercare' is a 1990s expression for old-fashioned neighborly concern. . . . The new focus is on emotional adjustment and meeting the needs of all family members. Because different people respond to death in unique ways, aftercare programs attempt to recognize and respect these differences in order to facilitate healing" [12, p. 12].

Aftercare may vary from simply making a telephone call to clients several weeks after a funeral to show concern on the one hand, to providing grief counseling by a certified grief counselor who is on staff on the other.

Weeks and Johnson provided a systematic outline of what needs to be done if you want to move into the area of aftercare in a responsible way. The first thing to do is determine needs by surveying clientele through a mailed questionnaire or by distributing a brief questionnaire at a grief seminar for the community. Assessing the resources already available also adds very important "data" to your fact-finding phase.

Then, it is very important to establish your goals. Are you most interested in educating the community, informing your clients about support groups, providing emotional support and/or individual counseling, or serving some other goal? To design your program, the extent of aftercare services and the source of materials and resources must be determined.

Weeks and Johnson referred to a lecture by Darcie Sims in which she categorized aftercare into the following: telephone calls, personal visits, cards, newsletters, brochures and literature, library services, community education, memorial services, holiday programs, support groups, referrals, and counseling. The nature of your program will determine the type of individual you will want to take on the mission of aftercare, be it full or part time. The Association of Death Education and Counseling offers a certification program for grief counselors and death educators. While certification does not guarantee quality, it certainly means that the person who is certified has met the criteria of this professional organization.

The most practical suggestions that Weeks and Johnson made are their general guidelines and recommendations on assessing the aftercare program once it is in place. In general, aftercare should seek: *staff cooperation* in the form of enthusiasm and support of all staff members, *flexibility* in the form of dynamic programs rather than static programs that never change, *maintenance of priorities* that separate pre-need sales from aftercare, and *assessment of aftercare program*. The formal assessment should: listen to the *positives* in the form of gratification and peace in the voices of those you serve, measure the numbers in terms of *quality* rather than quantity of people served, and recognize increased business *may or may not be related* to your aftercare program.

Bernadette Zimmermann of O. B. Davis Funeral Homes on Long Island, New York, posited several questions worthy of reflection by funeral directors in determining "How Funeral Directors Can Help":

1. What is feasible for your market? Is your area competitive?
2. If it is competitive, are there services your firm alone could provide?
3. Could your firm's existing services be enhanced?
4. If you have an aftercare program, do you provide services other firms in the area don't?
5. What programs can you implement staying within your existing budget? For instance, could some of your advertising/promotion budget be used for aftercare programs?

6. Will your aftercare programs be for the families your firm serves, or for the entire community?
7. Do you want your firm to be known as a resource for the community, or do you want to supplement existing services for the families you serve?
8. In terms of qualified bereavement specialists and facilities, is your area resource "rich" or "poor"?

Eloise Cole, a bereavement specialist who has been directing aftercare programs for fourteen years at Hansen Mortuaries in Phoenix, Arizona, summarized ABCs of evaluating aftercare as including: Assessment, Budget, and Commitment [14]. Bruce Conley of Conley Funeral Home in Elburn, Illinois claimed, in "Establishing Standards & Credentials Is No Small Task," that minimum criteria for aftercare programs should include: casual post-funeral follow-up, scheduled activities, programmatic educational events, group interactions, and professional bereavement care [15]. Barbara-Hirsch of Vincent Funeral Home in Simsbury, Connecticut, represented current thinking when she claimed that bereavement support groups are an integral component of an aftercare program [16].

Another source for aftercare guidelines is an article by Jennifer Hartenstein-McGraw who is public relations director and continuing care program coordinator at J. J. Hartenstein Mortuary, Inc., in New Freedom and Stewartstown, Pennsylvania. Her guidelines cover a wide range of topics, such as pricing services, involvement in community activities, local public relations, and establishing a presence on the Internet [17].

CORE VALUES AND ETHICAL SENSITIVITY IN AFTERCARE[3]

An *ethic of caring* and an *ethic of responsibility* are only two sets of core values that challenge our thinking, our conscience, and our integrity at times. An *ethic of caring* for people in need helps us to clarify our mission in well-thought-out aftercare programs. An *ethic of*

---

[3] A roster of core values may include a variety of moral virtues (i.e., honesty, respect, responsibility, compassion, self-discipline, perseverance, and giving). The author acknowledges that the source of this particular roster of seven core values is the School District of La Crosse whose core values policy was adopted by the board of education in September 1996. Readers are encouraged to claim these and/or other core values if virtue ethics is of value to them.

responsibility to the bottom-line drives us to calculate costs in time, money, and personnel. Aftercare providers may want to provide aftercare programs and to staff them with skilled bereavement care providers. Being a "good neighbor" is not always easy to do. At times, one's core values and ethical principles may be easy to recognize in a particular situation or dilemma, while at other times values of equal importance may be at odds with each other just because of the circumstances. Consider the following examples.

Funeral directors are in a special relationship with bereaved people, as it is the funeral director who deals with the body of a loved one that has died. In that unique way, a powerful bond may well be established between funeral directors and some bereaved family members. For instance, the courtesy of sending a card on anniversary occasions has resulted in expressions of appreciation, to which many funeral directors might testify. Some funeral directors report that the recipient of such a brief message of caring has led to a comment such as, "You are the only person who has mentioned the name of my son since his funeral!" The aftercare professional, and the funeral service organization to which he or she is accountable, is challenged to attend to details of how to set up an appropriate aftercare program. These details, at times, may include one's core values and a variety of ethical concerns.

Ethical sensitivity is a virtue that must be nurtured individually and organizationally in both at-need and aftercare situations. Organizational goals and objectives are not always easy to accomplish, especially when core values are being challenged (perhaps intentionally or unintentionally). Aftercare professionals must attend to how their own core values are addressed in a particular setting. Perhaps the best way to illustrate the importance of core values and ethical sensitivity is with several illustrative situations.

Please be aware that there are no "correct answers" to the following case examples and accompanying questions. Rather, the reader is invited to reflect on each of the following at-need and aftercare cases by identifying the core values (e.g., honesty, respect, responsibility, compassion, self-discipline, perseverance, and giving) that might apply. In the following case situations, ask yourself (and your aftercare colleagues):

1. What core values or principles are being challenged in this case?
2. How might I/we best respond to any apparent ethical quandary or dilemma present in each human situation?

AFTERCARE EXAMPLES

Case #1

What would you do if, with the best of intentions, you were visiting with a new widow whose husband you recently buried, and she offers to prepay for her own funeral at a time when she is heavy with grief and loss? Would you give a second thought to melding aftercare with pre-need sales knowing that she has yet to sort out her resources and plans?

Case #2

Sometimes funeral homes are made up of two generations of family members, or even several staff members who are very competent and caring. In what ways might you deal with a conflict in values over whether to initiate an aftercare program with a new staff member, even part-time, and the bottom-line needs of the firm? After all, you could afford a new hearse with the money you are going to spend, or are spending, for two to three years of aftercare counseling.

Case #3

A man who is participating in a grief support group sponsored by the funeral home and facilitated by the funeral home aftercare counselor mentioned in the support group that his wrongful death suit from his wife's death has been settled and he now has money from that settlement. The counselor knows that the bill for his wife's services is long overdue. Out of loyalty to his employer, should he break confidentiality and tell the accountant that the man now has money, or should he say nothing and allow his employer to take a big financial loss?

Case #4

The counselor hired by the funeral home on a part-time basis to facilitate their grief support groups is a counselor in private practice. Part of her agreement with the funeral home is that she will receive any referrals for individual counseling that arise from needs of the group members. Is this policy ethical and why?

Case #5

The funeral director who worked with Mrs. Smith on her daughter's funeral sees Mrs. Smith coming into the funeral home at regular intervals for follow-up services, e.g., counseling, participation in support groups, etc. The funeral director, genuinely concerned about Mrs. Smith, asks the counselor how she is doing. Knowing his genuine concern, the counselor shares information about Mrs. Smith regarding her difficult adjustment, lack of family support, and similar information. Is this a breach of confidentiality?

Case #6

The aftercare counselor has been an active member of a small, rural community for several years and knows Mr. Jones from working on several Rotary projects together. Mr. Jones is now seeking counseling following the death of his wife and daughter in an automobile accident. Should the aftercare counselor offer her services or should she refer Mr. Jones to another bereavement counselor?

Case #7

As part of a community education program the funeral home is offering a seminar on explaining the grief process. During the seminar the facilitator asks people to form small groups, assigns a group member to be a facilitator for each group, and has mini-support sessions. In one of the sessions, information is shared that could stigmatize the person who reveals something previously kept private. How might the seminar facilitator have prepared for such an eventuality?

Case #8

The aftercare counselor has been seeing Ms. Brown regularly over the course of the year since her husband's death. Ms. Brown is a competent woman in a professional job who is attractive and articulate, but at her last session she claimed that she no longer needed counseling. Should the counselor ask her for a dinner date and express his personal feelings for her? If so, when and under what circumstances would this be an ethical action?

Clarity in identifying core values and ethical principles is but a first, yet a very important step toward developing a strategy to assess ethical conflicts and practical solutions to problems such as those posed by the above practical case scenarios. Taking this first step may be easy for some yet most challenging for others. In either case, everyone involved is best served when aftercare professionals and their sponsors act on ethical principles of *respect for persons, beneficent care* to people in need, and *fairness and justice* for all concerned individuals and groups.

An *ethic of caring* (e.g., for bereaved individuals and families) and an *ethic of responsibility* (e.g., to the bottom line) may both be practiced in aftercare, but only when the aftercare providers attend to the core values and ethical principles assumed and practiced in particular organizations and settings.[4]

SUMMARY AND CONCLUSION

Clearly, aftercare as a part of funeral service care for the bereaved has grown in the 1990s from a general belief that what the funeral director contributes best in aftercare is a quiet presence. Others hold that providing a leadership role in death education remains the major mission of aftercare. Yet still others would view aftercare as a way to reach out to the half of our population that is not served by churches or synagogues. This chapter has attempted to view aftercare as a practical issue faced by funeral service personnel, as well as a broader issue involving institutional changes in society.

In the final analysis, it is up to each individual and each aftercare program provider to determine the extent and combination of what will work in a particular aftercare program. Attention to core values and ethical principles will build a sense of professionalism that leaders in the funeral industry have increasingly claimed in recent years. The paradigm shifts in health care and funeral service, as noted by Reynolds, are the sociological foundation upon which a quality aftercare program must be grounded. Acknowledgment of value conflicts and ethical dilemmas is but one step toward this important objective.

REFERENCES

1. E. Cole, Grief Relief, *Catholic Cemetery,* p. 14, August 1997.
2. R. Barrett, Mourning Lessons: Learning to Cope with Loss Can Start at an Early Age, *The Director,* pp. 24-26, 63, April 1995.
3. Steinbach, P. The Sanctuary: Detroit Program Meets Children's Needs Following Murder of a Family Member, *The Director,* pp. 28-30, April 1995.

[4] The values of autonomy, beneficence, and justice are central to medical ethics. Similarly, developmental psychology addresses issues of moral development and gender-based ethics. Readers interested in additional reading in ethics may examine the wealth of resources in any biomedical ethics or moral development bibliography. The author's experience in this area includes a year-long sabbatical on medical/ethical decision-making at the end-of-life. See: Robert Bendiksen, "Death, Dying and Bioethics: Current Issues in the USA," pp. 198-212 in *The Unknown Country: Death in Australia, Britain and the USA,* edited by K. Charmaz, G. Howarth, and A. Kellehear (St. Martin's Press, Inc., 1997).

4. S. Graves, No Silence About Violence, *The Director,* pp. 32-34, April 1995.
5. L. Nielsen, An Ageless Inspiration—An Aftercare Idea, *The Forum,* October 1996.
6. B. LesStrange, In the Long Run, Everybody Benefits: An Interview with Don Carson, *The American Funeral Director,* pp. 94-96, August 1997.
7. B. LesStrange, Meeting the Total Needs of Grieving Families is What Our Industry is All About: An Interview with Jamie Boles, *The American Funeral Director,* pp. 98-104, September 1997.
8. B. LesStrange, Our Services Don't End with the Delivery of the Register Book and Flowers, or When the Funeral Bill is Paid: An Interview with Tim Lockwood, *The American Funeral Director,* pp. 60-64, January 1998.
9. B. LesStrange, Funeral Service is Not Just About Arranging for the Service. It is About Helping Families Through a Very Difficult Time: An Interview with Barbara Fullerton, *The American Funeral Director,* pp. 40-44, February 1998.
10. V. Lensing, New Association Strives to Define Aftercare, *The Director,* December 1995.
11. V. Parachin, The Funeral Home: Business, Community Resource or Both? *The Director,* pp. 28-32, 1995.
12. O. Weeks and C. Johnson, Developing a Successful Aftercare Program, *The Director,* pp. 12-18, December 1995.
13. B. Zimmermann, What to Consider for an Aftercare Program, *The American Funeral Director,* pp. 44, 58, May 1996.
14. E. Cole, Evaluating Aftercare, the ABCs: Assessment, Budget, Commitment, *The Director,* pp. 20-22, February 1998.
15. B. Conley, Establishing Standards & Credentials is No Small Task, *The Director,* pp. 20-22, December 1995.
16. B. R. Hirsch, Bereavement Support Groups: An Integral Component of an Aftercare Program, *The Director,* pp. 29-31, February 1998.
17. J. Hartenstein-McGraw, 10 Tips for Promoting Aftercare, *International Cemetery Management,* pp. 22-24, September 1997.

CHAPTER 5

Multicultural Aftercare Issues

LaVone V. Hazell

As the initial support which was evident during the funeral gathering begins to dissipate, and family and friends return to other personal concerns, survivors may need maintenance from outside sources to sustain their strength during the long process of mourning. Americans of all ethnic groups and races tend to gravitate toward their own religious institutions and immediate families for support after a death. From a multicultural point of view, the way a family seeks and embraces aftercare services differs as greatly as the way the family grieves. Oftentimes however, the particularly grievous nature of the death, and/or the lack of a mainstream community whose culture is like their own, has forced many grieving individuals to turn to their funeral directors or mental health professionals for aftercare services. In light of this need, it is essential that funeral directors acquire knowledge regarding the varied aftercare needs of a diverse, multicultural society.

Aftercare, support, information, and encouragement following the funeral became widespread among funeral directors during the early 1980s. Since then, funeral directors have cared for hundreds of thousands of bereaved individuals, by helping them cope with their loss and express their grief, and by assisting them in practical and emotional ways to adapt to a new lifestyle [1]. After the completion of memorial services and burial, funeral directors provide numerous types of aftercare services. Contact in person or by phone, letters and cards to the bereaved, literature (e.g., pamphlets, books, audio-visuals), community educational programs, professional programs (seminars, workshops, guest speakers), and referrals to support groups or professional therapists are all examples of the aftercare services that funeral directors provide for their families.

The experienced aftercare professional will properly assess the needs of the mourner, and those needs may be met using the resources of those in the mental health, law enforcement, and hospital professions. Important issues that an individual providing aftercare must assess are varied:

1. What was the cause of death? Was it from a long-term illness, natural causes, or a sudden death, e.g., due to suicide or homicide?
2. What was the relationship of the survivors to the deceased? Was he or she the head of a household, a child, a sibling, or a parent?
3. What is the religious affiliation, if any, of the survivors? For example, are they Protestant, Catholic, Muslim, Jewish, or Buddhist, or by contrast, are they agnostic or atheist?
4. What is the racial and/or ethnic background of the survivors? Are they Asian Americans, African Americans, Hispanic Americans, Native Americans, Jewish, or European Americans?
5. What is the geographic location of the survivors in relation to that of the deceased—local, national, or international?
6. What is the status of the survivors in their grief process? Is it mild or severe, e.g., are they immobilized?

When these six issues have been explored, the aftercare facilitator will be able to select the appropriate method or technique to assist the survivors to move through their mourning period.

Facilitators who attempt to place an individual in an aftercare program must understand the great variety of reactions to loss. For some grief begins at the time they hear of the loss, while for others it is a delayed experience. In some cases grief goes on for a relatively brief period of time, while in others it seems to go on forever [2]. Depression, sleep disturbance, lack of appetite, anxiety, crying, forgetfulness, to mention a few behaviors, will become exacerbated by a loss and the way the behaviors are manifested differs from one culture to another. Grief is a universal emotion; however, the way an individual grieves can be as unique as a fingerprint as a result of cultural exposure or multicultural specificity. Behaviors which appear somewhat bizarre following a death may actually be quite normal manifestations of grief in a particular culture. In the Jewish culture the rending or tearing of clothing as a sign of grief would be considered a normal behavior. Overt displays of grief, such as pounding the chest and wailing, are normal manifestations of grief in the African and Hispanic cultures. Subdued and stoic grief responses would be normal for Caucasians of Irish descent. An understanding of the diverse grieving patterns from one culture to another is important for the aftercare professional to assess the needs of a variant community.

In spite of their use of valuable aftercare services and additional education, funeral directors can exacerbate an already difficult experience if they lack knowledge of the customs of the specific cultural group to which the grieving family belongs. Some examples of groups which accept or would avoid aftercare, and their specific cultural mourning customs, are described in Tables 1 and 2.

When assessing the needs of a family, the funeral director or other facilitators must be able to focus on each family's specific customs. A death in my own neighborhood illustrates the point with regard to the African-American community.

AFRICAN AMERICANS

In 1997, a young man was randomly shot by a sniper who fired a gun into a crowd from the terrace of a building. The tragedy left a family in crisis, a community outraged, and a funeral director immediately cognizant that there would be extensive bereavement aid required after the funeral: the loosely-tied community relationships would tighten for a brief period and then relax again as the terrible memories were submerged. The shooting took place in a racially-mixed, inner-city community. The boy's family was African American. The sixteen year old who died was a positive sports figure, an "exemplary student," who had no involvement in any criminal activity.

The appropriate aftercare referral, after the six issues described on page 58 were determined, required the help of the City's Victim Services Division and the Parents of Murdered Children and Other Survivors. Victim Services provides immediate assistance to families when it is determined that a homicide involving an innocent victim has occurred. This includes funeral compensation in most major cities throughout the United States. Parents of Murdered Children is an organization which offers specifically-oriented support groups, focusing on a sudden loss. A family would not ordinarily be aware that such services are available, but it is the responsibility of every funeral director to be knowledgeable about the many self-help organizations that exist in order to make helpful referrals.

In African-American inner-city communities, the senseless deaths due to violence have tragically increased, leaving the funeral director with the task of linking his or her professional services with those of

Table 1. Cultural Mourning Customs

Culture	African American	Asian American	Hispanic American	Native American	Jewish American	European American
Mourning Time:	6 mos.	Perpetual	1 year	4 days + age deceased	7 days + 1 year	3 days + 1-3 yrs.
Mourning Colors:	White	White	Black	Red/Black	Black	Black
Use of Candles	Yes	Yes	Yes	Yes	Yes	No
Body Preparation	Freezing Wrapping	Washing Wrapping	Embalming Dressing	Washing Dressing	Washing Shrouding	Embalming Burial
Sacrificial Offerings to the Spirit of the Deceased	Animals, food, money	Food, paper, gifts, money	Religious artifacts	Animals, food	Memorial gifts	Memorial & mass cards

Note: The information contained in this table represents data on urban American families who have had to relinquish many of their traditions to adapt to an increasingly secular society [4].

Table 2. Ethnic Variations Influencing Aftercare

Ethnic Background	Death Attitude	Death Ritual	Religious Focus	Funeral Rite	Aftercare
African American	Denying, embraced	Social function	Afterlife	Service, burial	Religious support
Asian American	Accepting	Social function	External existence	Service, cremation	Ancestral daily offerings
Latin American	Accepting, feared	Social function	Ancestral, spiritual	Mass, burial	Religious support
Native American	Accepting, cyclical nature	Social function	Spiritual	Chanting, cremation	Support—elders/ancestral
Jewish American	Accepting	Social function	Death final	Service, burial	Bereavement—religious support
European American	Denying, feared	Social function	Afterlife	Service, burial	Bereavement support varies

Eastern culture: Death accepting

Western culture: Death denying

Note: The information contained in this table represents data on urban American families who have had to relinquish many of their traditions to adapt to an increasingly secular society [4].

many other support groups. Unlike their rural counterparts, who generally have an intimate relationship with the family and the community at large, the urban funeral director is faced with hundreds of tragic deaths in families that often have very little or no prior relationship with their community funeral firm. African-American families traditionally shun any perceived interference from an "outsider," which further complicates the director's role. This distrust and resulting alienation, in addition to the intrusion of the police, lawyers, and other investigators seeking information and evidence regarding violent deaths, greatly challenges the funeral director's role as an aftercare facilitator. Rapport and trust must, therefore, be formed in a very short period of time. African-American funeral directors must exercise extreme sensitivity when dealing with families in this delicate situation or they will also be perceived as a part of the intrusive "establishment." In the tradition of their West African roots, African Americans place their trust in their own community and rely on their elders for direction. The most successful approach to assist families seeking aftercare services is to inform them that such help is available, while avoiding involvement in the process. This information should be shared at the grave site or through a follow-up phone call. There has also been a marked increase in bereavement ministries within African-American churches, which many grieving families choose when seeking help.

Funeral directors are also providing aftercare services in the form of commemorative gatherings for all the families they have served, either at the end of the year or during holiday seasons. The social network within the community is strengthened and the director has an additional opportunity to offer auxiliary support to the family. Many funeral directors also offer seminars and workshops in the community in educational institutions, law enforcement agencies, and at religious facilities and senior citizens' centers. One of the primary examples of the service to the seniors in community centers is Funeral Pre-Planning, preparing a Living Will and a Health Care Proxy, and explaining Estates and Wills. Funeral directors also conduct memorial services for the clergy, especially during the holiday season.

In spite of the tradition of handling mourning issues within the African-American family by the elders, major changes have taken place in the African-American community in the past ten years. For example, within the Muslim community, anticipatory grief and aftercare issues were originally addressed strictly within the sect. However, the New York Memorial Sloan-Kettering Hospital, a major cancer facility, hired the first Muslim *Imam* (Muslim religious leader) to assist Muslim patients and the survivors of cancer. This alliance opened the door for additional significant partnerships. Members of the leadership in the Muslim community are requesting workshops from funeral directors as well as grief counselors. During these workshops, they embrace the techniques to help them understand how they can assist the sect's survivors.

In the African-American community the religious leaders and the church play a major role in funeral customs and in the entire dying process. Death is a celebration of life, as clearly portrayed in New Orleans where a jazz band precedes the horse-drawn hearse or in New York where a band will accompany the rhythmic music of a full gospel choir during the funeral. However, when the services are completed and time cements the reality of the loss, many African Americans are faced with the difficult task of moving forward as they readjust their lives. It is during this period when aftercare services become crucial. Other groups, such as Asian Americans, generally remain very closed as they provide daily offerings to their dead at a prepared altar. They privately move through their grief within their own culture and rarely seek the assistance of support groups or other bereavement professionals.

ASIAN AMERICANS

As is often the case with African Americans, aftercare services are rarely sought out in many Asian communities; the Chinese-American community is typical in this regard. Traditional Asian customs dictate that funeral rituals and follow-up remain kinship-oriented. Each family member has a culturally-assigned role. Chinese death beliefs and practices in particular are based on a combination of Buddhist, Confucian, and Taoist principles. For the Buddhist, death marks the entrance in Nirvana or a new and better life. Ancestral worship, where the living owe everything to their departed ancestors, is the basis of Confucianism belief. As part of the world of the Taoist principle, the departed has specific actions by way of the soul and the spirit which affect the living. There is an intermingling of these principles in all three religious: Buddhism, Confucianism, and Taoism.

The death rituals of the Chinese-American mourner may last for years after the burial to insure the welfare of the deceased soul in the afterlife and the connection of the deceased with the family's ancestors. *Feng-shui,* or the fortuitous placement of architecture in internal spaces, is used by a geomancer to locate an appropriate place for the grave. The grave is then attended at least once a year, during the Ching Ming Festival in the Spring, when food, paper clothing, and paper money are brought to the grave and burned for the continual welfare of the soul. Many traditional Chinese will also create an altar (*butsudan*) in the home to honor the dead ancestor or set up portraits in a local temple to which prayers can be offered [3].

While such common religious functions help explain why in New York City the Chinese do not seek out aftercare services, some exceptions exist. For example, in 1998 a seventeen-year-old Chinese-American female was struck by a falling brick from a school building that was being renovated. Her grandparents did not attend the funeral because of cultural beliefs regarding the inversion of what is considered the "normal" cycle of life: the abnormal aspect of this trauma was that the child "died out of turn" with the parent. Given the implication that the basic function of the parent is to preserve the family and protect the child, there is an implicit expectation that the grandparents and parents will die before the child. Many cultures believe in the natural order of the life cycle, so that when a child dies before a parent or grandparent the sequence is disrupted.

LATIN AMERICANS

Latin Americans will turn to the church for solace after a death. An illustration is provided in the recent death of Junior Hernandez, a popular Latin-American radio show host of Puerto Rican descent. His popularity was evidenced by the outpouring of thousands of fans who revered his talent, and police estimated that as many as 12,000 people had filed by his fourteen-karat gold-plated casket. As frequently done in the Puerto Rican community, his casket was flown back to the island for burial.

Latin Americans celebrate the life of the deceased, consistent with their African-American counterparts. Generally, Latin Americans grieve openly and release their emotional pain without reservation. Crying and wailing are considered healthy experiences which are shared by the family, friends, and the community at large; children are included at all levels of the funeral ritual. Americans of European and Asian descents generally assume a more covert or quiet posture, which should not suggest that they do not also suffer the same intense pain of grief as other ethnic groups. Coping with a sudden death in the Hispanic culture does require some restrictions on the males in the family, however. What Latin-American men consider to be an appropriate image depends on a presentation of strength and emotional imperturbability, so their grieving often must be accomplished in private.

There is a specific delineation of roles following a death. The women prepare for the wake (which usually takes place over 2 days), and the men greet the guests and support the women. The extended family members and friends assist wherever they are needed. Distribution of death and dying literature which has been translated into the Spanish language is most beneficial as an introduction to aftercare services in this community, but it is the women who are most likely to or willing to take advantage of these services.

CULTURAL DIFFERENCES:
NATIVE AMERICANS

The roles of each participant in the rituals of Native Americans are very well-defined. Survivors are assisted with all duties, including bathing and dressing, which allows them the necessary time to grieve [5]. Unlike many other groups, Native Americans embrace death and life thereafter as a part of a cycle of nature. Rituals are specified for each part of the cycle, and the nature of these ceremonies are related to the tribe or nation to which the primary mourner belongs. Aftercare issues are addressed within the family, as opposed to the family reaching out for help to exterior support agencies. Viewing life as a circle, the fundamental philosophy of reciprocity—giving and taking mutually— is very important to the understanding of the Native American [6]. In traditional families, comprehension of and cooperation with the natural forces are a way of life. The focus is primarily on the afterlife as opposed to aftercare. Today, however, aftercare issues are addressed primarily within each tribal nation, unless one of its members seeks the education and skills and offers these services to the kinship. Aftercare and other forms of grief assistance can be practiced when the elders give their approval.

JEWISH AMERICANS

The Jewish mourner in contemporary American society also has specific rituals after a death has occurred. Traditionally, there are five stages of mourning which offer comforting guidance during acute grief. The first stage, called *aninut,* is the period between the death and the burial. With despair most intense at this time, all religious requirements for the mourner are suspended. The second stage, during the three days following the burial, is devoted primarily to lamentation and weeping in private. *Shiva* is the third stage—a period of seven days following the burial when the mourner accepts the condolences of family and friends in the home, and conducts prayer services. By contrast, in contemporary Jewish practice, *shiva* begins right after the burial, with the duty incumbent on close relatives and friends to bring food to the mourners, so they will not have to be distracted with the life-giving tasks of preparing meals. Not surprisingly, the period of lamentation of the second traditional stage was collapsed into one with *shiva*, since Jewish custom requires that burial should occur as close to twenty-four hours after the death as possible.

During the fourth stage, *sheloshim*, the mourner returns to normal social relations within the community, and tries to return to work. The final stage lasts for a twelve-month period, when the mourner returns to his or her customary functions. The observant Jew says the prayer for the dead, the *kaddish*, weekly at the synagogue. The day of death is celebrated annually on the *yahrzeit*, or anniversary date, when a memorial candle is lit in the home and burns all night. The grave site is, at minimum, visited during the period of the High Holy Days in the Fall. As a result of increased contemporary cultural approval of mental therapy, Jews increasingly welcome and seek out aftercare services when they feel it is appropriate, but primarily from co-religionists [7], and preferably within their own ethnic group. During the last stage, aftercare may become a necessity when family members find that daily living patterns are disrupted or seem stagnant as a result of intense, chronic grief. The realization that aftercare is needed may emerge in a few or in several months after the death of a loved one when support of family and friends begins to disappear.

CULTURAL DIFFERENCES: CAUCASIAN AMERICANS

Caucasian Americans of European descent comprise a not-so-well-defined "melting pot" of immigrants from all over the world who have had considerable intermixing among various cultures. As a result, their mourning practices encompass the greatest variety over all other migrant groups. With an attitude of denial toward death, white Americans have traditionally been the trained professionals in the bereavement area. An increased awareness of death and dying issues which surfaced during the 1950s led to the development of an interdisciplinary subject—Thanatology. The benchmark for systematizing the study of death and dying came in 1956, in the book "The Meaning of Death" by Herman Feifel [8]. Robert L. Fulton initiated the first regular program in death education at the University of Minnesota in 1963. He also discussed the double-edged sword that confronts the funeral director who must blunt as well as sharpen the reality of death. The funeral industry came under attack with Jessica Mitford's scathing critique in her book "The American Way of Death" [9]. Many other pioneers made major contributions to confront the subject of death. As a result of their efforts in developing the foundation for the study of the field of death and dying, other cultural groups were able to share their specific death rituals. Training programs and education curricula brought more sensitivity to the taboo subject of death. Aftercare groups became a part of the death and dying experience. Heart disease and cancer were, and still remain, the leading causes of death, requiring not only aftercare assistance but pre-need service as well. As a result of being diagnosed with a terminal illness and even being given a time limit to an imminent death, grief became a major issue for surviving family members well in advance of the actual event. Groups began forming which addressed the anticipatory needs of families. Sherwin B. Nuland, in his book "How We Die," describes what pre-need and aftercare is to dying individuals and to the survivors: To summarize, he states that the listening ear of merely two people can serve to soften the pain of grief [10]. When each family understands the severity of the assault of a life-threatening illness and the threat of death on the patient and his or her supporters, reaching out for help becomes a priority. Help in any form provides periods of respite as opposed to releasing the family from the misery and the draining effects of losing a loved one. A listening ear and sharing heart can abate the universal feelings of the survivor's anger and frustration. "The greatest dignity to be found in death is the dignity of life that preceded it. This is a form of hope we can all achieve and it is the most abiding of all. Hope resides in the meaning of what our lives have been" [10, p. 242].

With increased sensitivity and awareness of the need to extend aftercare to survivors, professionals have improved their knowledge and skills to relate most appropriately to the various populations they serve. The skills needed to relate to the different modalities whose underpinnings lie in the traditions that are exhibited by minority groups are being studied and improved so that we all can truly state that we are fulfilling the aftercare needs of all our neighbors.

SUPPORT AND REFERRAL RESOURCES

It is critical that, as aftercare professionals, we correctly assess the needs of our families. In assessing these needs, it is important to understand our own grief issues to avoid becoming "surrogate grievers" or becoming too involved in our families' grief. Family members expect aftercare professionals to be understanding, impartial, objective, and knowledgeable when they need direction about the resources that are available to sustain them through their mourning period. To this end, the aftercare professional should research available bereavement referral sources within the geographic areas of the families that they serve. It is also incumbent upon the funeral director and other after-care providers to research the cultural specificity of their families in order to maximize the available resources they can offer to adequately meet their needs. Aftercare professionals must additionally strive to impartially assess each family according to its cultural background, ethnicity, and tradition. Some of the referral agencies that have assisted New York funeral firms in aftercare are listed below.

1. Training Institute for Mental Health Practitioners
   40 E. 30th Street
   New York, NY 10016
   (212) 889-0870

   General mental health services provided by psychiatrists, psychologists, and social workers, on a sliding scale.

2. Calvary Hospital
   1740 Eastchester Road
   Bronx, NY 10461
   (718) 863-6900

   Bereavement Services offered for survivors of loss due to cancer and general grief issues. Six week sessions. No fee attached to services.

3. The Samaritans (National)
   P.O. Box 1259
   Madison Square Station
   New York, NY 10159
   (212) 673-3000

   Provides services for suicide prevention with a twenty-four-hour hotline. Support groups are designed for people who have also lost friends or family to suicide. No fee for these services.

4. LaGuardia Hospital
   102-01 66th Street
   Forest Hills, NY 11375
   (718) 830-4517

   Support services for general bereavement with referral resources available for other mild or chronic medical and psychological issues. Fee may be attached to special services.

5. Crime Victims Board
   270 Broadway, Room 200
   New York, NY 10007
   (212) 417-5160

   Financial compensation for individuals who are the victims of a crime. Support advocacy for families and victims. No fee for services provided.

6. Long Island Jewish Hospital
   270-05 76th Avenue
   New Hyde Park, NY 11040
   (718) 470-7000

   General support groups provided in bereavement and other issues. Suicide Van available for emergency services. No fees attached to services, unless hospitalization is required.

7. AIDS Support Groups
   Women's Center
   3320 Rochambeau Avenue
   Bronx, NY 10467
   (718) 920-4280

   Individuals, couples, group, and family counseling/therapy for those who have survived a loss from AIDS and those who are diagnosed HIV positive. Appointment necessary. No fee for services.

8. Real for Reality
   John F. Kennedy High School
   Marble Hill
   Bronx, NY 10467
   (718) 842-0200

   Support groups for students who have experienced the death of a parent or friend. No fee for support group.

9. Madeline Borg Community Services
   120 West 57th Street
   New York, NY 10019
   (212) 582-9100

   Provides bereavement groups for parents who have lost children. No fee.

10. Mothers Against Drunk Driving (MADD) (National)
    127 East 27th Street
    Brooklyn, NY 11210
    (718) 784-8469

    Support, guidance, and information available for loved ones who were injured or killed in alcohol-related automobile crashes. Legal referrals also offered. No fee for services.

11. I//WD Internet World Development
    www.thinkingofyou.com
    3070 Lawson Boulevard
    Oceanside, NY 11572
    1-888-839-2001

    Development and implementation of a personal World Wide Web page, prepared with information provided by members of the family, consisting of information, photographs, statements from the survivors, etc. The Web page may act as a life review of the deceased. A guest book is provided for friends and colleagues to e-mail condolences to the family.

As funeral directors, we assume many roles: advisors, community leaders, and administrators for our grieving families. Our services are indispensable, not only when a death occurs but long after the final rites are administered at the burial. Our responsibilities have increased over the past two decades as the families in our communities become more diverse. Death anxiety is an overwhelming emotion for most people and it is the funeral director who must help defray some of their fears. We are the caretakers of the dead as well as the living, which requires additional knowledge when the survivors need to move past the paralysis of their fear and grief.

Funeral directors are honorable professionals dedicated to the dignity of humankind in both life and death. Final rites, tributes, and the hallowed dignity of the funeral serve to honor a past life. Memorialization of the dead acknowledges the fact that a life has been lived and has now ended. Opportunities to remember and honor the dead are implemented throughout our profession. We must, therefore, always respect our families' time-honored traditions while giving enlightened and competent guidance and support to the bereaved [11].

REFERENCES

1. National Funeral Directors Association (NFDA), *Funeral Profession Helps the Living Cope,* 1 SAIC Internet Solutions, 1997.
2. W. J. Worden, *Grief Counseling & Grief Therapy,* Springer, New York, pp. 31-32, 1991.
3. R. Halporn, *Gods, Ghosts, and Ancestors: The Ching Ming Festival in America,* Center for Thanatology Research, Brooklyn, 1996.
4. L. V. V. Hazell, *Multicultural Perspectives of Death and Dying. Series of Four Workshops, Program Booklet 3,* Visiting Nurse Association of Brooklyn, Brooklyn, 1996. (The order in which racial/ethnic groups are listed reflects the author's experience with the types of services.)
5. T. A. Rando, *Grief, Dying and Death. Clinical Intervention for Caregivers,* Research Press, Champaign, 1984.
6. T. Tafoya, *The Widow as Butterfly,* presentation at the Conference of the Association for Death Education and Counseling, Portland, Oregon, 1994.
7. M. Lamm, *The Jewish Way of Death and Mourning,* K'tav Publishing, New York, 1983.
8. H. Feifel, *The Meaning of Death,* McGraw-Hill, New York, 1959.
9. J. Mitford, *The American Way of Death,* Simon & Schuster, New York, pp. 16-20, 1963.
10. S. B. Nuland, *How We Die. Reflections on Life's Final Chapter,* Vintage Books, New York, pp. 167-168, 242, 1995.
11. T. W. Van Beck, *Winning Ways. The Funeral Profession's Guide to Human Relations,* Appleton & Lange, Connecticut, pp. 211-214, 1999.

CHAPTER 6

Aftercare is Old Fashioned Caring

Darcie D. Sims
Sherry L. Williams

"Once I lived the American Dream. And with the birth of our son, our family was to have been complete . . . whole . . . two kids so no one would have to fight over a window in the back seat. Two kids because I had a lot of recipes that served four. We had two children because we couldn't figure out how to have the 1.6 which is the national average. We were the American Dream, at least for a little while." "And then, as it sometimes happens, it all ended. We learned you couldn't paint a rainbow on the wall and expect it to stay. The dream came to pieces and we were shattered. No longer the American Dream, we became the American Nightmare. We were bereaved."

"The world seemed so dark and silent. No longer did life seem worth living. The sun grew cold and the music died. Joy had been buried one afternoon in late fall and winter cam to reside in our house. We had entered a world we knew nothing about. We needed help. We needed understanding. We needed someone who could speak OUR LAN-GUAGE, the language of GRIEF."

"We discovered we were grieving, not just the death of our child, but the loss of close friendships, self-esteem and self-identity as well. We were SO alone! Left untouched by those around us who must have been afraid too. Perhaps death was catching or maybe no one knew what to say. I didn't know what to hear! But, as the months passed, it only grew darker and we began to wonder if we would ever know peace, joy, or love again."

> If I could just see HOPE. If I knew what to look for or how to act or how to feel . . . if I knew where the end was, I might find the beginning. If only the pain would stop . . . [1, p. 8].

And so you come, gently with quiet step, the aftercare provider, wanting to ease the pain wanting to help. . . .

What words are there that will bring comfort to the broken places within a soul? What songs can you sing that will hear the hurt? What threads can you weave that will hold me in my sorrow? How can you speak of hope in the midst of despair?

You, the aftercare provider, come with good intentions, a pocketful of skills and an outstretched hand. You define yourself as a caregiver, taking care and giving care to those who are hurting, sick, injured, dying, lost in grief, and to those who are struggling to find themselves. You come because you care . . . because you can do no less.

But caring is hard and who are you who dares to speak of hope in a world gone dark with despair? Why do you care? Why would a funeral home, a hospice, anyone, care about the survivor? Why would anyone risk caring about someone so devastated by the death of someone they love? What is aftercare and who are the aftercare providers?

AFTERCARE:
OLD-FASHIONED CARING

Aftercare is a recently defined profession, yet it has always existed. In every culture, in every civilization, in every tribe, band, camp, or group of people, there are always some who seem to be able to reach out beyond their own personal definitions and extend a hand of caring to others in need. Whether that was defined as a profession or was simply expected or at least acknowledged in a society, caring for others has always existed. But now we have created a profession, complete with titles, expectations, job descriptions, performance ratings, and potential credentialing procedures. We have become very sophisticated about caring as a profession and the professional care provider is appearing in a wide variety of settings.

From hospices to funeral homes and in all directions, the profession is growing, held in bounds only by the limits of available funding. It is an honorable and noble profession, but one filled with controversies and misunderstandings. Clear definitions for care providing have not yet been established that would allow the public to understand the role of care provider.

When we add the dimension of AFTER to the word CARE, it becomes ever more complex. After what? When does aftercare begin? After diagnosis? After death? After all else fails?

Whether aftercare occurs in a hospice, community-, or church-based program or is sponsored by a funeral home, there are some considerations which must be addressed before any care is delivered or received. Having a clear purpose and intent and a list of clearly stated expectations is essential for the success of any aftercare program. Without well thought out and clearly stated expectations, aftercare programs can dilute themselves and fail to support the bereaved and those who serve them. Poorly defined expectations are perhaps some of the greatest sources of program and personal stress in the world of aftercare.

THE FUNERAL DIRECTOR AS THE AFTERCARE PROVIDER

The funeral industry is part of the service system of a community. You are part of the backdrop of a community, often not really noticed until one needs your services, but depended upon to always "BE THERE" whenever you are needed.

We don't think much about the funeral home until it is time to visit one, whether for a pre-need visit or to pay our last respects. The funeral home is part of a community's invisible safety net, necessary, needed, but often not noticed.

The world is asking you for help, to be supported, to be rescued, to be healed of this terrible pain of grief. And many times, the world is impatient with the speed of healing and so demands of you the magic potion. It may seem as though everyone believes you have the answers and the magic wand, which will restore joy, peace, love, and hope to all. It is a BIG request and an even greater expectation. It is the hope of all who knock on your door . . . to be relieved of pain and sorrow and grief.

Funeral directors are seen as specialists in handling the details of death. It becomes natural for us to return to the funeral director for continued care and guidance (especially as families become scattered) because we have already established a caring relationship during a time of crisis and change.

The funeral home is also part of the mental health delivery system within a community and as such, has the opportunity to help or hinder the bereaved's journey through the valley of the shadow. Traditionally, a funeral home has been considered to be a place of sadness and grief, a place to come to say good-bye. It has been a gathering place where families and friends come together to support each other and to pay their respects to the deceased.

But can the funeral home be something more? It is already a social place. Many times the only reason family and friends get together is for a funeral or perhaps for a wedding. So the funeral home becomes a place to renew friendships and family ties and to console each other as well as a place to receive support.

If funerals are for the living, it seems reasonable to expect the funeral director to be able to help the survivor after the funeral, too. Caring does not stop at the grave.

We are not in the business of fixing broken toys. We do not have the answers or the magic potions. We can help more with the panic rather than the pain. It is standing beside someone in times of adversity, not walking through the fire for them. In that moment of being there, when someone cries out in pain, in fear, in grief, you become a symbol of hope. Caring is the first part of hope.

BUILDING A SENSE OF HOPE

How do you build a sense of hope? How do you build continued services and how do you set up an aftercare program? It would be easy if there could be a "cookie cutter" approach to the whole concept of aftercare. But no one person, death experience, community, or funeral home is the same as another. So, no one aftercare program will work for everyone.

As individuals, we all have different wants and needs. These needs and wants become more defined when someone we love dies. There are many variables that affect grief, such as: the relationship to the deceased, the circumstances of the death, our age and previous experiences with death, our support systems, our religious beliefs and our emotional and psychological makeup. These variables not only affect the grieving process, but also can dictate the types of aftercare services needed.

Our communities are different as well. Some are large, some small. Some have extensive grief support services available while others have few or no resources at all. Some communities are family and neighbor oriented, while others are very metropolitan and rather impersonal and detached. Each community will have different needs that must be filled by an effective aftercare program.

Wanting to help is an effective motivator for designing an aftercare program, but it will require more than a "good heart" in order to provide effective services to the grieving. What are your expectations for both your aftercare program and for yourself? Are you trying to eliminate pain? Are you trying to make "it" all right? Are you trying to make it easier? Or are you trying to make it less lonely, less frightening? Are you trying to help with the panic instead of the pain? Are you trying to restore control or are you trying to support others?

PLANNING

A good aftercare program begins with planning. You must first define your goals and evaluate your market. Are you in a very competitive market? Do you need more public relations? Do you want to enhance the service you already provide? Do you want to meet needs that aren't being met elsewhere in your community? What do you want your firm's image to be, not only with your families, but within your community as well? Is follow-up something that takes on a personal meaning for you? In other words, you have to decide what you want to accomplish with an aftercare program BEFORE you can start one. It is difficult to hit the bulls-eye unless you can see the target.

In addition to looking at your own personal goals and objectives, your business goals, your mission statement, and your community, you have to look at what resources already exist in the community. You must be budget conscious, so it is always a good idea to find out what resources are already available so you can network with existing services. This will help with your planning and it will also build good will with other community agencies and support services.

Is there a local hospice that provides some type of follow-up program for their families? If you helped sponsor or support their bereavement program, would they be able to accommodate others who were not hospice clients into their current bereavement support services? Help could be as simple as supplying the refreshments or as expansive as providing printing or mailing services or helping co-sponsor a community program or speaker.

Is there a local bereavement coalition of all grief support services in your community? If not, think about starting one as part of your aftercare contribution. Networking is a powerful way to assure the bereaved in your community do not fall through the service cracks and also increases the public's awareness of the extent of your services.

Contact the local clergy about support groups and activities that they might sponsor. YMCAs and YWCAs often have educational or awareness classes on coping skills that might be a resource for your families.

Then, you must take into account your own funeral home and your funeral home staffing. What is your business philosophy and work ethic? Your budget may be very limited or you might be focusing on growth and expansion. Your goals and objectives will impact what you want to do in terms of aftercare. What you want to do personally and how much you are willing to invest in terms of budget and employee time will influence the scope of your aftercare program. The willingness and enthusiasm of your staff to be supportive of an aftercare program will also influence the success of any program.

There are also a number of other factors to consider when planning an aftercare program:

> What are the number of locations and geographical boundaries of your service area?
>
> What is the average age, typical religion, and general ethnic background of your market area?
>
> Are you in a stable community or a very mobile, "bedroom" community?
>
> Is your funeral home perceived to serve a specific religious group?

These issues can greatly influence the types of services you provide. For instance, you will probably not want to include home visits as a part of your aftercare program plan if you are in a rural setting because much of your time would be spent in a car. Also, you want to make sure any information you use will fit the cultural, ethnic, and religious philosophy of the recipients.

You might not want to do a "Children's Grief" program in a retirement community or a "Planning for Retirement" program in a young neighborhood. And if you appear to be connected with a specific religious group, you might want to reach the other denominations in your area and offer programs and resources that can change that perception.

Begin to determine the scope of your aftercare program. Are you trying to develop an ongoing relationship with the family or do you want your aftercare program to be a "short or single contact only" program? How do you relate to your families now? Do you contact them following a death to supply information, education, and support? What kind of information do you supply now? Do you send informational brochures about the grieving process or do you make a personal call or visit? If you make a visit, how long do you stay? Is this an "educational" or "informative" visit or do you consider this to be a "support" visit, that may last several hours if the family wishes to talk?

Are you available for further contact, either by phone or personal visit? Can a family member contact you for continued information and support or do you help the family make contact with other local informational and support programs? Who makes the follow-up call or contact? You probably are already providing an aftercare program if you do any of the above mentioned items. But what else can you do?

A good aftercare program can be as simple as turning that courtesy call after the funeral into an information-sharing visit by sharing a few brochures with the family or perhaps telling them about additional resources. There is a wide span of services that can be provided. They include, but are not limited to:

- Library resources (books, magazines, brochures, video, and audio tapes). Either donate grief resources to your local library or start a small lending library at the funeral home.
- Newsletters
- Community education programs
- Handling the Holidays programs
- Community memorial program
- Grief support materials for a support group
- Grief resource directory of available community services
- Speakers' bureau
- Professional seminars on grief and bereavement
- Support groups

The list is only limited by your budget, commitment, and imagination.

If you run or are considering running support groups as part of your aftercare program, what kind of groups are effective? There are "open ended" groups with unlimited visits, based on a "drop in" type membership. There are time-limited groups, with a "closed membership," with specific agendas and "lesson plans" for each meeting. Or a support program can be a combination of these two very diverse kinds of groups.

Do you want to offer educational classes or study groups or monthly meetings where topics of the group's choosing are the focus? Groups can be educational focused or personal exploration themed.

Not all aftercare programs have a support group component to them, but all should have both educational and informational elements. Many programs simply are not able to provide a personal support program, but information and education may also be therapeutic [2]. It is extremely important, however, to have clearly defined boundaries and outcome expectations of the program.

What is your level of education and training? Are you an academically trained therapist or a "life trained" caring person? Does your aftercare program expect to provide therapy for its participants or is participation in the program therapeutic? Do you expect to provide therapy? The word counseling is still so controversial that it is not used here.

Accord Grief Management Services, in Louisville, Kentucky, suggests that funeral directors not open mental health clinics and provide counseling for the bereaved [2]. Do not confuse the role of an aftercare provider with the role of a therapist or "counselor." Giving information, education, and support are different than providing actual therapy. The scope of most, if not all, aftercare programs provided by funeral service should be the provision of information, education, and support.

Most funeral directors are not licensed counselors. Although you do, indeed, give counsel, it is not therapy. It is not necessary to provide therapeutic intervention or counseling services. Grief, as well as other types of stress, may intensify emotions and responses, but it is not a mental illness or an automatic reason for therapeutic intervention. If a family member requires such support, it should be provided by a licensed therapist in a clinical setting. These services are most likely to be available through a family's medical benefits package.

To the consumer, the term "counselor" implies that you are a professional therapist, trained to provide therapy. While any contact with a support person is therapeutic in nature, it is not therapeutic in the clinical sense.

Be extremely cautious about using the word "counselor," even if you do choose to employ a licensed therapist as an aftercare coordinator. The role of the aftercare coordinator should NOT be a clinically therapeutic one, as that implies liability as to services rendered. In many states there are licensing laws that govern professionals or practitioners who hold at least a master's degree in social work, psychology, expressive therapy, or guidance and counseling. A degree and license entitle them to use the term "counselor" or "therapist." Even if you live in a state with no licensure for counselors, there may be a professional counselor organization with some form of credentialing, certification, and/or registration approving practice. And even if the person you hire is, indeed, a fully credentialed therapist, remember the scope of your aftercare program should probably not be therapeutic intervention.

Many funeral directors shy away from providing aftercare services or abandon them because they fear liability issues. It is often support group and "counselor" terminology issues that create the misunderstandings about liability.

To be liable in a civil action, there are standards of care that are usually breached. The general rule of thumb is whether or not the action of the person was reasonable under the circumstances. Would the reasonable funeral director (aftercare provider, etc.), under like or similar circumstances, behave in a similar fashion [3]? In other words, what would your colleagues have done under the same set of circumstances? Would the funeral director have answered the questions to the best of his/her knowledge and ability? Would he/she have supplied a brochure or told a family about a support group or recommended a book?

Define the limits of your aftercare program. Be specific. List the services you will provide, such as help with insurance and paper work, telephone calls, a resource library, or listing of local support groups. This clearly tells people not only what you are doing for them, but what you are not doing for them as well.

Written materials given to families impart information for which the publisher or writer must assume liability. However, the publisher is not responsible for any promises about what the written material will do for the grieving person. If you or one of your employees tells a family that they will have specific outcomes from reading their booklet, article, brochure, etc., then you are going beyond the scope of the materials. You are, in essence, misrepresenting the content of the materials by giving a psychological prescription and prognosis.

A more effective (and safe!) way is to let families know that others have found certain information to be helpful and that they may too. In this way, you are offering them the choice to decide on their own whether the information will be useful for them. The difference is in providing information and advice giving, predicting outcomes or making promises.

BUDGETING

How will aftercare fit into your budget? Unless you have a bottomless well of cash, the money for your aftercare program will have to be pulled from other budget lines. Creating revenue streams for aftercare is often difficult, but with some thoughtful work and some creative budgeting, aftercare programs can be fully funded and operational with far less capital outlay than might be supposed.

Examine all of your budget lines for ways to create a budget for aftercare. Look at the money you are spending on advertising or public relations. Could you use your advertising and public relations dollars more effectively? Can some of that money be redirected toward aftercare?

Could you substitute photos of you and your staff in a newspaper advertisement with an ad slick about teen drinking and driving or drug use? An informational or educational advertisement goes a long way in selling the name of your funeral home and reminding the people in your community that you care about them.

Are there other groups in your community with whom you could work to create a community aftercare program, with each organization providing a portion of the funds? Are there groups that already serve as aftercare supports that could use sponsorship or a donation from your firm rather than duplicating services? Donations to existing support programs can also be seen as public relations.

What kinds of materials do you already have that could be used in an aftercare program? Do you have a collection of books, brochures, audio, and video tapes that you could make more accessible to the bereaved? Are you doing any kind of visits or letters to families after the funeral that could be redirected to include informational services about bereavement resources in your community?

Should you hire an aftercare coordinator or provider? Many funeral homes find the increased staff time taxes an already overloaded staff. Hiring a part-time aftercare person often makes the most sense of limited financial and human resources. Is there a volunteer who might be willing to oversee the program? If your aftercare program does not include personal visits or running support groups, often a volunteer can fill in quite well. If, however, you wish to have a support component, then you will need to look for a trained person or someone who is willing to obtain the training necessary to be effective.

If you choose to utilize a local professional who has volunteered to run a support group for you, please be aware of possible conflict of interest issues. It is strongly recommended that a professional therapist who volunteers to run a support group for a funeral home aftercare program NOT use the group as a source of referrals to him or herself [4]. This avoids liability and conflict of interest issues altogether.

Aftercare programs are often seen as costly with little or no immediate cash return on the investment. But long-term public relations establish you as an active part of the caring community. Many times funeral homes may experience a long-term increase in business. The increased awareness of the consuming public can be enough to justify funding a modest aftercare program.

There must be an overall plan, budget, and commitment to aftercare as a significant part of your business philosophy and service. Without a thorough and well thought out plan of service, aftercare may come across to your staff and community as just another "whim" or "advertising gimmick." Aftercare programs truly are a way to build and maintain a sense of community, a community of caring.

RESOURCES

Planning an effective aftercare program may seem like an overwhelming task, but you do not have to do this alone. Consider what resources are available in your community that you might work with in developing or expanding your program.

You might consider utilizing a grief management resource company to help you devote an aftercare program. These companies often provide printed materials such as cards, newsletters, and informational brochures as well as training, speakers, and special programming for holidays and educational seminars. A good grief resource company will help you tailor a program that suits your community rather than simply offer a package plan that does not take into consideration the unique needs and characteristics of your community and funeral service plan.

If nothing else is possible, you might consider coordinating and publishing a community resource guide for bereavement services. This guide is not a recommendation or referral list, but rather a listing of support services that are available to the bereaved in your community. You might wish to ask others in the community to help you compile the listings, perhaps even including a brief statement or two about types of services offered. Be sure to add a statement to this resource guide that explains this is not an endorsement of any service, but merely a listing of available resources within your community.

Sponsor an all-day professional workshop on grief or host a community awareness program. Plan a "Grief Relief Fair" or "Grief Awareness Day" at a local mall, with all the local support groups providing information about their services.

If your resources appear to be limited, do not look at this as a negative, but accept it as an opportunity for growth. You could begin to plan training for the professionals in your community so they can, in turn, become your referral resources.

FINAL THOUGHTS

Funeral service is about celebrating life and acknowledging death. Funeral service is about grief and grieving. Funeral service is about memorialization and ritualization. Funeral service is, indeed, for the living. And it is through information, education, and support, that the funeral director can provide a beacon of hope for the bereaved. One step at a time, you help lead the way to a new life for those left behind after someone dies. The funeral is one of those steps. Aftercare is another.

The funeral home does not have to be just a place for good-bye! Through an effective aftercare program, a funeral home can also be a place to learn to say hello, a place to learn to reassemble the puzzle that has been scattered by death.

THE LAST WORDS

Do you know what your true value is worth? Do you fully understand what you are giving when you stretch out your hand to find those struggling in the dark? Do you think it is your words of wisdom that bring light to a world gone dark? Do you think it is your action or perhaps your knowledge that brings hope to those who cannot imagine the horizon of another day?

Do you know all of your words, thoughts, knowledge, and action pale in comparison of your true gift? You and you alone are the GIFT you give to others. That's why we call you a present . . . You and your presence are the hope you bring. It's not your words, your actions, your knowledge . . . it's you. It is being there when the rest of the world shudders in horror, recoils in terror, flees in fright. It is being there when there are no words left to say, when there are no actions to be taken, except to move closer to one another and find the hands searching in the darkness. You are the light at the end of the tunnel. . . . You are the hope for a world grown silent with grief.

When you can dare to reach out across your own pain and grief and find the hands searching for the light, you become the voice of hope. Do not be afraid of the grief or the intensity of the pain. It is the right of the bereaved to hurt as deeply as they have loved.

The human spirit has an infinite capacity to endure, survive, and to grow. It requires laughter and tears to flourish. It requires love and faith, strength and support as well. It requires you and me and all of us together.

Hurt and pain have their lessons and we cannot rob ourselves of the richness of the tapestry that hurt and love weave together. To eliminate one from the loom is to break the thread and steal away the fabric.

The gifts within love are obvious. We do not dispute them. Yet, the gifts within hurt are as equal. I could not understand light if I had not known darkness. I could not sing sweet if I had not tasted bitter. I could not laugh if I had not cried.

Hope isn't a place or a thing. Hope isn't the absence of pain or fear or sadness. Hope is the possibility of renewed joy. It's the memory of love given and received. Hope is that magical moment when we reach out across our own hurt and pain and find each other, all searching in the darkness.

Hope is you and me and the person next to you and across the room and down the street and in your dreams. WE ARE EACH OTHER'S HOPE [1, p. 8].

REFERENCES

1. D. D. Sims, *If I Could Just See Hope,* Big A and Company, Wenatchee, Washington, 1994.
2. D. D. Sims, Can the Funeral Home be More than a Place to Say Good-Bye? *The Knight Letter,* p. 20, January-February 1997.
3. S. L. Williams, Don't Let Liability Become an Excuse for Not Doing Aftercare, *Today in Death Care,* p. 8, November 1998.
4. D. D. Sims and S. L. Williams, *Support Group and Grief Facilitation Manual,* Accord Grief Management Services, Louisville, Kentucky, p. 19, 1998.

CHAPTER 7

Intentional Aftercare:
After All, It's All Aftercare

Richard J. Paul

If we all lived in homes on stilts suspended above water, we would naturally teach our children to swim. It would be unthinkable to leave swimming lessons until after a child falls in the water. The human condition of mortality dictates that eventually everyone will experience grief. Just as it is the most difficult time to teach people how to swim after they have fallen into the water, it is not the most effective time to provide grief education when they have fallen into grief. However, "at times, helping happens simply in the way of things. It's not something we really think about, merely the instinctive response of an open heart. Caring is a reflex" [1, p. 5]. Caring is also, like mortality, a condition of humanity—so we have aftercare. What we do not have in response to life's myriad losses is all-encompassing, intentional aftercare.

Aftercare is the offering of two things—grief education and grief support to bereaved people. The same grief education that would be more appropriately introduced by parents, schools, and even churches over a lifetime—most frequently, if at all, is made available by various professionals, organizations, and businesses after a physical death. Aftercare as grief education is offered to help grieving people understand what has befallen them.

The second part of aftercare, grief support, is the provision of an environment, methods, and people which can facilitate the expression of grief or mourning. Even the phrase "expression of grief" is poorly understood in modern Western society. At best, mourning (the public or outward manifestation of grief) makes those not directly affected, uncomfortable. More frequently, grieving is not easily tolerated; it is perceived as an expression of weakness and it is discouraged for all but the briefest time.

The expression of grief is, in fact, a natural healing method of venting the stress, and eventually adapting to the change, caused by a loss. Grieving is a natural response to any loss. It is as natural as mother's milk. And just as it has become commonly accepted that "expressing" through breast-feeding is life-enhancing for both mother and child, it is my conviction that the bereaved who do not "express" their grief are at risk of life-limiting emotional and physical conditions. The gaps in aftercare can be held directly responsible for the bereaved failing to achieve a healthy adaptation to their loss.

AFTERCARE IS NOT A CULTURAL NORM

My pastor, placed in a Northern Ontario church for a three-year exchange period, commented on the lack of community in North America compared to his native Zambia. He specifically noted that everyone in his homeland was part of a community "family." "Third world" people not only develop a sense of personal, independent identity, but they also have a strong sense of themselves as part of the community. One way that this sense of identity as part of the larger whole manifests itself is how the whole community is touched and supports those who are most affected by a death.

We in the "first world" do not currently enjoy the same natural, social, and emotional interconnectedness in our persistent culture of "rugged individualism." And so we find the grief support of aftercare necessarily offered by the surrogate family support of aftercare necessarily offered by the surrogate family of hospital, funeral home, church, and bereavement outreach programs.

Aftercare as a deliberate intervention has been evolving in our society since the personal growth movement and encounter groups of the 1960s. During my funeral service education in 1980, as part of a self-designed project, I audited several grief support groups in Toronto. At that time the word aftercare was not familiar. However, I intended to learn as much as possible about post-funeral grief support before returning to my rural home town and assuming the responsibility of running a third-generation funeral home following my father's death. I hoped that I might be able to modify the aftercare which was available in that large urban center to accommodate the needs of my future bereaved clients in Northern Ontario.

Although I had the privilege of meeting several sponsoring organizations and support group facilitators I had been invited to attend only one meeting. As part of the introductions each person was encouraged to say why they were there and what they hoped to get from the experience. When it was my turn I explained my motivation and added that I wanted to learn more about how to support people in their grief because I believed that loss provided a powerful opportunity to grow. One of the bereaved mothers responded, "If you had told me during the funeral arrangements that I would grow from my son's death, I probably would have punched you." I learned a couple of things from that encounter. Specifically, that the concept of growing through grief is a delicate issue. While the philosophy behind providing aftercare may hold that growing through grief is a desired outcome, it is only with hindsight that the bereaved may be willing and able to see that growth. And secondly, I learned that aftercare does help people move through their grief as was evidenced in this case by that woman's acknowledgment that she could now speak out in public and state her point of view.

Over the past two decades the concept and practice of aftercare has developed from an increased understanding of both the power of grief, and the potential of education and support to facilitate grief work and reconciliation. However, there is still a strong resistance to or ignorance of the responsibility to provide some level of aftercare when a profession or enterprise involves serving the bereaved.

THE CHALLENGE OF AFTERCARE

Some funeral directors maintain that grief education, support, and counsel in general, and aftercare in particular, is not their job. These funeral directors demonstrate the cliche, "if you are not part of the solution, then you are part of the problem," and the problem for aftercare in our society is twofold. First, there is a general lack of understanding about the pervasive power and influence of grief in all our lives. Over the years I have heard quotations such as forty-eight hours to two weeks for the period that the general public feels should be expected for grief recovery. From the report of every grieving person I have spoken to, and from my own personal experience, grief is something that you get "used to," you don't get "over it." Therese Rando's list of some problem behaviors associated with complicated mourning include "antisocial acts, sexual acting out, alcohol and drug abuse, eating disorders, compulsive behaviors, accidents, suicidal gestures and acts, self-defeating behaviors, self-damaging behaviors,

self-mutilation, and acting out in social/interpersonal relationships
[2, p. 228]. These behaviors are prevalent throughout society and yet
rarely are they referenced as grief-related problems.

The second aspect of the problem of little support for aftercare is a
general lack of knowledge about bereavement which contributes to a
lower level of grief competency and sensitivity in our culture. Grief is
not limited to loss by death. Almost every day, human beings are
challenged by losses of varying degrees of intensity. However, individuals and society do not recognize nor respond supportively to the
fact of these losses. Duane Weeks, following his thesis study which
included extensive interviews with prison inmates, observed that the
incarceration of many inmates could likely be traced to prior losses of
different types that had not been understood and dealt with in a
healthy way.[1] Although research is currently limited on how grief
education and/or aftercare might positively impact every individual's
response to grief, it is my conviction that future studies and interventions in this area will demonstrate that people need the education and
support of aftercare to provide the necessary balance between life's joys
and life's myriad losses.

Part of the solution to grief incompetence is in naming and taking
ownership of the responsibility that funeral directors have to be grief
counselors, educators, and supporters. Every funeral arrangement
places the funeral director in counsel with grieving people. There is a
"segment of funeral directors who firmly believe that funeral directors
are not and should not be counsellors" [3, p. 4]. This group of funeral
directors confuse the role of a "counselor" with the work of a "therapist"
and do not want to stray into the latter form of interaction.

> Dr. Jackson, the noted psychologist, says, "Funeral directors do
> not choose as to *whether* or not they will be counselors. Their only
> choice is—will they be a good or bad counselor." He goes on to
> explain that by the very nature of the caretaking and caregiving
> services inherent in the duties and responsibilities of a funeral
> director he/she assumes the role of counselor not by choice but by
> his advice, direction and practice [cited in 4, p. 1].

In North America, funeral directors are the front-line caregivers with
whom practically everyone in grief will come into contact. More than
any other profession, funeral directors have the pivotal opportunity,
and responsibility, to facilitate healthy grieving by bringing a comprehensive knowledge of grief to their counsel. Besides the legal and

---

[1] O. D. Weeks, This was a telephone interview conducted Monday, May 3, 1999.

practical considerations of dead human body disposal, everything else the professional funeral director does needs to be viewed in the light of helping people with their grief or their is no point to the rituals and activities of the funeral process.

In consideration of the North American public's general lack of knowledge and understanding about death, loss, funerals, and bereavement, Dr. Jackson's statement might also be paraphrased, "Funeral directors do not choose _whether_ or not they will be <u>grief educators, grief supporters,</u> or <u>aftercare providers</u> only _whether_ they will be good or bad at it." Information about the grief process and how rituals can meet some of the needs of the bereaved must be disseminated by funeral directors in their role as a resource for grief management. Aftercare within funeral service begins with the funeral home and/or director's first contact with the bereaved.

The increasing numbers of funeral directors who recognize that their role includes grief education and support is the result of ever-improving curriculum and professors in funeral service education, more people with post-secondary education entering funeral service, and a general heightening of awareness about bereavement issues in the general public. The more that funeral directors bring an understanding of, and commitment to, grief education and support in their work, the more beneficial and valued will funeral service be in perception, and in fact.

WHEN DOES AFTERCARE BEGIN?

When aftercare is offered by hospitals, hospice, and palliative care it is introduced to the survivors following the death of a patient under the care of the organization. Where aftercare is offered by the funeral service provider, it is traditionally implemented following the last rituals and final disposition of the body.

In the medical care arena, the first news of a terminal prognosis has the potential to generate anticipatory grief, so perhaps aftercare should begin here. In this situation, both the family and the patient are potentially receptive for the education and support of aftercare. After all, it's "after" the news of an impending death. The coordination of the grief education for both patient and family which would form part of the hospital's aftercare program would be best led by the pastoral care department.

Unfortunately, it is a symptom of the prevailing lack of understanding about grief that pastoral care in general or more specifically aftercare is not considered a priority by hospitals, hospice, palliative care, and funeral service. There are still funeral directors who are adamant that they are not grief educators and counselors. And their absence from continuing education seminars on the subject of grief proves them right. I am certain that there are still many hospital administrators, doctors, clergy, nurses, social workers, and volunteers who feel the same way as do these "I am not a grief counselor" funeral directors. And the lack of support for aftercare will continue until these individuals and the corporate culture of these professions recognize the responsibility of providing aftercare.

ACCIDENTAL, INCIDENTAL, OR INTENTIONAL AFTERCARE

Aftercare, where it is provided, may be categorized as either Accidental Aftercare, Incidental Aftercare, or Intentional Aftercare. Accidental Aftercare is everything that happens when the bereaved are served by organizations or individuals that do not consciously consider aftercare part of their jobs. By its very nature Accidental Aftercare may accidentally help the bereaved. The understanding and compassion of exceptional individuals in the various helping professions are commented on by families when they are arranging funerals, but the comments are based on comparison with the majority of staff to which the bereaved are exposed. Where one individual may provide active listening and some relevant grief information and support, the majority of professionals are still not validating and supporting the grief experience. So, as long as caregivers who provide aftercare are the exception rather than the rule, Accidental Aftercare may leave the bereaved feeling confused, marginalized, and unsupported by the majority of caregivers.

Incidental Aftercare may occur from one of two sources. Out of a sense of obligation, because everyone else seems to have an aftercare program, some healthcare facilities and funeral homes may purchase pamphlets and make them available in the front hall. This half-hearted approach may be better than nothing, but not much. The second impetus for Incidental Aftercare can be considered as a thinly veiled marketing motive. If the drive is simply to sell prearranged funerals, or remind the client that your operation is the best, then the undisclosed purpose may come through loud and clear and contaminate any positive benefits that might accrue.

In the case of aftercare, the answer to the question, "What is in a name?" was demonstrated to me when I first started to see that everything I did as a funeral director could and should be viewed and judged as aftercare. After all, if the various rituals and activities associated with the funeral process are done to assist the bereaved in dealing with their loss, then it's all aftercare.

The epiphany which helped ratchet me through Accidental and Incidental to a perspective and position of providing Intentional Aftercare took place during a continuing education course I chose to take. To meet my need to feel more informed and more comfortable about grief and my role working with grieving people, I began what has become a life-long quest for education. In 1983, during my first course after being licensed, I attended a seminar called "Life Appreciation Training." This program was designed to equip funeral directors to assist their clients in appreciating the life of the deceased, their own lives, and life in general in the face of death. The originator and co-instructor of my training, Mr. Bill Bates, was a visionary who saw funeral service as a very powerful vehicle, in a momentous situation, to help people grow through their grief. One of his challenges to the participants was to ask, "What is your funeral home's grief education policy?"

It took me years after to realize that without a clear statement of what my intent was in working with the bereaved I wasn't getting anywhere. My aftercare was, at best, incidental. As Earl Nightingale said, "If you don't know where you are going, any road will get you there" [5]. Now I know where I am going as I function from the perspective that: "I am a resource, hired by people to consult with them in the development of a process to facilitate their transition from a physical relationship to a memory, spirit, love relationship with a significant person who has died." Now, my "education policy" and my mandate is, "To offer those I serve basic information about grief, and more specific insights as the situation compels, as well as creative process options for facilitating the ritualization, expression, and reconciliation of their grief." This mandate is "where I am going" and Intentional Aftercare is "the road" I am taking to get there.

With "Intentional Aftercare" the possibilities for providing aftercare are almost endless, but must be developed and implemented with a clear intent. With the genuine intention of assisting people to grow through their grief, almost any road will serve that purpose.

AFTERCARE OPTIONS

Aftercare in funeral service has parallels in hospitals, hospice, churches, and social organizations. Excuses for not implementing and maintaining an aftercare program usually fall under the department of: "It's not my job"; "I'm not qualified"; "It costs too much"; or "I don't know where to start." A cursory inventory of current practices in funeral service aftercare demonstrates that with the right intention it doesn't need to be rocket science, or therapy, it doesn't need to cost any more than a little of your time, and the best place to start is at the beginning.

The Initial Interview

I encourage everyone close to the person who died to participate in the funeral arrangement interview. At the outset, I set the tone for our relationship by saying that part of my role as a funeral director is first to identify issues of concern for my clients, then to explore the pros and cons of various options and finally to help them implement their choices and decisions throughout the funeral and after. I further clarify that I am constantly developing and expanding my knowledge of the issues surrounding death and grief with the intent of assisting them to make informed decisions.

Once I have addressed any pressing concerns of the family and housekeeping issues (such as where the washrooms are, how long we may be, etc.), I introduce my practice of gathering a brief life history of the person who died. I explain that this activity will: 1) provide me with information to create a keepsake memorial card that summarizes the person's life for everyone who attends; 2) the information will be used to draft an obituary or funeral notice to be placed in the newspaper following the funeral; 3) finally, I often will learn aspects of the dead person's life which can be symbolized or incorporated in the funeral process and ceremony (i.e., life symbols, pictures, music, people to speak, buildings or locations to use, activities that celebrate the person's life). The first time I began this practice, the wife said to me almost immediately after that part of the interview, "I am so glad we went through that. Ever since he died I have just been overwhelmed by the memory of his heart attack and worries about what am I going to do now, alone. And you helped me to realize that he had a good life and we had a good, long marriage together." From that time on, the life review has been an integral part of my funeral arrangement procedure, and my intentional aftercare.

The Second Interview

The second meeting with the majority of the family occurs during the private family time prior to public visitation hours. At this time, in addition to the housekeeping details of "who, when, where, and what"—I also introduce the "why" of viewing and visitation. I do this to give them an understanding, a context, a perspective from which to use the rituals of viewing the body and visiting with family and friends who come to support them.

The custom of viewing the body has been criticized as a primitive practice that has no place in the high-tech, highly-evolved intellectual world of today. However, it is just because viewing the body meets basic human needs that it's value transcends time and the dominance of logic over body and emotion. Physician and educator, Maria Montessori, explained her underlying philosophy of what has become known as the "Montessori method." It emphasizes that the more senses used in any learning situation, the deeper the integration of that learning. The bereaved have to "re-learn" the world as a place where the dead loved one is no longer physically among us. An obstacle on the path of adapting to this changed world is the desire for the fact of the death to be untrue. Viewing the body helps to use the senses in integrating on many levels the fact of death. Logic may try to overrule or underrate the use of the senses in accepting the death, but the logical level is just one connection that needs to be made in addition to the memory, emotional, social, and physical nexuses to the change. "Clearly the body of the deceased is the best symbol of the individual and, therefore, the most effective one to focus upon in attempting to perceive the deceased in a new relationship, as someone who is no longer alive and will only exist in memory [6, pp. 180-181].

I also use this opportunity to emphasize that they are in the process of moving from a physical to a memory relationship and while they are visiting with family and friends during the funeral process it is the ideal opportunity to gather new stories and reminiscences in order to strengthen the memory relationship. Finally, I introduce whatever additional information seems relevant to the people and the situation, i.e., it's okay to cry and laugh, to talk with and touch the deceased, etc.

After the Funeral. The Condolence Call

During the funeral process I arrange to meet with the family in their home one or two days after the funeral ostensibly to return pictures, deliver stationery, documents, and to help them with forms. I also use this time to take a closer look at the dynamics and needs of the family, remind them of our lending library and mention the local grief support groups and counselors available. We close off with the reminder that if they ever want to talk or would like more information about grief to give us a call.

Follow-Up Correspondence

A standard procedure for us currently is to send letters out once a week over the next several weeks following the funeral. The first is a questionnaire which invites the family to review the funeral process and comment on anything they found helpful or unhelpful. Not only does this gesture indicate that we continue to be accountable to them, but it encourages them to focus on and review, the funeral process to maintain their memory of the benefits that it provides.

The second letter reminds them of our library accompanied by one or two pamphlets that are most relevant to their bereavement. The third week the family receives a letter accompanying a laminated copy of the obituary as a gift and a keepsake. Each of these letters gently reminds the family that we remain available to them if they wish assistance in the grief process.

For years we regularly sent a letter just prior to the first anniversary of the death, letting our families know that we were thinking of them, that it may be a challenging time for them and that we are still available if they would like to talk or receive some information. We would also send a copy of the letter to the clergy who officiated at the funeral with a reminder of the details and a suggestion that the client might appreciate hearing from them. During that program I only received two comments, one from a widow who I just bumped into and she thanked me for the letter but thought she was doing all right. The other was from one clergy who asked me what he was supposed to do with the information, which demonstrates the need for further education in that profession.

We plan to reinstate this procedure because I am aware that almost everything about the first anniversary can conspire to rekindle the original feelings of grief—and yet the sense of isolation may be even more heightened at this time since very few people other than the principal grievers are even aware of the significance of the time. When we do start sending the clergy's first anniversary communication we will include some basic information at our next clergy breakfast meeting to ensure they know why, how, and with what they may wish to initiate contact with the bereaved.

Grief Support Booklets and Newsletters

There are a variety of programs available on the market that are designed to be mailed uninvited to the client at various intervals for reading in the comfort of their own home. Several authors and services offer different materials and programs to be purchased and implemented as aftercare. Bereavement Magazine even offers a program of gift magazines as a form of aftercare. One of my current goals is to introduce a funeral home newsletter, published three or four times a year that will include articles on bereavement as well as book reviews and announcements about grief education opportunities and support groups. The best equipped libraries mean nothing if they aren't used, and one characteristic of grief is an apathy or lack of motivation to reach out for help. All of these types of written materials which can be mailed have something of benefit to read and they take the onus off the bereaved to initiate helping themselves.

Grief Support Groups

It must be remembered that though a grief support group may be therapeutic for the participants, it is not therapy. It is very important for group facilitators to remember that they are not there as experts, with all the answers, to fix or change people. The leader is there to facilitate the support of the group by providing structure and format to proceedings. The importance of training facilitators is something that cannot be over emphasized, and yet it has to be acknowledged that many support groups have and do exist with leaders having little or no formal training in this field. However, many planned support group programs exist from how-to books and guided audio and video formats to local, national, and international organizations. All of the details regarding set-up and running grief support groups are usually covered, resulting in very little guess work for one with training in grief education and a genuine interest in helping the bereaved. Organizations and individuals will continue to set their own standards for training facilitators and the effectiveness of the leaders will ultimately be judged by the group. Like so many other aspects of responding to grief, the fear of doing the wrong thing should not prevent taking action, but should provide incentive for seeking the highest level of training available.

Grief Education Seminars

For the last ten years our funeral home has provided a lecture/ memorial service/support group type of program called "Holidays and Grief." Literally hundreds of people have attended and reported the benefit of feeling a little more in control of their situation as they approach the Christmas season by their increased knowledge of grief. If a funeral home or other organization was to do only one aftercare program a year, I would recommend this format.

The "how-to" informational seminar is an immensely popular form of aftercare for the bereaved. This format can combine any number of vocations and professions for a smorgasbord of advice to the newly bereaved. For example: 1) lawyer—on settling estates, rewriting wills, and power of attorney forms; 2) accountant—on filing tax returns for estates, avoiding unnecessary taxation now or in the future; 3) auto mechanic—basic car care and servicing information; 4) nutrition—on preparing healthy meals for one; 5) personal trainer—to encourage physical activity; 6) physician—to educate about personal care and encourage a physical; 7) funeral director—provide information about funerals and bereavement, etc. From the perspective that "knowledge is power," the bereaved will have the opportunity to learn both how to deal with their new situation and feel empowered to do something.

Over the years I have had some very well-known names in grief education come and provide an evening lecture for the general public and a day-long seminar for caregivers. Bill Bates, Alan Wolfelt, Earl Grollman, and Doug Manning have each spoken to approximately 500 local grieving people one evening and about 100 caregivers the following day. I have always charged admission to these programs but regrettably have never broken even. This seminar format is very time-consuming and costly but also very rewarding if it is well advertised and well attended.

Memorial Services and Activities

Monthly, quarterly, or annual memorial services provided for the families of someone who has recently died are a fairly common form of aftercare among some hospitals and funeral homes. These services may be held around the holidays, but are just as often held at other times of the year. Some organizations include the planting of a tree(s), decorating a tree, taking home a candle, contributing to a local food bank, or some other activity to involve the participants as part of the memorial service. The numbers that attend attest to the continuing need for ritual as a tool in the reconciliation of the losses in their lives.

CONCLUSION

In the spirit of working with the whole person, health care and funeral service professionals must consider the ongoing needs surrounding the patient, including the family and friends. Unresolved grief has been blamed for much of the emotional, behavioral, and/or physical problems that plague the bereaved later in life. This alone should be an impetus for society to sanction aftercare. But, since caring is a reflex, the knowledge of the pervasive lack of support for their bereaved client should be the strongest enticement to try to fill that void and meet those needs.

The motivation to provide aftercare must come from a higher place than the bottom line. Offering aftercare must be it's own reward. It is of the utmost importance that caregivers remember that you can lead a horse to water, but you can't make him drink. With "Intentional Aftercare" the investment must be in the offering of quality aftercare, not in the client's acceptance of the offer. The return on that investment must be in the giving, not in whether or not it is accepted. Just as no two people grieve the same, so no two people will be in the same place to receive the offer of aftercare. Aftercare provides the grieving person with the opportunity to help themselves understand their grief when they may have felt dangerously close to being out of control, or even worse felt nothing at all. The issue remains that it is our job to plant the seed, not insist that it grow on the spot.

There no longer is a traditional, predictable safety net of extended family, church family, or neighborhood family to catch the bereaved. Because of this the onus is on every profession that deals with grieving people to recognize the need for aftercare and identify how they will choose to respond to that need. After all, for the professional, from death on—it's all aftercare. The question is only, "Will we offer Accidental, Incidental, or Intentional Aftercare?"

REFERENCES

1. R. Dass and P. Gorman, *How Can I Help?: Stories and Reflections on Service,* Alfred A. Knopf, New York, 1988.
2. T. A. Rando, *Treatment of Complicated Mourning,* Research Press, Champaign, Illinois, 1993.
3. A. D. Wolfelt, *Interpersonal Skills Training: A Handbook for Funeral Service Staffs,* Accelerated Press, Muncie, Indiana, 1990.
4. H. C. Raether and R. C. Slater, *The Funeral Director and His Role as a Counselor,* National Funeral Directors Association, Milwaukee, Wisconsin, 1975.
5. E. Nightingale, *Audio-Lecture, "Lead the Field,"* Nightingale-Conant Corporation, Niles, Illinois, 1989.
6. T. A. Rando, *Grief, Dying, and Death,* Research Press, Champaign, Illinois, 1984.

CHAPTER 8

Finding "Fire and Joy" in Your Work–An Autobiographical Perspective

Paul V. Johnson

"How did you get involved in your position as a funeral home-based Aftercare Services Director?" That question is asked of me at least a couple of times a month, and for that reason I have decided to share my answer with the hope that it will encourage others who may have similar aspirations. My response relies heavily on past experiences in my life, but it also encourages others to spend some time reflecting on important experiences in their life which may already have helped prepare them for a career in aftercare.

Had anyone told me fifteen years ago that some day I would be employed by a funeral home and directing an aftercare program that I had developed for use in such a facility, I would have politely disagreed and indicated that I was perfectly happy in my position as an associate professor of sociology at a local college. My likely response to such a suggestion would have been, "I prefer to work with people who are happy about their lives, excited about their future, and in good emotional health. There may be some chaplains, clergy, or social workers who may be interested in such a position, but I am perfectly happy doing what I am doing."

Now, after serving as the Director of Aftercare Services for the Bradshaw Funeral Homes in the Twin Cities area for the past fourteen years, I feel called to the work of aftercare the same way we often think of clergy or missionaries being called to their work. A quotation kept on

101

a bulletin board above my desk describes my feelings well: "You know that God is calling when the 'fire and joy' you find in your work meets the world's needs." I have the luxury of having people tell me nearly every day that they are grateful that someone "still cares about them," and for this they express great thankfulness to me. That in itself makes the position very rewarding.

So how did this position come about? Did I just wake up one morning having decided that I wanted to work at a funeral home? No, it was a series of things which pointed me in this direction. Things which had occurred earlier in my life, now in hindsight, loom as significant experiences which were preparing me for this position. Let me mention at least three things which helped prepare me for the position I currently hold.

LIFE AS A FUNERAL HOME ATTENDANT

The first happened longer ago now than I really like to remember. It happened when I was a junior in college and, like most college students, needed a place to live and a place to work. I found both of those when I applied for and received a position as a "funeral home attendant" at the Listoe-Wold Funeral Home in St. Paul, Minnesota.

As a funeral home attendant it was my responsibility to be "on duty" every other evening, every other weekend, and every other holiday. Always dressed in a white shirt, tie, and dark suit, I greeted people who came for visitations, directed them to the family whom they had come to see, and cleaned up the facility after the visitation was over.

If a death call came anytime during the night, it was my responsibility to call the funeral director who was on call that evening and accompany him (in those days it was always a "him") to pick up the body of the individual who had died and bring it back to the funeral home. Upon our return I was free to go back to bed, but often I stayed up and talked with the funeral director as he embalmed and did other preparation work with the body.

During the year spent as a funeral home attendant, I learned a lot about death, grief, and funeral service. I learned about how people acted when they came to a funeral home for a visitation. I learned how family members dealt with the death of their loved ones. I learned what funeral directors did and early on decided that I did not want to do that for my career. In other words, I learned a lot, but at the conclusion of my year as a funeral home attendant I simply chalked up the year to experience, never thinking that I would ever have anything to do with funeral service as a career.

LIFE AS A MILITARY INDUCTEE

A second experience which helped prepare me for the position I now hold occurred when I was drafted into the United States Army. All through my undergraduate college career and through two years of my Masters program, I stayed one step ahead of Uncle Sam. Everyday of my college and graduate school experience threatened to be the day that I received my induction notice, and finally in the spring of 1970 it arrived. This was the height of the Vietnam War and I was convinced that I would go to Vietnam and be killed. Needless to say, this turn of events was not something about which I was very excited.

Being quite naive about the inner workings of the U.S. Army, I had the audacity to request the position of chaplain's assistant and thought the Army would actually meet that request. Little did I know that if you request something from the Army, they will typically respond as opposite as possible so as to confirm that they, indeed, are in charge of everything.

Well, the Army made a "mistake" in that they actually gave me what I had asked for in terms of a military occupational specialty. I have yet to meet anyone else who actually got the position they had requested. So, upon completing basic training at Fort Bragg, North Carolina, I continued on with advanced individual training and Chaplain's Assistant School at Fort Dix, New Jersey and Fort Hamilton, New York.

As we neared the completion of our training at Fort Hamilton and waited to hear about our first duty assignment, the staff at the Chaplain's Assistant School one day announced, "Men, be prepared to go to Vietnam. We have obviously had casualties there which we need to replace and all of you can expect to be assigned there." You can imagine my surprise when the orders came on the following day and mine did not say "Vietnam," but "Snelling Air Defense Site, St. Paul, Minnesota." Not only had the army given me the position I requested, but now they were sending me back to my home area to work at a base that was so small we didn't even have enough personnel to hold services on Sunday. As a result, Sunday, a day that should have been among my busiest, was like another day off. Talk about great military duty—it couldn't have been any better!

So what does this position in the military have to do with developing and directing an aftercare program within a funeral home setting? It was in my position as a chaplain's assistant that I experienced the most difficult work I have ever experienced. You probably know that when there is a death in the military, whether it comes as a result of combat, a car accident, homicide, suicide, or any other reason, the survivors of the deceased individual are not notified by letter or over the telephone, but in a face-to-face meeting with a representative of the military service. It was the chaplain's responsibility to bring such news and as his assistant, I accompanied him on each of these calls.

During the six months that I was stationed in the Twin Cities, I made about twenty of these calls with my chaplain and to this day I can drive the streets of the Twin Cities and remember what happened at particular houses. I don't remember individual names but I do remember what happened at certain houses.

One of these visits, in particular, stands out in my memory. We drove up to the house in our olive drab U.S. Army vehicle and, of course, were wearing our uniforms. As we knocked on the door, it opened. But before we could say a single word, that door slammed shut in our faces. The woman, who seconds before had been standing inside the screen door, was now running out the side door of her house and heading for the back yard. We ran after her, grabbed her, and held her down on the ground. She was kicking, screaming, and flailing her arms all over. We had not gotten a chance to say a single word, but she knew why we were there. Her son was in Vietnam and we were coming to share the news of his death.

Not all of our "first calls" were as dramatic as that one, but not a single one of them was easy. Never once did Chaplain Olsen and I return to our office after one of those calls and say, "Boy, didn't we do a good job communicating with that family. We really shared that information well." No, I know that I came back to the office each time hoping that this would be the last one of these in which I would have to participate.

In my current position at the funeral home I do not bring news to people that a loved one has died. If they are dealing with a funeral home, they already know that someone important to them has died or that death is imminent. I am, however, often involved with a family while they are still trying to accept the fact that a death has occurred. Often I will watch the 10 o'clock news at home and see a news story about a traffic death, suicide, or homicide and come to my office the following morning and learn that we are serving that family at one of our locations. Little did I know that my work as a chaplain's assistant would help prepare me for this aspect of my current position.

LIFE AS A COLLEGE PROFESSOR

A final experience which helped prepare me for my current aftercare position occurred after I left the military and was invited to join the faculty of the private, liberal arts college where I had earned my undergraduate degree. After teaching there for a couple of years the Academic Dean requested that I develop a new course of my choosing that I would teach during the month-long, January interim term.

I do not remember what led up to my decision, but the course I proposed to teach was entitled "Living With Death and Dying." I do remember meeting with the administrator in charge of new courses whose first response was, "Do you really think that college students will sign up for a class on death and dying?" She continued, "You know that students take only one course during the interim term and January is the bleakest, coldest month of the year around here—do you really think anyone will want to take this course?"

My reply was that I didn't know what the response would be, but that I thought the course should be taught. I shared information with her about other colleges in our area that had courses similar to the one I was proposing and encouraged her to approve the proposal. She finally did.

That term, as well as every subsequent term the course was taught, the course filled on the very first day of registration. Students were very interested in issues related to loss and grief and were excited to explore such issues in the class. Some students took the course because their parents had gotten a divorce and that was the loss on which they personally wanted to work.

Other students took the class because they had experienced the death of a loved one and wanted to deal with it. I will never forget a young man named Mark whose father had taken his own life two years earlier. Mark used his journal, in which I required students to make daily entries, to tell me some of his thoughts and feelings about this very difficult loss. It was the first time he had opened up with anyone and shared his innermost thoughts about his dad's death.

On another occasion a student followed me back to my office after class and as we got there she began to cry quite uncontrollably. Assuming that something quite serious was the cause of her tears, I asked if someone close to her had died. She said that no one had died, but that the previous day she had gone to see her physician. Thinking that maybe she had been diagnosed with a serious or terminal illness, I asked her about that but she said that was not it either. Observing that whatever was causing her tears was obviously quite serious, I asked her what it was. She replied, "Yesterday when I saw my doctor, I found out that I will never be able to bear my own children." Her lifelong dream of being a natural childbirth mother that she had had since childhood ended at that point and it was this serious loss which she was grieving.

As a part of my class I always took my students to visit a funeral home. It was my belief then, and it is an even stronger belief now, that everyone should visit a funeral home before they *have to* visit a funeral home. It is one thing to be in a casket selection room with a group of friends as part of an educational experience, and a totally different experience when one is there because one's parent or spouse has just died.

To arrange for these funeral home tours, I would always call the same funeral director, Jim Bradshaw. When I had been the funeral home attendant at Listoe-Wold Funeral Home during my college years, I had worked with Jim who was in his first position as a funeral director following his graduation from the Mortuary Science Program at the University of Minnesota. Over the years as I had gone on in the academic world, Jim had gone on in the funeral service world and was now the owner of six funeral homes in the Twin Cities area. He was always happy to come to speak with my classes and following his presentation we would tour one of his facilities.

One day after one of those tours he and I were having lunch together and without having spent the previous night planning a presentation for him or developing a business plan, I simply said, "Jim, you need a bereavement follow-up program in your funeral home." I shared how some research (unpublished) I had been doing at a local hospice program indicated that as difficult as it was during the time leading up to an individual's death, and as difficult as it was around the time of the death and the funeral, that it can be even more difficult in the weeks, months, and years after a death if an individual or family is not getting the kind of help they need.

In response to my statement Jim replied, "That's an excellent idea. You know, I've been thinking of offering something like that, but I've never found anyone who either thought they could do the job, or even wanted to do the job. But it sounds like you do. When would you like to start?"

Because we often joked with each other, I thought he was kidding so I replied, "How about tomorrow?"

"You're on," was his reply and, just like that, my position started.

I continued teaching at the college, but now was working part-time at the funeral home developing an aftercare program. It went this way for about eight months until one day Jim approached me with the following question.

"Would you ever consider leaving your position at the college and join us full-time?" I was extremely excited about the possibility of doing just that, but needed to weigh the pros and cons of such a potentially life-changing move.

I felt a "pull" to accept his offer, but at the same time I had everything one could want in a teaching position. I was a tenured Associate Professor, I had great faculty colleagues, great students, as well as the three best things about being a teacher—June, July, and August off! To give up all of that would certainly be a major change.

I remember confiding with a faculty friend about what I was thinking of doing and his immediate response was, "Are you crazy? How can you give up the stability you have here at the college for something so uncertain? What if Jim Bradshaw sells his business or dies unexpectedly? The next person who owns his company could care less about aftercare."

In spite of this advice, as well as that of others, I followed my "gut level" feelings and accepted Jim's offer. That was fourteen years ago and during these years I could not have had a more fulfilling career.

AND HOW ABOUT YOU?

So why have I shared this lengthy discussion of how I got involved in aftercare? Well, a partial reason is just to tell my story. The main reason, however, is to be an encouragement to you, the reader, as you consider your involvement with aftercare.

If you are already involved in some aspect of aftercare, I encourage you to spend some time reflecting on what brought you into this position in the first place. We call can benefit from thinking back upon our earliest motivations and experiences to help rekindle a passion for the work we do. Years of experience as well as other demands that may have been placed upon us have a way of diverting our attention from that work we feel called to do. By thinking back on what got us interested in caring for grieving individuals in the first place, we are encouraged to commit ourselves again to this important work.

For those of you who are considering a possible aftercare position within a funeral home setting, have you spent time looking back into *your* past and reviewing both the experiences as well as the relationships which have been important in shaping you into the individual you are today? Maybe someone or something in your past can help open a door to a new career that will provide you with the same sense of accomplishment and satisfaction that I have experienced.

If you are interested in pursuing a position in a funeral home-based aftercare program, I would encourage you to speak with funeral service professionals in your area and let them know of your interest. The more information you can provide about your qualifications for such a position, as well as examples of related experience you have had, the more likely your chances of obtaining such a position. Your skills at relating to people, especially when they are in difficult circumstances, are also critical to being successful in such a position. Nothing is more basic, however, than finding a funeral home owner who believes in the concept of aftercare as a way of extending care to people who need it.

CHAPTER 9

Aftercare: Past, Present, and Where Do We Go From Here?

Vicki Lensing

Answering the question of what constitutes aftercare is difficult enough without bringing in the issues of who can provide it and how these caregivers are trained and supported professionally. Yet there is growing concern about training and education related to aftercare, both from the institutions providing it and the individuals doing it.

To address these issues and understand where aftercare may be going, it is important to understand how aftercare began and the various forms it has taken.

PAST

As far back as 50,000 years ago, man exhibited concern for the dead. Neanderthal burials included food, ornamental shells, and stone tools, which implies a belief in an afterlife and a human concern about beliefs and rituals. Ancient civilizations such as the Egyptians, the Greeks, and the Romans also demonstrated beliefs and rituals surrounding death and an afterlife. During the Middle Ages, rituals of mourning emerged. Through the seventeenth and eighteenth centuries, death was romanticized, yet more focus was given to the bereaved and the emotional aspects of grief. By the late eighteenth and nineteenth centuries,

> the center of attention now shifted to the bereaved. Mourning became profoundly important, and people again became apprehensive, not about their own death, but about the death of their loved

ones. Exalted and dramatized, death became important because it affected the loved one, the other person, whose memory was perpetuated in the ornate cemeteries of the eighteenth and nineteenth centuries [1, p. 83].

In the 1800s, as Philippe Aries points out in his book, *The Hour of Our Death,* early American settlers were stoic and accepting of death [2]. He also states that the current death customs practiced in Western world emphasize denial. Mourning rituals are no longer observed, life is to continue as if untouched by the death of a loved one. He continues,

> It is quite evident that the suppression of mourning is not due to the frivolity of survivors but to a merciless coercion applied by society. Society refuses to participate in the emotion of the bereaved. . . . From now on, the denial of death is openly acknowledged as a significant trait of our culture. The tears of the bereaved have become comparable to the excretions of the diseased. Both are distasteful. Death has been banished [3, pp. 579-580].

This is where, in baseball jargon, aftercare has stepped up to the plate. When death occurs, those people affected are looking for answers, direction, and support. As Aries stated, this support is difficult to find in today's society. This is why most aftercare programs began: to fill those needs for grievers as best they could.

Aftercare started in many funeral homes as a way of helping a family or individuals cope with the death of a loved one. The scenario is fairly common: no one was providing the services needed by the grieving individuals so the funeral home decided to fill those needs. There was no organized program to follow. Funeral homes responded in a variety of ways that seemed natural in assisting with the grief process: listening, trying to provide support and information, and helping to normalize the grief responses experienced by the individual. Grievers felt, to some degree, a comfort level at the funeral home.

When a death occurs, the emotional impact and ensuing post-death experiences may vary from individual to individual. However, the interactions of the griever with the funeral home following the death begin the relationship. The funeral home becomes a resource of information, options and support.

> The survivor usually exhibits an inability to meet problems that accompany and follow a death. Emotions must be dealt with at the time they are being experienced. The catharsis of talking about emotions is essential. In counseling the survivor there is no model or format to follow. No single method offers a magical single answer. The diversity of methods is matched only by the diversity of the crisis situations [4, p. 247].

Funeral home staff members are often put in the position of hearing intimate details of a family or relationship, of normalizing a situation that feels strange and abnormal to those involved and of providing unique options to assist the family in choosing their own personal ritual of saying good-bye. Grief and the individual's own method of expressing it are accepted with understanding.

> The funeral director must accept irrational behavior, expressions of hostility, and acts of disappointment as natural phenomena in the acute grief process. He must realize that logic and reason are not always solutions to acute grief. He recognizes that impractical notions and unusual behavior are justified components of grief work [5, p. 231].

That grief work begins at the funeral home. No matter what type of ritual that family chooses to say good-bye, the grief work has begun and the funeral home has been a part of it. Hence, the feeling on the part of some individuals that the funeral home is a safe place to return to pursue other paths on the journey of grief.

What those other paths might be and what types of support might be helpful to the bereaved were left to the funeral home to discover. And what many funeral homes found was that there were no support groups, no books, no brochures, and no programs available to help grievers on their journey. So resourceful funeral homes took up that challenge and developed what have now become extensive aftercare programs.

This seemed to happen gradually but it appears that by the 1980s, funeral homes that had or were beginning to provide aftercare services began to look to their colleagues for more information and support. Firms varied greatly in the types of aftercare programs offered. This seemed to depend on the community they were serving, the dollar and time commitment given to such programs by the firm, other resources available in the specific community and the creativity of the person(s) doing the aftercare.

These programs ranged from home visits to newsletters, from support groups to lending libraries, from follow-up notes to educational seminars. These programs were carried out by funeral directors, funeral home staff members, and volunteers.

Questions began to arise about liability, training, cost, and budget. Funeral home owners were concerned about adequate training for those persons facilitating support services and the legal consequences for the funeral home in providing such services. Who would pay for these services and how they would be budgeted into the expenses of running a funeral home were also concerns for funeral home owners. Those who were providing these services were also asking questions: What else can be done and where do I learn how to do it? Most aftercare programs began on a shoestring budget by someone who volunteered to develop the program and was trained by their own personal loss experience or through the few seminars and books that were available at the time.

Just as aftercare programs sprang up in the mid-1980s, resource services for aftercare also began to emerge. These services offered a range of products, including training workshops and seminars, brochures, video and audiotapes, publications and newsletters, mail pieces and anniversary cards, and speakers' bureaus.

Likewise, many funeral home suppliers saw an opportunity to offer aftercare materials such as books, videotapes, cards, and brochures. Some suppliers contracted with nationally known experts in the field of grief and others developed a series of materials specializing in different types of losses.

Professional funeral service associations also got involved and offered materials for purchase. Some included aftercare seminars at their meetings and conventions. However, many of these associations required membership in order to participate. This was sometimes a problem for those persons providing the aftercare programs in funeral homes but who were not licensed funeral directors. These programs or materials were not always available to them.

There were several venues that brought aftercare providers together—either through activities, such as the National Funeral Directors Association (NFDA) Pursuit of Excellence Program,[1] courses such as those offered by the National Foundation of Funeral Service (which has since merged with the NFDA) or through workshops and conventions, such as those offered by Association for Death Education and Counseling (ADEC).[2] These types of functions provided networking

---

[1] National Funeral Directors Association (NFDA) Pursuit of Excellence program, created in 1981, is a national quality recognition program for progressive funeral directors whose businesses exhibit outstanding and innovative customer service and community relations. Areas of emphasis include compassionate service, educational programs, community and professional service and maintaining a library and media resources. (From the NFDA Pursuit of Excellence 1998 cover letter and brochure.)

[2] Association for Death Education and Counseling (ADEC) was established in 1976 to provide a forum for those interested in improving life through facing the realities of dying, death, and bereavement. An organization of both lay persons and professionals, it offers an opportunity for those of like interest to share mutual concerns, cares, and direction about death education and/or grief counseling. (From ADEC membership application form.)

opportunities for aftercare providers. They were able to receive new information, exchange ideas about creating and maintaining different types of aftercare programs, learn how to sustain existing programs and in effect, find a support system of colleagues who were blazing the same trail.

By the 1990s, aftercare was gaining momentum. More funeral homes recognized the opportunity to further expand their service base by providing aftercare programs. They saw the value in becoming a community resource. Many programs were networking with local schools, hospitals, churches, and hospices to provide a balance of bereavement support and information.

Simultaneously, questions of expense, liability, and training also continued to grow. Articles in a variety of trade journals addressed this new wrinkle in funeral service. In "A New Definition for Funeral Service," authors John Borgwardt and Dan Isard addressed not only what aftercare was but also the cost and return of offering such a program [6]. The entire issue of *American Funeral Director,* August 1994, was devoted to the debate on the pros and cons of aftercare in "Aftercare Services—The Debate Continues on Aftercare's Role in Funeral Service" [7]. In the December 1995 issue of *The Director,* aftercare was also featured. Attorney T. Scott Gilligan, general counsel for NFDA, discussed liability and legal issues concerning after in his article, "Aftercare: The Legal Perils of Aftercare" [8]. How to set up an aftercare program as well as the concerns for training the individuals providing those services were addressed in "Developing a Successful Aftercare Program" [9]; and "Establishing Standards and Credentials is No Small Task" [10].

Aftercare providers were frustrated—where did they fit into funeral service? Individuals who ran successful aftercare programs struggled with where to go for additional training. Associations such as ADEC offered certification, but often at a higher professional level than appropriate for all aftercare providers. Those who were just beginning a program looked for a place to learn the basics. Funeral home owners were questioning the dollars and sense of having an aftercare program as well as the liability issues. Funeral homes who already had existing aftercare programs saw the value but also worried over conflicting liability information. Professional counselors queried over offering counseling without appropriate licensure.

In 1994 and 1995, two conferences were held to address some of these issues. The National Conference on Aftercare, meeting each year, raised the same concerns and spawned a task force to examine aftercare in detail. That task force reported back to the conference in 1995 and at that meeting, the National Association of Bereavement Support

Providers in Funeral Service (NABSPFS)[3] was born. However, the challenges of determining standards of practice and a certification process are yet to be tackled by the association.

PRESENT

Having now looked at the history of aftercare in funeral service, it is necessary to also look at why bereavement support is important in today's world before examining some possible options to the current questions and challenges of aftercare.

Grief, as defined by William Worden, is a normal reaction to loss, and mourning is the adaptation to that loss which the griever experiences [11]. Alan Wolfelt adds to that by saying, "By definition, mourning is the outward, or public, expression of your many thoughts and feelings regarding the person who had died" [12, p. 1]. Furthermore, Sandra Graves explains, "Grief is experienced physically, psychologically, socially, and spiritually, to a greater or lesser degree with each loss" [13, p. 2]. All three agree that each unique grief experience must be acknowledged and worked through in order for the individual to emerge from his/her mourning in a healthy manner.

Aftercare has supported these tasks of mourning with a range of programs. Many of these programs were begun based on the knowledge, experience, time, and resources available. There were no manuals to outline a bereavement program. Most aftercare providers have created their own programs, educating themselves, soaking up training where they could, and networking with others to glean more information.

This brings us back to the dilemma of what type of programs are being offered by whom and how are they qualified. There seems to be some consensus among providers that there are levels of aftercare being offered. The difficulty is in defining those levels as illustrated in the following examples of aftercare programs.

The first level or beginning of an aftercare program starts with the first contact with the family, often by a variety of staff members while performing everyday responsibilities in a funeral home. It may be

---

[3] "National Association of Bereavement Support Providers in Funeral Service (NABSPFS) recognizes that death is a part of the life cycle and grief is a normal response to that loss. We are committed to informing, education and supporting individuals, organizations and communities, emphasizing and affirming the importance of ritual closure, funeral service and memorialization of those who have died. We develop, implement and provide a continuum of care with the intention of encouraging optimum healing and growth." (NABSPFS mission statement.)

listening to a family member recount the circumstances of the death or explaining death and funerals to the children in that family. It may be casual conversation made while flowers are being delivered after a funeral. It may be in the suggestions and information shared with a family after the funeral: from dealing with various aspects of paperwork to writing thank you notes.

The next step is more active: communicating with the family personally or through written materials. Some aftercare providers make phone calls or home visits to check on the needs of the family. Information on support groups, community resources, and other materials can be provided at this time. Some programs provide a newsletter to the bereaved. Other firms have a follow-up program whereby notes are sent out at scheduled intervals or on certain dates (birthdays, holidays, wedding anniversaries, or the anniversary of the death). These tasks are usually the work of one particular person on staff.

There is also a plethora of material available today on the various aspects of grief, such as brochures, booklets, video and audiotapes, as well as many books. Many aftercare programs include a lending library of these materials that can be borrowed for a short period of time. Usually the aftercare coordinator is charged with overseeing the maintenance of the lending library as well as being aware of current materials.

Some aftercare includes outreach programs, scheduling several events during the year related to grief. These events include coping with the holidays programs; memorial services; informational seminars with local or national experts; social gatherings at difficult holidays such as Valentine's Day; holding a commemorative service for Easter, Mother's Day, Father's Day, Veteran Day, or Memorial Day; or educational programs for children. These outreach programs appear to be limited only by the creativity and resources available. They are usually designed to address a specific need and often become an annual event. Again these events are usually under the responsibilities of the aftercare coordinator.

Support groups are another facet of an aftercare program. These self-help groups may be operated by or funded through an aftercare program. If these are already support groups available, the aftercare program may be a referral agent to existing groups. If the group is sponsored by the funeral home, the purpose of the group needs to be clarified: is it peer support or is it group therapy?

According to Peter Rebold, an attorney and licensed funeral director, each state has legal definitions for "counselor," "professional counselor," or "social worker" [14]. Some states may prohibit unlicensed persons from being identified by one of these terms and may have

penalties for violating the law. Rebold suggests aftercare providers
check their state's statutes to see if a "saving statute" is listed, such as
the following example from Florida:

> No provision of this chapter shall be construed to . . . prevent
> qualified members of other professions from doing work of a nature
> consistent with their training and licensure, so long as they do not
> hold themselves out to the public as possessing a license or certifi-
> cate issued pursuant to this chapter . . . [15, p. 393].

This example supports Rebold's suggestion that aftercare providers
act within the parameters of individual state laws and regulations and
learn to recognize survivors who need professional help and encourage
them and their families to seek it. Commenting on the history of
liability for aftercare, Rebold said that as of 1995, there were no
reported cases in the fifty states of a funeral home being sued for
aftercare functions. He said the advances of aftercare in funeral service
have not stopped because of potential liability and insurance will
always be available to cover such situations.

T. Scott Gilligan of Keply, MacConnell & Eyrich, in Cincinnati,
Ohio and general counsel of NFDA agrees with Rebold's findings.
While his research failed to uncover any malpractice lawsuits against
funeral directors in regards to aftercare programs or support groups,
he cautions,

> If a funeral home has a licensed professional operating its program,
> it should carry malpractice insurance. If the aftercare program is
> run by a funeral director, he or she should check with the funeral
> home's insurance carrier to ensure that its malpractice insurance
> would cover any claims involving grief facilitation [16, pp. 10-11].

Recognizing when support group participants need professional
help is key. Knowing how to identify when a griever needs professional assistance is another instance where training is important for
an aftercare provider who facilitates a support group. Also knowing
which professionals provide grief counseling in a community is helpful
as a resource for group participants. However, it is recommended that
a list of professional counselors be given rather than specific referrals
be made.

Gilligan suggests,

> The funeral director must not hesitate to recommend professional
> counseling to those having difficulty in the grief recovery process.
> The referral should be made to the affected individual and also to

his or her family. It is also a good idea to follow up to ensure the individual is consulting a professional grief therapist [16, pp.10-11].

Licensed professional counselors run some aftercare programs. They may be hired as a staff member of the funeral home or the funeral home may have a contract with a particular counselor to provide specific services for them. Obviously, the scope of what they can provide is based on their license. They may do one-on-one counseling as well as small groups. Some may see individuals privately and be compensated. The arrangement is dependent upon the funeral home, the counselor, and health insurance today. Other funeral homes may have a professional counselor on retainer to see their clients. Again, this arrangement is between the funeral home and the counselor.

The benefit of support groups also needs to be noted. Psychotherapist Marylou Hughes has said,

> One reason bereavement support groups abound is that there are a lot of bereaved. But the main reason for their popularity is that they work. The commonly held definition of a bereavement support group is that it is a group of people who get together on a regular basis and, with the help of a leader, discuss their problems adjusting to a world in which their loved ones no longer live [17, p. 15].

The formats of support groups vary. Some are informal discussions, some have a speaker, and others may have a social event alternately with discussions. Again, Hughes concurs. "Bereavement support can be called an activity, a class, a spectator event, an entertainment or a special occasion. People in grief give each other support while they are learning, enjoying themselves, developing new skills and giving help to others" [17, p. 15].

Aftercare is also education. Everyone (unless they die first) will be a griever someday. Educating the public about grief is a valuable piece of aftercare. This may be through speaking to clubs and organizations, offering tours through the funeral home, working with the local school district, or participating in local health and business fairs. These are opportunities to teach people about grief.

Schools are another place where aftercare providers can participate. Helping develop and implement grief and loss curriculums, assisting teachers and faculty with classroom activities, responding to school needs when a death occurs, and serving as a resource are also components of an aftercare program.

Another aspect is in networking with other agencies: hospitals, hospices, churches, and nursing homes. Often these groups are in need of training on aspects of grief. Joining with other agencies to present or sponsor an educational event is a way to reach more people in addition to working as colleagues. Such networking provides an excellent opportunity to exchange information and understand one another. It serves as a building block for future endeavors and creates a relationship.

TRAINING AND CERTIFICATION

It should be evident that the scope of an aftercare program can be from very basic to all encompassing. Each program has been designed to fit the particular community it serves. Because of that, the questions of training and certification present some problems. How much training is needed to run a basic aftercare program? Does the training increase at each increment of an aftercare program? Who provides this training? Who trains the trainers? How is training measured? Who oversees the certification? How frequently is one recertified? What is the ongoing expense of such training and certification?

Today an individual can take a five-day class and be certified as a grief counselor from the American Academy of Bereavement. What does that mean? Professional counselors take issue with those aftercare providers who use the title counselor when they are not licensed or trained. It can also create confusion for the public. Aftercare coordinators engaging in active aftercare programs should use the term "grief recovery facilitator to describe themselves and their roles," recommends Gilligan. "This label eliminates the possible problem of misrepresentation while aptly describing the role" of the coordinator [16].

This underscores the need to create some standards of practice that can be accepted by all. Networking with others may be critical to reaching a consensus. This is also where professional associations can be helpful.

Associations such as the NFDA, ADEC, NABSPFS, the National Hospice Organization, and state funeral director associations may be the starting points. Talking, sharing ideas, and reaching an understanding of what aftercare is about is critical. Data needs to be collected on what is currently available. These organizations are natural places for the debate and mechanics, standards, and certification to take place.

However, funeral service is not the only place where aftercare is happening. Collaborating with social workers, counselors, clergy, and other mental health practitioners may also be beneficial. There may be models in place that can serve as an example. Currently, ADEC and NABSPFS are looking at these issues. But it is a monumental task and it will take time and research before universal standards are accepted. Aftercare providers should engage these associations in taking a hard look at how to proceed.

FUTURE

The benefits of training and certification would be far reaching. For the aftercare provider, this would give clarity to what skills they have and what additional training is needed. For the funeral home sponsoring such a program, it would give the parameters of aftercare by establishing levels and standards. This would help in hiring as well as address some of the expense and liability concerns. Organizations that provide training would also know what to teach and how to develop curriculum. Professional counselors would have a clear understanding of the limitations of the various levels of aftercare and how they also fit into the program. Lastly, the public would be on the receiving end of competent services.

The result would be a pool of certified aftercare providers that would be an asset to a funeral home and a resource for grievers and the community. Annual conventions and regional meetings would not only provide education but also an opportunity for networking with other aftercare coordinators. Coordinated training efforts, the development of new resource materials and the cooperation between other related professional colleagues would only enhance aftercare as it is now known. Referrals to appropriate support for grieving individuals could be made across the country through the networking efforts.

This is where the future of aftercare lies. Continuing efforts by aftercare providers to network with one another, with associations and other professionals, and their joint commitment to establishing standards and training will carry aftercare into the next century and beyond.

LIST OF BEREAVEMENT RESOURCES
(This is a partial list and is not meant to be complete.)

BEREAVEMENT TRAINING PROGRAMS

Accord Aftercare Services
Sherry Williams
1941 Bishop Lane, Suite 202
Louisville, KY 40218
(800) 346-3087

The American Academy of Bereavement
Division of Carondelet Management Institute
2090 North Kolb Road, Suite 100
Tucson, AZ 85715

The Canadian Centre for Bereavement Education
and Grief Counseling
49 Gloucester Street
Toronto, Ontario, Canada
M4Y 1L8
(416) 926-0905

Center for Loss & Life Transition
Dr. Alan Wolfelt
3735 Broken Bow Road
Fort Collins, CO 80526
(303) 226-6050

King's College
Center for Education About Death & Bereavement
Dr. John Morgan, Coordinator
266 Epworth Avenue
London, Ontario, Canada
N6A 2M3
(519) 432-7948

National Center for Death Education
Mount Ida College
777 Dedham Street
Newton Center, MA 02159-3310
(617) 536-6970

RTS Bereavement Services (Resolve Through Sharing)
Gunderson Lutheran Medical Center
1910 South Avenue
La Crosse, WI 54601
(608) 791-4747

LIST OF ASSOCIATIONS

The Association for Death Education and Counseling (ADEC)
342 North Main Street
West Hartford, CT 06117-2507

The National Association of Bereavement Support Providers in
Funeral Service (NABSPFS)
P.O. Box 167
Iowa City, IA 52244
(319) 338-8171

LIST OF RESOURCES

Accelerated Development
3808 W. Kilgore Avenue
Muncie, IN 47304-4896
(800) 821-8312
(Catalog of books available)

ADM Publishing
P.O. Box 751155
Forest Hills, NY 11375-8755
(718) 657-1277
(National Directory of Bereavement Support Groups and Services)

A Place to Remember
DeRuyter-Nelson Publications, Inc.
1885 University Avenue, Suite 110
Saint Paul, MN 55104
(612) 645-7045
(Cards and booklets for the death of an infant)

Aquarius Productions, Inc.
35 Main Street
Wayland, MA 01778
(508) 651-2963
(Videotapes)

AfterLoss AfterCare
Drawer 599
Summerland, CA 93067
(800) 423-8811
(Newsletters, printed materials)

Beacon Press Order Dept.
25 Beacon Street
Boston, MA 02108
(Books by Dr. Earl Grollman)

Bereavement Publishing, Inc.
8133 Telegraph Drive
Colorado Springs, CO 80920-7169
(719) 282-1948
(Booklets, cards and Bereavement Magazine)

Centering Corporation
1521 North Saddle Creek Road
Omaha, NE 68104-5064
(402) 553-1200
(Catalog of books and videos available)

Compassion Books
477 Hannah Branch Road
Burnsville, IN 47006
(704) 675-5909
(Catalog of books and videos available)

Grief Support Services
2400 86th Street, Suite 13A
Des Moines, IA 50322
(800) 843-3496
(Publications and cards)

NFDA's Educational Foundation Marketplace
P.O. Box 2764
Milwaukee, WI 53227-0641
(800) 228-6332
(Catalog of books, brochures and videotapes available)

Pregnancy and Infant Loss Center, Inc.
1421 E. Wayzata Blvd., Suite 30
Wayzata, MN 55391
(612) 473-9372
(Resources for death of an infant, miscarriage, stillbirth)

Thanos Institute
P.O. Box 1928
Buffalo, NY 14231
(800) 742-8257
(Videos, brochures)

Willowgreen Productions
P.O. Box 25180
Fort Wayne, IN 46825
(219) 424-7916
(Videotapes and books available)

LIST OF SUPPLIERS

Batesville Management Services
P.O. Drawer 90
Batesville, IN 47006
(800) 457-9756
(Catalog of books, brochures and materials available)

The Dodge Co.
165 Cambridge Park Dr.
Cambridge, MA 02140
(617) 661-0500
(Book and resources available)

Guideline Publications
P.O. Box 1141
Madison, AL 35758
(800) 552-1076
(Booklets and brochures available)

Medic Publishing Co.
P.O. Box 89
Redmond, WA 98073-0089
(Booklets and brochures available)

The Sometimes Line
P.O. Box 638
Greene, IA 50636
(515) 823-4361
(Bereavement cards)

RESOURCE MATERIALS: BOOK LIST
(This is a list of suggested reading for aftercare providers.)

Bereavement—Counseling the Grieving Throughout the Life Cycle
by David Crenshaw
Continuum Publishing Co., NY 1991

Life After Loss—A Personal Guide Dealing with Death, Divorce, Job Change and Relocation
by Bob Diets
Fisher Books, Tucson, AZ 1988

Disenfranchised Grief—Recognizing Hidden Sorrow
by Kenneth Doka
Lexington Books, MA 1989

The Mourning Handbook
by Helen Fitzgerald
Simon & Schuster, NY 1994

Expressions of Healing
by Sandra Graves
Newcastle Publishing, North Hollywood, CA 1994

Living When a Loved One Has Died
by Earl Grollman
Beacon Press, Boston 1977

Death Etiquette for the 90's—What to Do & Say
Different Losses Different Issues—What to Expect and How to Help
Grief in the Workplace: 40 Hours Plus Overtime
Using Grief to Grow—How You Can Help—How You Can Get Help
by Johnette Hartnett
Good Mourning, VT 1993

Bereavement and Support—Healing in a Group Environment
by Marylou Hughes
Taylor & Francis, Washington, DC 1995

Helping People Through Grief
by Delores Kuenning
Bethany House Publishers, MN 1987

The Helper's Journey—Working with People Facing Grief, Loss, & Life-Threatening Illness
by Dale Larson
Research Press, Champaign, IL 1993

Aspects of Grief—Bereavement in Adult Life
by Jane Littlewood
Routledge, NY 1992

No Time for Goodbyes—Coping with Anger, Sorrow and Injustice after a Tragic Death
by Janice Harris Lord
Pathfinder Publishing, Ventura, CA 1988

Empty Arms
by Sherokee Ilse
Wintergreen Press, Maple Plain, MN 1990

Don't Take My Grief Away
by Doug Manning
Harper, San Francisco 1984

All Our Losses—All Our Griefs—Resources for Pastoral Care
by Kenneth Mitchell and Herbert Anderson
The Westminster Press, Philadelphia 1983

Loss & Anticipatory Grief
by Therese Rando
Lexington Books, MA 1986

Treatment of Complicated Mourning
by Therese Rando
Research Press, Champaign, IL 1993

Grief—The Mourning After Dealing with Adult Bereavement
by Catherine Sanders
John Wiley & Sons, NY 1989

What to Do When a Loved One Dies
by Eva Shaw
Dickens Press, Irvine, CA 1994

Men & Grief
by Carol Staudacher
New Harbinger Publications, Oakland, CA 1991

Understanding Grief—Helping Yourself Heal
by Alan Wolfelt
Accelerated Development Publishers, Muncie, IN 1992

Grief Counseling and Grief Therapy
by William Worden
Springer Publishing Co., NY 1991

REFERENCES

1. L. A. DeSpelder and A. L. Strickland, *Perspectives on Death: Cross-Cultural and Historical, The Last Dance—Encountering Death and Dying,* Chapter 2, Mayfield, Mountain View, California, 1992.
2. P. Aries, The Age of the Beautiful Death, Chapter 10, in *The Hour of Our Death* (First American Edition), Alfred A. Knopf, Inc., New York, pp. 446-450, 1981.
3. P. Aries, Death Denied, Chapter 12, in *The Hour of Our Death* (First American Edition), Alfred A. Knopf, Inc., New York, pp. 579-580, 1981.
4. C. Novitzke, What A Funeral Home? Chapter 27, in *Acute Grief—Counseling the Bereaved,* O. S. Margolis et al. (eds.), Columbia University Press, New York, p. 247, 1981.
5. K. Edison, Having the Courage to Care, Chapter 24, in *Acute Grief—Counseling the Bereaved,* O. S. Margolis et al. (eds.), Columbia University Press, New York, p. 231, 1981.
6. J. Borgwardt and D. Isard, A New Definition for Funeral Service, *American Funeral Director,* October 1993.
7. X. Cronin, The Debate Continues: Some Practitioners Question the Reasons for Aftercare While Others See a Need to Help with Grief Resolution, *American Funeral Director,* 117:8, pp. 18-19, August 1994.
8. T. S. Gilligan, The Legal Perils of Aftercare, *The Director, LXVII*:12, pp. 10-11, December 1995.
9. O. D. Weeks and C. Johnson, Developing a Successful Aftercare Program, *The Director, LXVII*:12, pp. 12, 14, 16, 18, December 1995.
10. B. Conley, Establishing Standards and Credentials is No Small Task, *The Director, LXVII*:12, pp. 20, 22, December 1995.
11. J. W. Worden, Attachment, Loss and the Tasks of Mourning, Chapter 1, in *Grief Counseling & Grief Therapy,* Springer, New York, p. 10, 1991.
12. A. D. Wolfelt, The Ability to Love Requires the Necessity to Mourn, Chapter 1, in *Understanding Grief—Helping Yourself Heal,* Accelerated Development Inc. Publishers, Muncie, Indiana, 1992.
13. S. Graves, *What is Grief? Expression of Healing—A Compassionate Workbook,* Newcastle, North Hollywood, California, 1994.
14. P. Rebold, Rebold & Son Funeral Directors, Cincinnati, Ohio, *Liability and Aftercare,* presented at the National Conference on Aftercare, Louisville, Kentucky, September 14, 1995.
15. *West, Section 491.014.* (2), Florida Statutes Annotated (Fla. Stat. Ann.), 1991.
16. T. S. Gilligan, The Legal Perils of Aftercare, *The Director, LXVII*:12, 1995.
17. M. Hughes, The Why and Wherefore of Bereavement Support Groups, Chapter 2, in *Bereavement and Support, Healing in a Group Environment,* Taylor & Francis, Washington, D.C., p. 15, 1995.

SECTION 2

Aftercare in Other Venues

CHAPTER 10

Aftercare and the Schools

Robert G. Stevenson

Everything that lives will one day die. Death is, after all, a part of life. However, a look at our schools could make one question this basic fact. The topic of death is one that is seldom discussed in schools and some educators labor under the mistaken belief that it is not a subject which they need to address. Schools often do not have a procedure for coping with student grief. Teachers are, for the most part, still unaware of the role they can play in helping grieving students. The reality is that students do experience the death of loved ones and their grief can have an impact on their learning and on the learning atmosphere which can be real, immediate, and profound.

When dealing with grief, students may react in any of a variety of ways. Both these students and their schools must learn to cope with behaviors which may include:

- emotional numbing—This can vary from a brief period of shock to a reaction where children believe, in effect, that if feelings hurt this much, they will withdraw into themselves and refuse to feel anything at all.
- guilt/anger—These two feelings are often linked in grieving people and may result in apathy (a withdrawing from life) or in acting out. This acting out from guilt and/or anger may be directed at others through verbal or even physical attacks. It can also be directed back at the student him/herself in a pattern of "accidents" or as punishment-seeking behavior.
- inability to concentrate—Grieving students may work on assignments, at home or in school, in the same way as they previously did

but with results that are far less satisfying. Their minds are, to put it simply, "on other things." Their loss is paramount and academic work takes a back seat or may be dismissed entirely because it has become meaningless in the face of death.

• fear of the future—The future is unknown and children may fear they will be unable to cope with additional losses that could arise in this unknown future. Examples of this fear may be seen in students who resist any further changes in their lives or their environment. This can be taken to a point where a student may even deliberately fail to avoid the change and losses which could accompany graduation. These fears, if unaddressed, may even develop into a type of free-floating anxiety where every change requiring action on the part of the individual becomes an immediate crisis.

Grief, although a healing process, does produce anxiety in the grieving individual and may impact friends and classmates as well. The effects of anxiety on school work have been demonstrated by a number of researchers, including Gaudry and Speilberger [1] (this work was among the first to identify the link between level of anxiety and student achievement) and Behrens et al. [2] (this study was among the first to describe the impact of loss on elementary school children in a school setting). Students experience a shorter attention span and difficulty in concentrating which may be accompanied by a drop in grades. In varying degrees, many of these students perceive themselves to be "helpless" in coping with crises. They may show signs of depression, increased episodes of daydreaming, or they may withdraw from socialization with peers. These students also report somatic complaints more often than their peers. All of these possible disruptions in the learning process and classroom routine make a teacher's role more difficult. Ignoring these very real difficulties being encountered by students will only magnify their effect. Aftercare is not only important for those in funeral service, it is a concept that clearly has a place in schools and the education process as well. However, although many of the tasks of aftercare take place following a death, the time to prepare to carry out these tasks is before the death occurs.

AFTERCARE GUIDELINES FOR TEACHERS

The following guidelines can help teachers to provide helpful aftercare for grieving students. They can be implemented now by educators and parents to prepare for the time when such a situation will occur.

Know What Local Support Systems Exist

In many areas there are now organizations with programs that provide assistance for just this type of situation. There are countless programs across the country which now offer help to schools. Concerned adults should learn what programs operate in their area, where they are, and how they can be contacted should the need arise.

Have a Procedure to Inform the Class As Soon As Possible When a Death Occurs

The National Association of Secondary School Principals has established a system for informing the school community of a death [3] (this protocol has been adopted by schools throughout the United States, Canada, and Europe; it can provide a good starting point for teachers and administrators who wish to have guidelines in place for dealing with such an event). The news will be painful no matter what is done; however, prior planning for such an event can help keep that pain to a minimum by avoiding mistakes—usually well-intentioned—that could make the reaction worse. This is important for children of all ages. A detailed discussion of the teacher's role in helping elementary school students to cope with the death of a classmate appeared in *Instructor* magazine [4] (this article discusses the role of the elementary school teacher in helping a child to understand death and grief), and the author, Dr. Janice Cohn, has worked as a consultant for the New York City Board of Education helping New York elementary schools which have experienced the death of a student.

Encourage Parents to Deal with Issues of Death at Home

In most cases, children will feel more comfortable discussing the topic of death with their parents who, after all, know their own children better than any "experts." This is an area where the home and school should cooperate to reinforce each other as all parties try to help the children involved. This is not an "either . . . or" situation. Many children need care in all areas of their lives when trying to cope with the death of a loved one. It is always appropriate for a parent to tell a child what s/he believes about an afterlife and to pass on personal and family traditions of faith. This cannot be done in a public school setting without the risk of violating the personal beliefs of many families. Students can speak of their beliefs, but that is not the same as a presentation by a caring adult who can answer the "Why?," which often follows such explanations. One of the best examples of such a parent-child talk was shown in the David Suskind film, *All the Way Home* [5] (this is David Suskind's production of Mosel's play (screenplay by Philip Reisman, Jr.), which is based on James Agee's Pulitzer Prize winning book *A Death in the Family*, Jean Simmons and Robert Preston play the parents and their child is played by Michael Kearney). A mother tries, with varying degrees of success, to explain to her little boy what death is as they discuss the illness of his grandfather. This film can be a valuable tool to facilitate discussion in a classroom or home setting. Another resource is the series on child development called, "Footsteps. . . ." In the episode entitled, ". . . And we were sad, remember?" two mothers take different tracks in explaining the death of a grandmother to their children. The video presents the effects of parental choices on children but stops short of telling parents how they should act toward their own child. That decision is still one that is best made by a parent. However, if parents avoid facing this issue, children may call upon educators for answers to their questions.

Be a Role Model

Grieving parents, teachers, and other concerned adults model ways to deal with sadness. They can show children that grief hurts, tears are "normal," and that emotions need not be "avoided." Such an experience can reduce fears of both children and parents and is really effective teaching. This task may be complicated if teachers have unresolved grief from a prior loss, or if they believe that their role as caregiver precludes them from dealing with personal issues related to a loss. In the first instance, it is most helpful for educators to examine their personal feelings about loss and grief before a crisis occurs. This can make them more aware of their feelings and help them to avoid unexpected emotional complications when helping students.

If a school community is to respond effectively to the grief that follows a death, all members of that community must be able to obtain assistance if needed. This includes educators and staff. In one school system, a teacher died in a tragic accident. The administration and teachers were there to support the students, families, and community members who looked to them for leadership in establishing aftercare programs. However, there was almost no thought given to the needs of the educators themselves. After a stress-filled year, their personal need to grieve caused many of them to become emotionally overwhelmed and, in some cases, physically ill. With proper "care" available to the caregivers throughout the aftercare process, this sort of trauma can be minimized. Both of these issues have been successfully addressed as part of professional in-service programs preparing school leaders to implement aftercare.

Cooperate with Parents

Myra Lipman of the New York Parents League has stated that schools cannot assume the entire responsibility for a child's death education nor can they ignore the matter entirely [cited in 6] (the editors assembled a group of authors to show the benefits of having death education in schools, based on practical examples drawn from courses offered over the previous 25 years). There should be effective home-school communication so that parents know what information is being presented to their children. Successful death education courses exist across the country and can make the school a focal point for helping concerned parents with specific needs to contact appropriate support groups in their community.

Avoid Silence

Social critic Phyllis Schlafly has been quoted as saying, "Anything they (teachers) do is apt to be far worse than doing nothing at all" [7] (a balanced discussion of the pros and cons of actual courses on death education which take a proactive approach rather than waiting to react to a crisis). It has been shown that silence can magnify the feelings of helplessness, hopelessness, and loneliness which are part of all grief reactions and can add feelings of worthlessness [8] (this article discusses the differences between fear and anxiety and the role that each plays in the child's understanding of death; it also presents implications for a school curriculum). In this way "silence" may actually strengthen all four of the emotions present in many suicide attempts. The silence which Ms. Schlafly sees as preferable can cause children to feel they must confront alone the topics of dying, death, and the feelings they generate.

Be Aware of the Importance of Nonverbal Communication

All of us must be aware of the many ways in which we communicate. Our attempts to speak with children can be influenced by location (where we speak), time (when we speak), and space (distance between us as we speak). We should be aware of all of the factors which have an impact on our communications with children. Location should be one in which children feel most comfortable or least threatened. In school, this is typically the child's classroom, not an auditorium, cafeteria, or assembly hall. The best time to speak about a death is as soon as the entire staff has been informed and knows what to tell students about what has happened. It is not good to postpone such communication, but it can also be a mistake to speak out too quickly and spread misunderstanding or rumor.

Memorialize After a Death

Memorials need not be traditional or formal, but it is important to show students that a change such as a death does not simply happen without other changes taking place as well. By taking time to mark that change with some ritual, some rite of passage, we confirm that this change has happened and that the child's reactions to that change are justified. If we try to "deny" that a change has taken place, we should not be surprised when children adopt coping mechanisms which attempt to do the same and continue that "denial." In some cases, students may act out to block "business as usual" until some recognition of the death takes place in the school. There are some who believe that such memorials should not take place when a suicide has occurred. There has still been a change for students. One must be careful not to romanticize the method of death but a rite of passage is still essential both to acknowledge the change that has occurred and to validate to students that *every* life has meaning and their absence would be noticed because their life in that school is so important.

When rituals take place in a school following a death, parents should be kept informed of all that takes place so that they can remain the primary support for their children. Classroom rituals have involved lighting candles, drawing pictures, sharing memories, or, in the case of a student death, creating a memory book as a gift for the parents and family. Other rituals may involve the planting of a tree, donation of books or other equipment to the school in the name of the deceased (with an accompanying ceremony), or a gift to charity in the name of the deceased.

My students used to raise money with candy sales in school. The money was regularly sent to local charities, such as the Tomorrow's Children's Fund or the Emmanuel Cancer Foundation, in the name of deceased loved ones. A notification was then sent to survivors that a gift had been made in their loved one's name. This ritual had benefits at many levels and continued at the students' request for several years.

It was important enough to my high school students that they continued it even after my retirement.

Offer Support for All Ages

Before my retirement, my students published several articles discussing what schools could do for students—from a student perspective. We regularly received calls from parents and organizations throughout the area. They sought assistance in providing help for bereaved children and families and wanted me to ask my students (high school juniors and seniors) to suggest or to evaluate a particular response. It is clear that schools do not have all the answers to any problem, but they do have information which many parents have found useful. When the school can act as a clearinghouse for such information, there is no need to reinvent the wheel.

Provide Security And Structure

With one part of life "out of control" because of a death, students need to be able to feel that they still have some control in other areas of life. It is not unusual for students to attend class immediately after a loss and to try to go through the day in as "normal" a manner as possible. This gives them a feeling of "control" over this part of life. However, to force children to behave in a routine manner after a death when they do not wish to do so, removes the very feelings of control we are trying to reinforce. The "individual" child is ALWAYS more important than a "general" policy.

Plan To Cover A Full Range Of Responses

Planning should be aimed not only at school-wide response after a death but to things a teacher may do with an individual student. Teachers should know that an individual child may have an increased need for attention. If asked questions by students, teachers should be honest and avoid platitudes, avoid speaking of blame for the death, listen (and not feel the need to try to solve all of the grieving student's problems or to make everything "all right"). Help students to understand grief and to set priorities. Lower grades do not necessarily make someone a "bad" person. They are easier to face and overcome when the student begins to understand the factors that may be causing them.

Help Each Child at His/her Own Developmental Level

There are many materials available to use with students when a death has occurred. Books about death and grief exist in abundance. They are geared to many ages, developmental levels, and even to specific cultural/ethnic groups. A book that is very good for a middle school student or class may miss the mark entirely if read to second graders. Teachers and parents should know *in advance* what is contained in any story they share with a child. There are death/loss curricula for high schools, middle schools, and elementary schools. These are not automatically interchangeable. Material aimed at younger students can be used with older students, but the reverse is not equally true. A classic book that pointed out the developmental differences in student grief and highlighted possible ways of dealing with grief in ways appropriate to the level of the student is *Discussing Death* by Gretchen Mills et al. It does not provide a curriculum, but offers instead the information that can be the basis for creating classes to aid grieving students.

Acknowledge the Impact of a Child's Death on Teachers

As time passes, most members of the school community will grieve, recover, and move on from a loss and its aftermath. It may seem that, since the death of a student has a clear impact on that child's teacher, to stress this point is only to belabor the obvious. However, teachers in the roles of caregiver and educator may have difficulty taking time to tend to their own needs. When a child dies, teachers often spend long hours helping children and parents and in seeking training to be more effective in that role. Such a death also places an emotional strain on teachers as well as on students and parents. It is important that schools acknowledge this situation and that they take time to acknowledge the change that has occurred for staff as well as for students.

Assume a Partnership Role in Aftercare

The partnership of parents and teachers is vital in assuring a caring atmosphere for students in which learning can flourish. In addition, every teacher and school should have another "partner" when called on to assist students following a death. Each school should develop a "partner" school that can be called upon for help when a death effects a school community. Typically such a partnership involved joint staff development so that the educators in both schools get to know each other before some crisis occurs. They then can work out ways in which the school coping with the aftermath of a death can draw on needed support from the partner school. Teachers too may at times need a partner. A teacher coping with personal losses may not be able to give full attention to the needs of grieving students and may require the assistance of a colleague at such a time. Partners can also discuss and evaluate attempted interventions and constantly improve their ability to assist students.

REVIEWING THE MAIN POINTS

In looking back we can see that the following points should be kept in mind when attempting to help students deal who are grieving a death:

1. Know before the need arises what local support systems exist.
2. When a death occurs in the school "community," inform the class and share the facts that are known in an age-appropriate manner.
3. Since parents are the primary support of children, schools should do all they can to assist parents at this difficult time and continue to work with parents throughout the year. Children are helped most when home and school cooperate.
5. In the long run, silence about death and grief is more likely to hurt a child than speaking about it in a caring manner.
6. Nonverbal communication conveys more than words alone.
7. The memorials and rituals which follow a death show children that each of us is important and validate their feelings by confirming that a change has occurred.
8. With proper preparation, schools can offer support for students of all ages, but each child must be helped in a manner appropriate to his or her developmental level.
9. Aftercare plans and procedures should cover a full range of response, from school-wide to specific responses used with individual students.
10. In times of bereavement, feelings of "control" are important.
11. A student's death has an impact on teachers and educators and we must remember to take time to help the helpers.

RECOMMENDATIONS

Children who have suffered the death of a relative or friend clearly have special needs. A well-known psychologist once said of her own grief, that knowing why you hurt won't make you hurt less. It should be added, however, that it could keep you from hurting more than you have to. If this is true for adults, it is even more so for bereaved children who have lost someone precious to them. To keep the hurt from being worse than it has to, schools and parents have found it helpful to create procedures to employ when the need arises. In this way, plans are formed when the pressures of time and emotional distress are at a minimum. School policies, staff training programs, and even appropriate readings for use by (or with) students can be put in place in advance of need. There are things which can be done by parents and educators now to help children faced with the need to cope with a death. If, as a parent or educator, you had been faced with the situation described above, what would you have done? If you are able to take the time now to think of an answer to that question, it may be the first step toward helping a student in the future.

REFERENCES

1. E. Gaudry and C. Speilberger, *Anxiety and Educational Achievement,* Wiley and Sons, Sydney, Australia, 1971.
2. R. Behrens et al., A Descriptive Study of Elementary School Children Who Have Suffered a Major Loss, master's thesis, Simmons College of Social Work, 1964, cited by H. Moller in *Explaining Death to Children,* E. A. Grollman (ed.), Beacon Press, Boston, Massachusetts, 1967.
3. R. G. Stevenson and H. L. Powers, How to Handle Death in the School, *Education Digest,* May 1987.
4. J. Cohn, The Grieving Student, *Instructor,* January 1987.
5. T. Mosel, *All The Way Home,* Paramount Pictures, 1963.
6. R. G. Stevenson and E. P. Stevenson (eds.), *Teaching Students about Death: A Comprehensive Resource for Educators and Parents,* Charles Press, Philadelphia, Pennsylvania, 1996.
7. F. M. Bordewich, Mortal Fears, *The Atlantic,* February 1988.
8. R. G. Stevenson, The Fear of Death in Childhood, in *Children and Death: Perspectives from Birth through Adolescence,* J. E. Schowalter et al. (eds.), Praeger, New York, 1987.
9. G. Mills, *Discussing Death: A Guide to Death Education,* E.T.C. Publishing, Palm Springs, California, 1976.

ADDITIONAL REFERENCES NOT CITED IN TEXT

Fassler, J. *Helping Children Cope: Mastering Stress Through Books and Stories,* New York, The Free Press, 1978. (Joan Fassler's book examines children's literature by topic and age and is considered by many parents to be a very important aid in helping them select books with which to help their children deal with developmental problems, including death in an age-appropriate way.)

Levin, S. Lessons in Death, *The Dallas Morning News,* April 17, 1998, Section F. (This is a beautifully written, balanced discussion of the growing area of death education in public schools.)

Nagy, M., The Child's View of Death, in *The Meaning of Death,* H. Feifel (ed.), McGraw-Hill, New York, 1959. (This brief article gives an excellent overview of the developmental process the child goes through in reaching a mature understanding of death. It describes the results of one of the first studies conducted in this area.)

Stevenson, R. G., *What Will We Do? Preparing a School Community to Cope with Crises,* Baywood, Amityville, New York, 1994. (This book offers an overview of the ways in which schools can assist children and parents in a time of crisis, including the period of grief following a death.)

CHAPTER 11

My Journey to the Dougy Center . . .
. . . A Support Center for Grieving
Children and Their Families

Beverly J. Chappell

AFTERCARE?? Aftercare for families who have had a loved one die is a fairly new concept. In 1948 through 1951, my student nursing days, even adequate care of the patient who was in the process of dying was not the rule. This patient was almost always placed in the room farthest away from the nurses' desk and his call-light the last one to be answered. Frequently the student nurses were told by the nursing instructors, head nurses, and the staff doctors to give more attention to the newly admitted and post-operative patients for whom we could do something worthwhile. We were told, "there isn't anything you can do for that patient to make him better."

This was precisely the patient to whom I wanted to give my attention. On one occasion I was almost expelled from nursing school because I sat with a woman, a former industrial nurse and one of my favorite patients, holding her hand and wiping the uremic frost from her face until she died. At another time while working nights on the small west wing of the hospital, I let a young mother and her two small children in the emergency exit door to spend nights with her husband, dying of leukemia, after the night supervisor had made her early rounds. I pushed her out again before the supervisor returned in the morning. The little ones slept curled within their daddy's arms. This was at a time when no one under sixteen was allowed in the hospital. It was said that they might bring in germs. And, true, that was very likely. At that point, however, it was the leukemia that would cause his death, not a germ.

The mom had told the children that Daddy was going to die soon. I only hope it made letting go a little easier for all of them because someone had done the unthinkable. The daddy had not just disappeared out of their lives never to be seen again. That kind of thing has happened through the years. It is still happening today—with all of our sophistication.

This was the same hospital where I met my pediatrician husband (then in internship and residency), a man whose mother died when he was fourteen. He and his twelve-year-old sister had been sent to a movie that afternoon with their two cousins while their mother died and was moved to the funeral home, then were taken to the cousins' house after the movie to spend the night. At dinner, almost as an afterthought, they were told, "Oh, by the way, your mother died this afternoon while you were gone." My husband was so angry about being sent away and not being told that his mother was dying that he refused to go to the funeral—and then felt guilty for not going. He lived with that anger and guilt for forty-five years before he finally dealt with it and became reconciled to his mother's death.

Because of the death of his beloved mother while he was an early teenager, it was his greatest wish for me to stay at home and be a full-time mother after our first child was born. With his $125.00/month residency salary, giving up my larger salary made it difficult. It was worth the financial struggle and a joy to be a constant part of our children's lives. It seemed like no time at all before our firstborn had "flown the nest" and our other child would soon follow. Without all of their activities and my taxi-driving rituals, where would the next lap of my journey take me? Did I want to return to my nursing profession?

During our son's junior year in high school, the mother of his best friend died after a thirteen-month struggle with cancer. His mother and dad were divorced and his two much older siblings were no longer in the area. Since Brian was not old enough to drive, often either our daughter or I drove him to the hospital and stayed with him while he visited his mom. It was unbelievable. In 1972, this many years later, her doctor and the nurses on this unit were very little different from my student nursing days—"scared to death of death!" Will it always be considered a failure for a patient to die, for the treatment not to work?

I held Brian's and his sister's hands at their mom's bedside as she died and spent much time with them during their agonizing period of raw grief. Brian came to live with our family for a time until he graduated from high school. He became one of my greatest teachers about teen grief—from those days until the present.

This experience increased my interest in working with the dying patient, but how did one get preparation for that type of work? Often I had heard, "when the student is ready, a teacher will appear." And appear she did.

In the fall of 1973, a course "Issues of Death and Dying" was being offered by Ecumenical Ministries of Oregon. It was not too difficult to persuade my pediatrician husband to attend with me. He had very recently had two little girls die—one who was three of a Wilms' kidney tumor, the other who was four of leukemia. The text for this course was Dr. Elisabeth Kübler-Ross' book *On Death and Dying.* The course assured me that this was the direction I wanted to take on the next portion of my journey.

In April of 1974, we met Dr. Ross at a lecture and in June went to one of her One-Week Workshops. Following this workshop, reading, seminars, and workshops on dying, death, and bereavement became the air I breathed. My husband was a great sport and accompanied me most of the time. By September I was doing lectures for college psychology classes at Portland State University, at the University of Oregon Medical School for medical and nursing students, at hospitals and nursing homes for staffs, and two-day workshops in isolated communities for hospital personnel and clergy.

In 1976, I coordinated, as well as taught in, a winter term course at Warner-Pacific College. For many years I regularly taught classes on death and dying, including Children and Death, for student nurses at the Walla Walla School of Nursing. I co-taught a course, Dying and Surviving, for three terms at Portland State University out of the Department of Urban Studies. Several of the students in that class had a life-threatening illness and continued to repeat the class for the support they received from each other. When the class ended, a number of these students continued to meet in our home on an every-other-week basis. I also began working at a hospital with dying patients and their families, although the hospital of my choice really did not know what to do with an advocate for the dying. People found out about my work more by word of mouth than by doctors' or hospital referral.

Even though my observations of families with a loved one dying gave me great insights as to how the children or grandchildren in these families were or were not prepared, it wasn't until two or three years later that my work narrowed almost exclusively to families who had a dying child. In many cases the mother took the ill child from medical center to medical center in search of a cure. Dad was working two or even three jobs to pay the bills—and the oldest child in the family, sometimes only eight, was parenting the younger children of the family. There were school lunches to make, laundry to do, and, more difficult, disciplining the littler siblings.

Occasionally this little "mommy" would share with me that she wished her ill brother would die and that the rest of them could finally be a family again. "I don't want to be the mommy! I just want to be the little girl!" And when the brother did die, this little girl felt totally responsible for his death. It was then that I learned first hand about the perils of "Magical Thinking" and how it put surviving children, and often the parents, on tremendous guilt trips.

At that time the siblings were very seldom included in the funeral or final ritual. After the burial the parents tried to pretend everything was the same as always. Seldom was the name of the child who died mentioned in front of the other children. Their photographs mysteriously disappeared. The children might ask questions about the "missing" sibling and mom or dad would get teary. After the third time they did not ask again. But the questions were always a part of their wondering. Frequently I held surviving children in my arms trying to assure them that they definitely were not responsible for the death and that their parents still loved them very much even though their sibling had died. Many times the children could not be convinced of that. Some of the parents were so deep in their own grief that, secretly, I was not convinced either. Often the family closeness was totally destroyed. Many of these grieving parents divorced.

Schools, funeral homes, and hospitals started calling me for advice and/or consultation: should Sally go to the funeral? Jimmy should not see the body, should he? Georgie is misbehaving terribly on the playground. The other children are not safe around him. Kyle is running away all the time. When he is home he kicks and bites and fights. He has even put his foot through his bedroom wall in several places. Annie is over-eating. Johnny is not sleeping. Beth has always been a good student; now her grades are falling and it is a fight to get her to go to school. And, often I was told "Molly-4, Kevin-10, or Tony-15 has been caught shoplifting. They are stealing things they have no use for, not things that they need, or even want."

In May 1980, I was called to a nearby grade school to do a workshop with a small group of mostly ten-year-olds who had experienced the death of a parent or grandparent or had a loved one in the process of dying. I had previously worked only with one-on-one situations—one family, one or both parents, or the child or children of the grieving family. I called upon my friend, Cheri Lovre, in Salem, who had been working with children for several years and asked her to share her expertise with me and give me the courage to go into this unfamiliar experience. It took much more courage for the school and the parents to allow this workshop to happen even though the children were eager to try it.

When the day arrived, we sat in a circle on the floor in the resource center. The children were full of anxiety and showed it in many different ways. My fears and discomforts were hopefully more well disguised. It took quite a while to find a comfort level for sharing their feelings, but when it began and as it continued I witnessed the miracle of children helping children with the pain and agony of their grief—until now not a hint of it recognized by anyone I knew. They taught me more that day about children needing to share their feelings with other children of comparable ages and experiences in a safe environment, away from their grieving parents—and without judgment—than anything I had experienced before or have since.

It was shortly after that I received a letter from Elisabeth Kübler-Ross, "Dougy is coming to Portland for some new experimental treatment. I told his family that you would meet them at the airport and look after them while they are there. Give Al a hug for me. Love, Elisabeth."

Doug and his family became the next powerful teachers to impact our lives. He was in the final stages of an inoperable brain tumor and, while in Portland, the radiation treatment could not shrink the tumor so that he could be given the experimental treatment being developed by Dr. Edward Neuwelt at the Oregon Health Science University. The chemotherapy, which hopefully was to pass through the blood brain barrier, could not be given because anything else added to the overly swollen brain would press on the medulla and kill him instantly. I watched as Doug reached out to another dying child and told him not to be afraid to die. I continued watching as he comforted other dying children and as he did everything he could do to prepare his family, the staff, the chaplains, and me for his death. He told the chaplain that he was too tired to fight any longer, but he could not die yet, not until his family could make it without him.

Dougy's death came in December 1981, less than three months after he returned home to South Carolina from Portland. I kept in touch by phone, letters, and through a manuscript written by his mother, but was too far away to be of much assistance as his parents, his four brothers, and two sisters responded to that death with dances of denial, blame, anger, and helplessness. Although unable to help Doug's family with their grief at that time and distance, the spirit of that caring, loving, early teen filled my being. I knew that there must be something I could do to allow his spirit to live on.

In April 1982, my husband announced to me that he was planning to take a week away from his practice to attend a one-week workshop, "Introduction to Interpretation of Spontaneous Drawings," being put on here in Portland by Dr. Gregg Furth. Taking a week off from his pediatric practice was unheard of and to take a workshop that he had shied away from for many years totally stunned me—even though I had hoped for ages that he would take it and possibly (at long last) deal with the feelings he had carried all these years over the death of his mother. These were feelings which he definitely had no desire to look at or discuss.

Gregg had been a family friend for many years and was very aware of Allan's "hang-ups" concerning death, especially the death of his mother. I had organized the workshop here in Portland, but made myself as scarce as possible so I would not inhibit Allan in any way as he participated in this workshop with Gregg and twenty-seven other searching adults. This major step that was so hesitantly taken became the longest, most painfully wrenching, difficult week of his life. It also brought about the most tremendous healing—the first healing for him in forty-five years. He was freer, more relaxed than I had ever seen him. It was almost like being married to a different husband.

I mention this workshop and change in Allan only because it led to his being open, from that time on, to the fact that children needed to address their grief to enable them to go on with life and become all that they could be. And this led directly to the next step toward forming a safe place where children could talk with other children in grief and realize they were not alone in their feelings and pain.

In August, a young boy who had just celebrated his eighth birthday came to the office for a physical so that he could play school sports. After his check-up and he had left the room for the playroom, his mother, who as a child had also been a patient of my husband's, said to him, "Dr. Chappell, I need to talk to you. Michael has become a monster and we don't know what to do with him. It is terrible! He kicks and bites. He runs away from school and from home. His grades are poor— he has always been a good student. I don't know what to do!! Can you help me?"

Dr. Chappell asked her when this unusual behavior began and she responded, "Last October." Then he asked if anything might have happened at that time to precipitate these reactions. Her reply was, "Yes. His father died."

The story continued that Dad and his best friend had gone to the store for milk about 10:30 P.M. and not returned. She had called hospitals and police all night long, but got no help. At noon the next day a police officer and family member came to the door to tell them that both Johnny and his friend were dead. While the officer was talking to the mom, Mike's aunt was talking to him. She did whatever so many well-meaning people have done for centuries, patted him on the head and said, "Mike, now you are the man of the family. You have to be strong and take care of your mother and little brothers. Don't cry or it will make them sad. It will make them cry, too." (What does "be strong" mean to a seven-year-old child?)

Before they left his office, Allan called me and asked if I would be willing to work with Mike. I told him I would be delighted and then reminded him that we planned to be out of town for ten days starting the next week. "Tell them to stop by the house on their way home and I will loan them some appropriate books from my library to read while we are gone."

I loaned them two books about children having a parent die and talked with them for quite a while. Soon after we returned home from our trip, Mike and his mom dropped by and brought back one of the books saying he had not found it very helpful. They asked if they could keep the other one longer; that it really spoke to both of them. This was Eda LeShan's *Learning to Say Goodbye* [1]. Mom said Mike had been ill and had stayed home from school. While the next younger son was at school and the youngest son down for a nap, she and Michael would sit and read this book. She would read until she started crying and then Mike would say, "I'll read, Mom, while you cry and then when I start crying you can read again."

Mike kept the book until late January, reading parts of it to his best friends when they came to his house to visit or play. He worked hard to make sense of his loss. (It was only recently that I was told by Mike's mother, "For quite a while Mike spent one or two evenings a week at Dr. Chappell's office after Dr. Chappell had finished with his patients. He and Mike drew pictures, made paper airplanes and flew them, and talked about how much it hurt to have a parent die 'when you are just a kid'.") And while Mike was working on his grief, my husband and I were on a quest to find anyone in the city of Portland who would support our belief that children needed help with their grieving. They needed to talk, rage, and cry with other children who had suffered comparable losses. They had to know they were not alone in having a parent, sibling, grandparent, or best friend die.

Who would listen and agree that we might be aware of something important? My physician husband was able to open doors for a friend and me that we did not have the clout to arrange. With him at our side we visited the neo-natal intensive care unit at the medical school, the chiefs of pediatrics and pediatric oncology, child psychiatrists and psychologists, family therapists, and counselors. No one—not one person—was willing to step up and say, "I think you may have something here. I would be willing to refer children to you." One person did write us a note after our visit and said he would like to have us keep in touch with him, to let him know if we did something and it worked. (That, in itself, was encouraging!)

The friend, another Bev, and I sought out people who could tell us what needed to be done to start an organization where grieving children could tell their stories, listen to others, and support each other. Who should be on a Board of Directors? What about incorporating? How do we get a 501(c)3 tax exempt status? It all seemed so overwhelming. Where should we begin? As we left the office of this person who had been most helpful, who had been the founder and director of an early hospice just outside of Portland, I said, "You know all these things. We are starting from scratch and don't know anything. It is scary, but I guess we will learn as we go." As we were walking to the door she put an arm around each of us and said the most profound thing I had ever heard, "Bev and Bev—that is God's protection for you. If you truly knew the struggle ahead for you, I'm afraid you wouldn't take the first step." No truer words were ever spoken!

November and December were spent gathering a Board of Directors. We had been given good information and most of the people who agreed to serve on the board were fantastic. By December we had four little boys and a fourteen-year-old girl waiting for us to begin a group. The first meeting was held in our home the 29th of December, 1982. In no time at all two little girls (sisters) and two pre-teen boys (not related) joined the group. All of these children had experienced the death of a dad.

The next question became, "How often should we meet?" We tried once a month, but the children said that was not often enough. Then we tried meeting weekly. That was too often and became invasive in their school, sports activities, and family life. Once every other week was perfect for the children and their parents—and for the facilitators.

Several of us facilitating the children had trained at the Attitudinal Healing Center in Tiburon, California, on children's group dynamics, but no one suggested that the mothers bringing these children to the group needed more assistance than the children. They sat in the living room and studied their feet, not interacting with each other at all. Conversely, once the children were in a safe place and could talk without making their moms sad or cry, they did and said what they felt was important for them to share. From the first night the children taught us, as facilitators, what they needed to do to heal. AND THEY KNEW!!

One evening at a post-group meeting, it was suggested we split up the facilitators and send some of them upstairs to work with the mothers. That was one of our best decisions. As parents shared their fears and concerns and the children did likewise, the facilitators could use the information gleaned at pre and post meetings to gently guide both the parents and the children in their healing. Something we had not anticipated and we learned immediately not to question, sometimes siblings remembered their loved ones and the facts surrounding the death differently. As one would speak, the other would say, "That isn't the way it was!!"

It was, we realized, truly different for each child, as was the relationship each person—child or adult—had with the loved one who died. The children continued to teach us exactly what they needed. One wanted to draw pictures. Another needed to race around making lots of noise. And often one would just snuggle up to one of the facilitators needing to be held and loved.

By word of mouth the groups upstairs and downstairs kept growing. Before long we had outgrown our home. February 29, 1984, we moved into a house on the periphery of Warner Pacific College campus where almost immediately we began a second Sons and Daughters Group (loss of parent, grandparent, primary care person) and began the first Sibs and Friends Group (loss of sibling or best friend). We had room to expand and also have office space. The college allowed us use of the gym for expending the kids' excess energy and the auditorium for trainings of our volunteer facilitators and for workshops.

Valentine's Day, February 14, 1985, Dr. Elisabeth Kübler-Ross came to Portland and did an evening benefit lecture for us. That afternoon she helped us celebrate the Grand Opening of The Dougy Center for Grieving Children and Families, named for Doug Turno, the lad from South Carolina we had both known and loved. He had endowed us with his legacy and loving spirit before his death at age thirteen.

The next day, Bonnie Strauss from *Hour Magazine,* in Portland with Gary Collins for another purpose, came to The Dougy Center (TDC) with cameramen and for more than eight hours videotaped TDC at work. This program was aired on April 15, 1985—our first of many national exposures.

In August of 1985, we did our first training on a national level for people from other states wanting to begin support programs in their communities based on what we were doing. From that training came our first "spin-off" center, Fernside: A Center for Grieving Children, in Cincinnati, Ohio. They opened their doors in December of 1985 with Rachel Burrell as founder and director.

Bonnie Strauss had been deeply touched by The Dougy Center, but especially by eight-year-old Jenny whom she had featured on *Hour Magazine.* She returned to Portland and did a follow-up story on Jenny and TDC for *Good Morning America.* This aired in July 1987. From this program came hundreds of responses from across the United States. By overwhelming request we held our Second National Training that October for more people wishing to start groups for grieving children in their communities. From this training came almost immediately new support centers in Tacoma, Washington; Fort Worth, Texas; Portland, Maine; Charleston, South Carolina; and Scottsdale and Tucson, Arizona.

By this time we had many requests to add another group. It started with the staff quite apprehensive, certain that it wouldn't work. This group was for pre-schoolers, three- to five-year-olds. Once again, at the very first meeting, the children proved us wrong and we continued to learn from them what they needed for their healing. The first day a four-year-old girl stood beside the chair where her mother was sitting and said, "My sister died on the mountain. That is why I am here. I need to talk about how I feel."

The experts thought we were crazy when, in April 1988, we put on a concurrent session at the Orlando, Florida, ADEC Conference (Association for Death Education and Counseling) about our newly formed groups for LITTLES (three- to five-year-olds). We had been doing these groups for more than a year and seeing amazing results. A university faculty member was so intrigued with our success with grieving children, especially that young, that he came to TDC to witness what we were doing firsthand—and was convinced. At that time the concept of grieving children sharing feelings and supporting other grieving children in comparable age groups was entirely new.

It wasn't long before we added a group for children and teens who had experienced the death of a parent, sibling, or friend by suicide. Two years later another group was added for those suffering a death loss by homicide—and we outgrew another facility. In July of 1988, we were fortunate to locate and move to a perfectly wonderful huge, old home which we have since purchased. The mortgage was burned in April 1997.

Within the Portland Metro Area the most difficult group to reach was the teens. They wanted no part of a "little kids' center." Suddenly they began, one by one, to come for support. We had started a Monthly Meeting Group for overflow families on the waiting list because of temporary lack of space. We did not want these people to feel abandoned until space opened for them in the smaller, ongoing, every other week groups. This group was open to children of all ages, and their parents, with different types of death losses. Strangely, this once a month meeting was attracting more and more teens. Now there are so many teens wanting to be a part of a teens only support group that there are three ongoing groups for teens at the Center.

TDC reaches out to the community and has trained crisis teams in many schools. The Center has been available for any crisis and tragedy that happens in the Metro-Portland area—as well as across the nation. Hundreds of people from the community have taken the Volunteer Training and some volunteers have continued to serve the Center as long as ten and twelve years.

Referrals to the Center are received primarily from hospice programs, hospitals, physicians/pediatricians, school counselors and teachers, the Department of Justice, personnel departments, mental health workers, Services to Children and Families (SCF), and previous participants and volunteers.

In 1992, the name of The Dougy Center for Grieving Children was changed to include the addition, The National Center for Grieving Children and Families.

Let me share with you where The Dougy Center is now and what hopes there are for the near future. In conversations and written communications from Donna Schuurman, Executive Director of The Dougy Center, this is what I have learned.

For the first time in the Center's history it is financially stable. The director has had many sleepless nights and has worked diligently with the Board of Directors and others to get it to this point. Because a support program for grieving children was such a new concept and because, at the beginning of this journey, specialists caring for children did not see the need for such a program since "children do not grieve," it was very difficult to obtain financial backing to keep the doors open. Now that grief support has become a service demanded by families, schools in crisis—those across the nation and around the world wanting to form such programs—and acknowledged and supported by specialists working with children and teens, funding is more accessible than ever before.

The Dougy Center currently serves approximately 275 children and teens between the ages of three and nineteen and over 120 parents or other adult caregivers in thirty ongoing grief support groups. These groups include:

- six groups for children ages six to ten who have lost a parent
- one group for children ages six to ten who have lost a sibling
- two groups for pre-schoolers ages three to five
- one group for children ages eleven to fourteen
- one group for children who have experienced a murder or violent death
- three groups for teenagers
- one group for those who have experienced a suicide in their family

Adult (parents/primary caregivers) groups meet separately, but at the same time as each of the above groups. There are 125 adults in these groups.

In addition, a varying number of children/teens and their families are served in our Monthly Meeting support group. TDC receives five to ten phone calls per day from parents, teachers, school counselors, or family members in the Portland area and across the country seeking help or advice in dealing with a child or children in grief.

Since its inception, The Dougy Center has served more than 8,000 individuals in direct and indirect grief support services. The number of children and adolescents has increased over the last two years, from 250 to 325 each month. TDC continues to have more people than space in the ongoing, smaller every-other-week groups at the Center, although all new families preferring placement in a smaller group can attend the Monthly Meeting until space is available. The policy has always been for the groups to be open-ended and each family may stay as long or as short a time as deemed necessary by them. The average length of participation at TDC is twelve months.

Since the very beginning of the Center, groups have been formed to fill specific needs and requests. There has been a need for an expanded program for those in the Portland area experiencing violent deaths, many gang related. A satellite program, The Dougy Center, N/NE is now functioning in that area of Portland in a rented house. It has been suggested by dads whose wives have died that it would be helpful to have a group just for men. It is especially difficult for most dads to take moms' place with their daughters. Many areas find dads needing special help. One dad found out his daughter was having her teacher re-do hair each morning when she arrived at school because Daddy couldn't do it right.

An old garage behind TDC main house will be torn down. In its place will be built a two-story facility with a full basement to house a resource center containing a library with books, video players, and tapes—a comfortable place to be. This facility will provide much needed extra group meeting rooms.

In 1997, we were privileged to receive national coverage in *Newsweek, U.S. News and World Report, Parenting,* and other news magazines. More than 100 communities in the United States and Canada (and most recently, The Rainbow House in Kobe, Japan) have developed grief support programs for children based on The Dougy Center's model after receiving our national training. The "Ripple Effect" has been amazing. As TDC continues to do National Trainings, the centers formed from those trainings are also doing National Trainings.

This means that our spin-off "children" centers are giving us "grandchildren" centers and they are perhaps begetting even "great-grandchildren centers.

People have come for training from England, Ireland, South America, Australia, Germany, Canada, Jamaica, and Japan for a National Summer Institute. Presently there are FAX and e-mail communications to and from South Africa and Athens, Greece, about support programs for grieving children.

In 1993, the death of my husband left me with the loss of my greatest support system. Family and friends from across the United States sent contributions to TDC in his memory. Information about TDC was included with thank-you letters acknowledging those gifts. One of these packets of information was seen in the home of one of my high school classmates by a friend of hers from Tobolsk, Russia. Rosa, a teacher of English, asked her about TDC and its services and told her of conditions and the poor health of the people in her area. "So many of our children have had siblings, parents, and grandparents die—and are not in good health themselves. Can you get me information so that I might begin a support group at my school?"

The WARM Place for Grieving Children in Forth Worth, Texas, was close by and I asked their Founder/Executive Director, Peggy Bohme, if she could get information to them immediately. Peggy told me it would be like getting it from TDC, that their copies of support group materials still carried TDC name. A letter in December 1997 from my high school friend said she has heard from others that Rosa is doing a children's grief support group, but she has not yet heard directly from Rosa.

When TDC was humbly begun, none of these amazing developments were a part of our agenda. They were not a part of our wildest dreams. All that we wished was to offer support, caring, and love to as many grieving children as was possible. But the pebble that was gently dropped into the water has rippled across the state of Oregon, the nation, Canada, and now the world. It has rippled and rippled—and with each additional child and family that is supported in their grief I feel more humbled and blessed by those believing in, and expanding, this dream. There aren't words to adequately express my gratitude and delight. Dare I just way, WOW!!

In closing, may I leave you with something that captures the heart of what happens when children have an opportunity to share and help others with their grief in the safe, warm "nests" provided by these grief support centers for children and their families. In a recent newsletter from Fernside: A Center for Grieving Children in Cincinnati, Ohio, is a poem written by Jerome H [2]. It expresses what many of the Centers' children feel. He has given me permission to share it with you.

> MY FERNSIDE by Jerome H.
>
> I came to Fernside, not long ago
> I was a boy, just about 8 years old
> and sat in a circle.
> And there were others just like me.
>
> I saw it in their eyes
> and in their hearts,
> they hurt just like me.
>
> Oh, not just a scrape to the knee,
> but a bruise to the heart,
> a hurt that will always be.
>
> For no one can replace him or her
> or either of them.
> That's just the way it is,
> and will always be.
>
> But I came to Fernside.
> That's the difference,
> and sat in a circle,
> for there was a place for me.

Yes, the grieving child and teen continues to be—and will always be—the greatest teachers we will ever have. And we must always continue to listen and to learn!

REFERENCES

1. E. LeShan, *Learning to Say Goodbye: When a Parent Dies,* Macmillan Publishing Co., Inc., New York, 1976.
2. H. Jerome, My Fernside, in *Inside Fernside, XI*:6, November/December 1997.

CHAPTER 12

A Hospital-Based Grief Support Center: The Nuts and Bolts of Development

Ben Wolfe

Comprehensive, coordinated programs and services offered under one "roof" for individuals, families, staff, and communities dealing with an impending death or who are bereaved are rare. St. Mary's Medical Center's Grief Support Center (GSC) in Duluth, Minnesota, however, has been such a center for the past fifteen years. An umbrella for various support programs and services and located within the Medical Center's Social Services Department, the GSC provides a comprehensive program of counseling, support, advocacy, education, and research for individuals who are dealing with, or affected by, an impending death or who are bereaved (as a result of ANY type of death). Programs and services are not only for adults, parents, children, and families throughout the Duluth, Minnesota and Superior, Wisconsin area, but also for health and educational institutions, community members, and specialized groups in northern Minnesota, northern Wisconsin, and northern Michigan.

Originally developed in January 1985 as an extension of St. Mary's Medical Center's mission and services, the GSC was the first in the state and possibly one of the first in the nation to develop such a hospital-based grief support program. At this time there are still no other existing centers similar in Minnesota.

I am a strong advocate for the development of grief support centers located within the hospital versus a bereavement facility offered off the hospital grounds. This grief support center model also demonstrates acknowledgment by the hospital that the issues surrounding death are important and need to be talked about and "seen." Having the grief support center within the hospital facility also offers the opportunity to create a truly collaborative, hospital-wide approach to grief support. Within this model, GSC staff see and work with their fellow employees daily and as a result can appreciate some of what these employees are experiencing.

Additionally, this model provides the GSC staff "hands on" with patients and families and true collaboration with other health care personnel, physicians, residents, and volunteers. The model clearly provides opportunities that would not be possible if the bereavement center were not located within the medical facility. It is one thing to "talk" with families blocks or miles away from the hospital about a youngster in a hospital's pediatric intensive care unit (if the family could find the time to get away from the unit), while it is an entirely different approach to be able to be with the same patient, his or her family members, friends or nurses, chaplains, physicians, and other health care personnel who are caring for this family. "When does grief begin and when does it end?" is truly a question one needs to think about when given the opportunity to create a model concerning bereavement programs and services within a hospital.

The Grief Support Center is a unique model offering an opportunity for complete care. The primary goal of this chapter is to examine the "nuts and bolts" of developing a grief support center and, in particular, some of the challenges and opportunities a grief support center can provide.

St. Mary's Medical Center's administration took a chance initially in investing money and time into a program that had not existed elsewhere. Originally, I was asked to help develop, implement, and facilitate a program at the hospital for bereaved children in 1983. The Young Person's Grief Support Program was well received in both the hospital and the community. Because of the success of the children's program, I approached the director of the hospital's social service department in the fall of 1984 regarding a grief support center and she said, "put a proposal together and let's see what happens." I remember typing the first draft for the hospital administrators to review and thinking to myself, "will it really happen? Will St. Mary's really start a program that had no track record of being done elsewhere?"

The proposal was submitted to administration in late December 1984, and the director of social services and I then discussed with them the value of the program. They listened. They asked very good questions and then said, "We'll get back to you soon to let you know our decision."

All I could think about was how long would it take for them to get back to us and what would their decision be? Within a few days I clearly remember the social services director calling me and saying, "welcome on board . . . Administration liked it! They are going to take a chance and want you to start as soon as you can. You will be under the umbrella of the social services department and are on a one-year contract. We will just have to see what evolves over the next year before we know where to go from there!" Although it's been fifteen years, it still seems like just yesterday when I received that phone call!

Initially, it was up to just me to develop, implement, and coordinate the programs and services conducted by the GSC. Currently, the GSC consists of one full-time program director/grief counselor/death educator, two part-time (.6 FTEs each) grief counselors/death educators, with one counselor also serving as the volunteer coordinator, two graduate-student interns each year at twenty hours per week each, and an additional fifteen individuals who facilitate the various GSC support groups. The facilitators are employees at the Medical Center, from another local hospital, the University of Minnesota, Duluth, and the community in general. We have been fortunate to have outstanding facilitators over the years and have had different facilitators for some groups, while other facilitators have been with us for the entire time.

In addition to counseling, we have given over 1,300 inservices, training programs, or presentations on dying, death, grief, loss, and bereavement at the local, regional, state, national, and international levels to literally tens of thousands of individuals. Some presentations last only thirty minutes to one hour, while many others have been two days in length. The audiences have ranged from kindergarten children and their teachers to physicians, residents, school superintendents and principals, clergy, hospital administrators, social workers, marriage and family therapists, psychologists, volunteers, hospice, funeral service and nursing home personnel, bereaved persons, nurses, and emergency service personnel.

The GSC also consults on bereavement issues with elementary and secondary schools, universities, churches and synagogues, hospitals, hospice programs, physicians, funeral directors, community groups and agencies, private industry, etc., from not only the region, but from across the United States, Canada, and countries overseas. We have been on television and radio on numerous occasions and articles have been written in various newspapers and journals on our programs and services. We circulate our free newsletter, *Grief Notes,* to approximately 3,000 individuals, organizations, physicians, churches, and institutions, regionally and in other parts of the United States and Canada.

While it was not initially, nor is it now, our intent to be a "crisis center," over the years the GSC clearly has been put into that role numerous times when there has been a death of a student or teacher at any educational institution, from kindergarten to university, as well as when a significant death takes place in the region. Our role has been to try to be available when called upon, but more important, to try to teach others how to cope with crisis events in their own communities and to help them prepare for such events as best as they can in a proactive manner.

Throughout the fifteen years we have done individual, family, and group counseling with the focus on impending death and/or bereavement issues. We try not to spread ourselves too thin and "be all" to everyone. Rather, it is our hope to be especially good at what we do and know when to refer individuals to others in our region who can assist them with issues we do not work with (i.e., divorce and separation, sexual abuse, chemical dependency). We have learned a great deal at the Grief Support Center from those who were dealing with life-threatening illnesses, who were dying, or who were bereaved. We have also learned a great deal from the many professionals and volunteers who cared for these individuals.

In addition to individual and family counseling, fourteen grief support programs are currently offered to those who are dealing with an impending death or who are bereaved. One of the programs, the GSC's Bereavement Follow-Up Program, has for the past thirteen years followed-up with every family who has had someone die at St. Mary's, except deaths within the hospice unit. The Bereavement Follow-Up Program is a collaborative effort between the GSC, Chaplaincy, and departments within the Medical Center. Another program, the GSC Volunteer Program is also an integral part of the GSC and provides not only many hours in assisting the GSC directly with our programs and services, but also includes the Person-To-Person Volunteer Program and the GSC Widowed Person Service (WPS) which utilizes trained bereaved GSC volunteers and matches them, upon request, with persons who are bereaved from any type of death within the community.

Following are some ideas and suggestions to consider.

1. Steps Necessary to Begin the Development of a Hospital-Based Grief Support Center:

Who should be on a grief support center development committee or task force? Think of persons who represent a wide range of services now offered within the hospital, including physician(s) and administrator(s) if possible. If the center hopes to serve not only the hospital but also the community, consider community members who could also serve on the committee or task force to get a "wide range" of input and support.

A. Needs assessment in the hospital: The goal of the needs assessment in the hospital itself would determine if there is interest and a need for a center, and will also determine how much "enthusiasm" staff and administration have for the project. How is the hospital now dealing with end-of-life issues in particular and serving the needs of the patients and families and staff who care for them? Is this an area the center can assist with and how has the hospital up to this point dealt with families of patients who have died concerning bereavement follow-up procedures? Who are the individuals that should be on the needs assessment task force and, after the form is completed, who within the institution should complete it? The goal of this needs assessment would help determine if there is a need for a center and also what programs and services could such a center provide or assist with.

B. Needs assessment in community: As the hospital develops a grief support center, what additional programs and services are already being offered in the region and how will the center affect or be affected by programs already in place? Is the center being broad in nature regarding serving the needs of both inpatient and their families and hospital employees, or will it also serve as a regional center for anyone interested in the programs and services offered? Who is best to design the assessment form and who should receive this form? What is the time frame you have to work within if you have already received money for the center prior to the needs assessment? A major question that will need to be determined is not only where in the hospital should the grief support center be located, but also, will the center be a department of its own or under the umbrella of another department? If the center is under another department, which department would be the most appropriate for your institution?

2. Determine Philosophy, Mission Statement, Goals and Objectives:

As a result of the needs assessment or committee/task force outcomes, a philosophy, mission statement, goals, and objectives will need to be determined. These will need to be revised periodically, but there needs to be a clear direction for everyone involved to know what the center is and what it will and will not provide. Our GSC approach to these areas indicate the GSC is an extension of St. Mary's Medical Center's mission and services and is an umbrella for various support programs and services, providing a comprehensive program of counseling, support, advocacy, education, and research for individuals who are dealing with, or affected by, an impending death or who are bereaved.

Regardless of any needs assessment or meetings that do take place, review and share with others the tremendous amount of research now available on dying, death, grief, and bereavement. This literature review will also add tremendously to the need for establishing a grief support center. The articles you identify, either in professional journals or articles and books written by and for lay persons, will all indicate dying and death are experiences known in all human societies and will report that bereavement is one of the most difficult of all life's changes. They will indicate individuals in a state of bereavement, whether child or adult, go through a grief process, including various times of physical, emotional, psychological, behavioral, and spiritual concerns. Additionally, how health care professionals and volunteers respond and how they can be affected by those we care for in health care institutions is also very well-documented in professional literature and needs to be discussed.

Our Grief Support Center operates according to the following objectives:

A. To provide in the Medical Center through guidance of professional facilitators, supportive, small group settings for children, adults, and parents to work through their feelings of grief and develop coping skills to assist them during the crisis prior to and/or following the death of a family member, relative, or friend.

B. To counsel in the Medical Center children and adults on an individual and/or family basis as requested by them.

C. To counsel Medical Center patients, families, relatives, and/or friends as requested.

D. To identify and train Grief Support Center Volunteers to serve in the GSC's Person-to-Person Volunteer Program and the GSC's Widowed Persons Service Program and to assist with various other Grief Support Center services and programs.

E. To provide bereavement follow-up, in collaboration with other appropriate departments within the Medical Center, on all deaths (except hospice) through the Grief Support Center's Bereavement Follow-up Program.

F. To serve as a resource and provide leadership, defusings, and debriefings to administration, department heads, and staff within the Medical Center regarding bereavement or critical incident related issues.

G. To be available at times of critical incidents or related crisis events in the region and serve in a consultative or participatory role.

H. To act as a regional resource center for those needing information and assistance concerning impending death or bereavement.

I. To provide a comprehensive GSC Library on topics related to dying, death, grief, bereavement, and loss issues for both lay persons and professionals.

J. To collect data and do research on impending death or bereavement.

K. To produce educational materials, both printed and audiovisual, regarding impending death or bereavement issues.

L. To develop and promote specialized conferences, seminars, workshops, and training programs as a form of continuing education for target groups who work with or are interested in grief, loss, and bereavement.

M. To provide professionals for speaking engagements on topics related to impending death or bereavement at the local, regional, state, national, or international level.

N. To collaborate with and/or serve as consultants to educational and religious institutions, community health professionals, and agencies and organizations who are interested in grief and bereavement.

3. Funding

A. Budget: Will the center have its own budget or will it be part of another hospital cost center? The budget will need to take into account the programs and services being offered and will also need to look at where the funds will come from. Will the budget be supported by funding from the hospital budget or will the center be expected to raise its own funds from a variety of sources ranging from grants and donations to presentations and income from counseling and consulting? Funding initially needs to take into account the "development" of the center and the fact there will be a number of "unforeseen" factors, especially advertising to get the word out that the center exists. Will the space at the hospital be given to the center to use and what initial costs for "start up" (computer, phone, etc.) will be needed? Will the Hospital Bereavement Committee/ Task Force be asked to create a board to supervise the center or will it be on its own as a department or under another department's budget?

B. Salaried or Volunteer Staff/Facilitators: How many staff positions do you feel you will need or can financially afford to have? Will the coordinator of the grief center be a volunteer position and occupied by someone already on the staff of the institution but working "extra," or will it be by someone from outside the institution who is volunteering to coordinate the services and programs? Will secretarial assistance come from within the grief center's budget or will it be "donated" to the center by another department? Each salaried position needs to also look at health insurance, vacations, and sick leave, etc. If the salary of the coordinator is based on a contract, which means the person is hired "from outside the health care institution," how will the contract be written regarding "coordinating the center's programs and services?" How will facilitators be selected? Will facilitators be paid for their work, or if employees of the hospital, will they receive comp time (leaving a few hours early to compensate for the time they've facilitated groups)? Will job descriptions indicate they are to facilitate specific groups, or will these facilitators serve only as grief center volunteers, receiving no financial reward for their facilitative work? What about liability insurance for counseling or facilitating groups (check with your hospital's legal consultants and also with the hospital's volunteer department)? What about contractual arrangements with individuals "from outside the hospital" to provide individual or family counseling services for a specific amount of money per client, etc.? What type of job description will exist for any persons involved with the center to provide any type of service?

C. Physical space for the center and also for individual counseling and support groups: Where in the hospital will the center be located? Will the center be visible and available for people or will it be tucked in a back corner of the hospital as an "afterthought?" Space needs to be allocated for counseling and support groups. Will there be enough space during the day and during the evening for the support groups or will there be competition for space? Will the rooms offered for the groups be easily accessible or hard to find? What about signage within the hospital informing individuals where the center is or the location of the various support group rooms?

D. Supplies (*Grief Notes*/brochures/paper, etc.): What supplies will you need? There are brochures, newsletters, printing costs, mailing costs, paper for duplicating, telephone expenses, etc. that need to be taken into account. Will these be under the budget or will the center be asked to find "donations" to print the brochures, cover the cost for mailings, etc.?

E. Travel and Education: What education will be needed by the center's staff and volunteers and where will they be able to receive it? Some training can be done locally and within each state, while some training will need to take place with other bereavement professionals from across the United States at national conferences and seminars.

F. Advertising: Working with the hospital public relations department will help in this area to determine the best approach, not only in initially getting the word out about the center but also the important part of maintaining visibility.

G. Books/organizational affiliations: What journals and books will need to be purchased for the grief center library or for reference for the staff and other health care professionals and volunteers within the hospital? The hospital library may already have a good selection of books and journals, so check with them to avoid duplication of costs.

H. Miscellaneous: What about coffee and cookies for groups? Who will pay for these costs and what about meetings that community members are invited to? Will they expect to be fed or will they pay for their own parking and food to attend a meeting you are requesting them to attend? Who will pay for your travel to regional communities if they have a crisis and you offered to assist? Will you pay out of your budget for travel or will you expect to be reimbursed by the people who called you for your assistance?

I. Comp time for some staff (other hospital departments): What arrangements can be made with other departments within the hospital if you utilize their staff for some of the grief support groups? Will it be part of their job description as talked about previously, thus they will be "paid" by being given comp time for hours put into groups "after hours," or will they be given time out of their scheduled day to lead groups? What about programs that are conducted on weekends? Will the union play a part in this if nurses are utilized?

J. Parking/Picking people up to participate in groups: Where will the individuals who participate in individual, family, or group counseling park their vehicles? Will parking be free or will they be expected to park and pay like any other person utilizing hospital services? Will your institution offer to pick up people and bring them to the support groups offered or will they be expected to make their own arrangements to attend the groups? What could you see as issues that would arise if you did offer to pick people up for counseling or for support groups?

4. Income (Where Will the Dollars Come From?):

A. St. Mary's Medical Center: The GSC budget is created with funds from the Medical Center budget and also utilizes funds from other sources to provide its programs and services.

B. Individual/Family Counseling (Third party reimbursement/ self-pay and St. Mary's/Duluth Clinic Community Care Program): There has never been a fee for the GSC support groups offered by the Medical Center, however, there is a fee for individual, couple, or family counseling. (Initially when the center was developed, all individual and family counseling was free, however, after a few years a fee for service was added.) Additionally, there has never been a fee for seeing patients or patient's families within the medical center, even when we are requested to see them by a "doctor's order." For individual, couple, and family counseling there is a fee and clients register for counseling when they arrive at the medical center with the medical center's registration department. All client billing is taken care of by the medical center after the charges have been submitted by GSC staff.

C. Presentations by GSC staff: The GSC is reimbursed for staff presentations outside of the medical center. Presentations within the Medical Center to specific departments are free as is crisis intervention or consultation. In addition to an honorarium for outside presentations, all additional expenses are also paid for by the requesting agency or organization.

D. Consulting: Reimbursement for consulting is requested along with any additional expenses such as travel, accommodations, and meals.

E. Donations: These are placed into the St. Mary's Foundation special account for the GSC which can be used by the GSC as needed for special requests.

F. Grants: For special circumstances grants have been applied for to support programs or conferences benefiting certain populations or topics.

G. Special events by other groups ("Tree-of-Lights"): This is an example of a fundraising program conducted by the Medical Center's Auxiliary to help support and enhance the programs and services conducted by the GSC. Individuals purchase a light on a holiday tree for $10 in memory of someone who has died or to honor someone special. An official tree lighting program is conducted the second week of December with children's readings, songs, and a short program. Refreshments are provided after the program.

H. Special programs conducted by GSC: When we conduct programs for the community which provide surplus dollars these are also placed into the St. Mary's Foundation special GSC account for future access as needed and approved for their use.

5. GSC Staff/Personnel:

As mentioned previously, currently the GSC consists of one full-time program director/grief counselor/death educator, two part-time (.6 FTEs each) grief counselors/death educators, with one counselor also serving as the volunteer coordinator, two graduate-student interns each year at twenty hours per week each, and an additional fifteen individuals who facilitate the various GSC support groups. The facilitators are employees at the Medical Center, from another local hospital, the University of Minnesota, Duluth, and the community in general. Our GSC Volunteers also consist of a wide variety of interested community members and medical center personnel. All receive ongoing training in a variety of ways and are covered by the medical center's liability insurance. The GSC Volunteers, in addition to the GSC training, also go through the medical center's volunteer training.

6. Public Relations:

A. *Grief Notes:* Our newsletter (produced 3 times a year) is mailed to 3,000 persons while we also circulate another 3,000 every three to four months at presentations or through requests for them. There is no charge for our newsletter and its purpose is to educate and also provide information about the GSC programs and services.

B. Brochures: For each of our groups a brochure has been designed and is available to advertise the program.

C. Ads in papers: These can be costly and we have not done many in the past few years as we have relied on the media and word-of-mouth to spread the word about the programs and services offered.

D. News releases: These are sent out to the local media as appropriate by our Medical Center's Public Relations Department.

E. St. Mary's Foundation: They advertise the GSC in some of their promotional materials as a way of seeking donors who want to know what the Medical Center is doing to meet its mission.

F. Media interviews (TV/Radio/Print media): This happens a great deal and obviously is one way to get the word out quickly and broadly to a wide audience.

G. Monthly letters to various groups: We send out a monthly "reminder letter" for a number of our support groups which comes from the facilitators. Some smaller support groups such as our SIDS group or our Infertility Support Group may also receive handouts that may be important to the members along with the "reminder letter."

H. Publications by Medical Center: These also share periodically what the GSC is offering.

I. Medical Center/other agencies newsletters: Due to collaborative programs, other hospitals and agencies also advertise what we are offering.

J. Church/Synagogue bulletins, etc.: As we get information to the churches and synagogues, many of them also place the information into their weekly or monthly newsletters.

7. Programs Offered:

The following programs are currently being offered by the Grief Support Center. (The first eight groups listed are all "open groups" and free of charge, while our young adult and children's groups are "closed groups" and require pre-registration.)

A. Adult Grief Support Group

B. Senior Grief and Loss Support Group

C. Parent Support Group (Miscarriage and Stillbirth)

D. Parent Support Group (Birth to 10 years of age)

E. Parent Support Group (Over 10 years of age)

F. SIDS Support Group

G. Infertility Support Group

H. Suicide Family Members Support Group

I. Young Adult Grief Support Group (closed group)

J. Young Person's Grief Support Groups (Ages 5-8, 9-13, and 14-17) (closed groups)

K. Kids Can Cope (Ages 8-16 years of age) (closed groups) For youngsters who have a family member, relative, or friend with cancer or any other serious medical condition.

L. SIB's Day (A full-day program/workshop offered once a year for siblings whose brother or sister is chronically or terminally ill or has a special need. Ages 5 to 13 with youngsters older serving as "junior staff.")

M. GSC Volunteer Program

N. GSC Bereavement Follow-up-Program

O. Parents of Murdered Children (POMC)—Our Grief Support Center does not "officially" sponsor this group, but supports its presence in our facility and helps provide training and consultation to the facilitators.

8. Volunteer Program:

A. GSC Person-to-Person Program and the GSC Widowed Person Service (WPS): Trained GSC Volunteers working with bereaved persons with supervision from the GSC staff.

B. GSC Bereavement Follow-up Program: Collaborative effort in following-up with all deaths at St. Mary's Medical Center, except deaths within hospice.

C. GSC Library: Library open to the community and the medical center staff with books and audiovisual materials related to death, dying, and bereavement.

D. Bereavement packets: Packets of information developed and handed out to medical center patients and families, and anyone inquiring from outside the facility requesting information on specific deaths (i.e., childhood death, SIDS, violent death, suicide, etc.), or how to support someone who is now dealing with a life-threatening or terminal illness. Literature is also available for medical center staff as requested. Some departments such as

Emergency and Newborn Intensive Care have information available and distribute to families as needed.

E. GSC "Helpers": Help with GSC Library, community programs.

F. Give talks when asked: Volunteers often are asked to share "their stories" with others in the region.

G. Special Projects: Assist with a WIDE VARIETY of projects as they arise.

9. October Awareness:

A. White Ribbon Campaign: Small white ribbons are made by volunteers and distributed free of charge throughout October to promote Infant and Child Loss Awareness Month.

B. Exhibits at Malls: Displays are conducted at various malls to promote the child loss awareness month activities and hand out literature.

C. Walk-For-Remembrance: This walk is to promote October Awareness Month and is conducted in a highly visible city location with good response from the media.

D. SMMC Lobby Display: Display of materials and handouts relating to infant and child death. We also include brochures for all of our programs at this display.

E. Memorial Service: Offered once a year in October for parents whose child has died from any cause of death and at any age. This GSC service, conducted in the Medical Center's Chapel, has roughly 150 attendees each year and is not open to the media. In addition to this service, hospice also conducts quarterly services for those who have died within the hospice program, while previously the Chaplaincy Department also provided a quarterly memorial service for families and friends of anyone who died in the medical center.

F. Presentations in region: These are offered by the volunteers and also by the GSC staff throughout the month focusing primarily on infant and childhood death.

10. "Honoring Our Children" Monument:

On October 29, 1994 a stone was dedicated at a local cemetery which has been used ever since for burials of children who have died as a result of a miscarriage at St. Mary's if the child's parents chose not to have the child buried, cremated, or donated to science. All families who have experienced a miscarriage between the last burial and the most current burial are notified regarding the time of the burial and what will take place. Some families choose to participate in this non-denominational service, while others just thank us for letting them know.

11. Speakers:

Not only does the GSC provide speakers for other organizations and groups, but we also host speakers to educate our own community and region on grief-related issues. These programs have been conducted generally two times a year with attendance ranging from over a 100 to 2,400 for Rabbi Harold Kushner.

12. "In-House" Counseling/Education:

A. Individual/Family Counseling for patients/families (as indicated previously)

B. Facilitated a Hospice staff monthly support group for a significant period of time and currently facilitate an oncology nurses support group.

C. Employee Assistance Program (EAP) (if appropriate): Although the Medical Center utilizes outside sources for EAP, it is not uncommon for employees to utilize our services for individual or family counseling when an impending death or bereavement issue exists, in addition to their participation in the GSC support groups offered. There is NO charge for employees to see any of the GSC staff or graduate students.

D. Nursing and new staff orientation: GSC staff previously participated in nursing orientation and now materials are made available for new medical center employees.

E. Educational Training: For St. Mary's Medical Center departments and other hospital departments such as Hospice, Burn Unit, Mental Health, Oncology, Clinical Pastoral Education, NICU, Emergency, Volunteer, Home Care, Orthopedics, Lab, Dialysis, plus physicians and residents.

13. Crisis Intervention:

A. In the Medical Center for Staff/Patients

B. Schools/Universities

C. Critical Incident Stress Defusings and Debriefings for First Responders in the region

D. Communities-at-large when requested

14. Gabriel's Gifts:

For a number of years, through the GSC's Gabriel's Gifts Fund, children who have died from either miscarriage, stillbirth, neonatal death, or childhood death at St. Mary's have had their feet and hands placed in special material which is then used to make a plaster casting of their feet and hands for parents. These are given to the families and there is no charge for this service. Donations are given to the GSC to provide this service. The plaster castings are completed by social workers, nurses, and GSC staff, and after the Medical Center's Prosthetics Department completes the castings they are then given to the families.

15. Caskets for Miscarriages:

For many years small wooden caskets have been provided at no charge by the GSC to families who have experienced the death of a child due to miscarriage and who would like to use them to bury their child. The small wooden caskets are made by a local artist and paid for with funds donated to the GSC by the Medical Center's Auxiliary. For stillbirth, neonatal deaths, or older children who die, caskets are purchased by the families at their own expense from the funeral home they have chosen. The small GSC caskets are also used when burials are done at the GSC monument when the miscarriages are buried by the GSC staff, families, and medical center staff. Some caskets are plain on the top lid while others are carved.

16. Consultation/Program Development:

A. Grief center development, program, and services development: The GSC staff consults on a regular basis with agencies, organizations, and therapists. Fees are arranged depending on the request, time, travel, etc.

B. Crisis (prevention/intervention/postvention training): Consultation and trainings range from working with schools, universities, churches, and industry to correctional institutions, hospitals, and city employees.

17. Research:

Provide opportunities for professionals doing research to utilize the GSC if appropriate. Additionally, the GSC also requests periodically those who have utilized our services to also participate in question-naires and quality improvement research.

18. Benefits to the Medical Center:

A. How does the GSC serve the Medical Center directly?: The GSC provides a resource and leadership in the Medical Center regarding bereavement-related issues to administration, department heads, and staff.

B. GSC staff are available at times of crisis: Staff is available to try to meet employee/administrative needs as requested during times of crisis, or after.

C. GSC staff provide end-of-life and bereavement training as requested by departments for employees.

D. Provide services for patients/families and after a patient's death maintains contact through the GSC Bereavement-Follow-Up Program.

E. Provides individual counseling opportunities to employees and their families as appropriate.

F. GSC staff serve on committees: Staff serve on various committees within the medical center ranging from organ donation and end-of-life decisions, to the Volunteer Department "Tree of Lights" Committee. Staff also serve on various types of committees locally, and at the regional, state, and national levels.

G. How does the GSC benefit the Medical Center's "public image?": The GSC has demonstrated "out-reach" by the Medical Center regarding impending death and bereavement issues is appropriate and well received in the region. The GSC also demonstrates the commitment by the Medical Center to its mission as it provides services and programs to the community and region.

19. Evaluation of GSC:

Over the past fifteen years, a variety of ways have been utilized to evaluate the GSC and also assess its value and "customer satisfaction." Some of the ways this evaluation has been accomplished are by:

A. Quality Assurance by Medical Center: The Medical Center's Marketing Department used questionnaires to evaluate the GSC regarding individual, couple, and family counseling, our GSC support groups offered, and the persons who organized and requested training from the GSC.

B. Letters of appreciation from clients, staff, administrators, patients, physicians, residents, and the community-at-large.

C. Evaluations on presentations by our staff given within the Medical Center and in the community/region/and at the state, national, and international levels.

D. GSC staff/facilitator "gatherings": Staff and graduate student interns meet on a regular basis to evaluate how we are doing. The GSC facilitators and staff meet periodically to assess the needs of the facilitators and also discuss issues related to facilitating bereavement support groups.

E. Meetings with the Social Service Department Director: These are held on a regular basis to assess and evaluate how the program is doing. Additionally, the Social Services Department Director is also responsible for the supervision of the GSC Program Director.

F. Evaluation of GSC staff, graduate interns, and facilitators: The GSC Program Director is responsible for the supervision and evaluation of the GSC staff, graduate interns, and facilitators.

G. Attendance at programs/presentations offered, etc.: Through "word of mouth," written evaluations from different programs offered such as the GSC Facilitator Training Programs, the Young Person's Grief Support Programs, volunteer evaluations of trainings, and evaluations completed by attendees at training programs conducted by GSC staff locally, regionally, and at state, national, and international levels.

In conclusion, the opportunity for community growth through a comprehensive, progressive grief support center within a hospital has proven, beyond a doubt, it truly benefits not only its customers, but also the hospital itself. I feel fortunate to have had the opportunity to develop and implement the St. Mary's Grief Support Center model, yet without the support of our social services department director, our GSC staff, interns, facilitators, secretary, volunteers, and all the St. Mary's Medical Center staff and departments who have supported us, none of this would have happened. I would especially like to thank those St. Mary's administrators who took a chance to create something unknown and untested at the time. And finally, a very special thanks to the patients, clients, families, and all those who I have had the privilege and honor of working with and learning from over the years.

CHAPTER 13

How the Military Family Copes With a Death

Bonnie Carroll

CNN has just announced a breaking story. A fighter aircraft has gone down over water, and the pilot failed to eject. Nothing has been recovered, no plane, no crew, no sign of anything. The headline story mentions the price tag on the multi-million dollar aircraft, relays the statistics of the casualty count, and pinpoints the location on an ironically cheerful map. We all feel informed and sorry, shake our heads at the price paid in taxpayer dollars, yet feel no connection since this story has no bearing on our lives. We have heard it before, military training accidents happen as a consequence of maintaining combat readiness, and the public has become almost numb to these losses.

How often have we seen a military funeral portrayed in a movie or on television? It is usually the last time we see the family as their character fades away . . . the widow dressed in black gracefully receives the folded flag, sheds a tear, and takes her children by the hand and leads them off into a life we never see. In reality, the military family usually deals with two funeral homes, and often a third location when they move from base housing. In one such case, the death occurred on deployment in Korea, the widow and children were living on a base in San Diego, the burial took place in Chicago, and the family moved to Florida to live. The close-knit community that exists for most Americans is not a part of the military dynamic, and this impacts the aftercare and complicates the grieving. As Karen Hilliard, a young Navy widow put it,

> After a few months, I finally let go of that part of my life that was
> so important to me—being a military wife. My focus began to shift
> and my identity became an issue. How could I no longer be a part of
> the military community other than wearing the label of the woman
> who will always have to put "active duty—deceased" on checks
> written at the exchange or commissary? The question seemed too
> hard to answer or maybe it was just that the answer was one I did
> not like [1].

When we hear of these deaths, we may ponder for a moment the
impact, but they occur so frequently it would be overwhelming to really
calculate the emotional price paid each time one of these deaths occurs
in military service. As a society, we could not possibly mourn each loss
or care about each death since there are approximately 2,000 each
year. This is a staggering number, considering we are at peace. During
the duration of the Vietnam War, the death toll was well over 57,000.
Where are these hundreds of thousands of family members now, what
happened to them after the funeral, when the final note of taps drifted
out over the rows of white headstones, and who was there to support
them in the immediate aftermath? Where did they all go? And where do
they find support, or continuing emotional care, as their grief journeys
begin?

This chapter will tell the story of one tragedy, but it was out of this
particular military air crash that a group of survivors worked together
to create an aftercare organization that would reach out to all who were
to follow them and change the way this segment of our society would
cope and heal.

On November 12, 1992, I could not have been more content with my
life. I had a blissful marriage to the youngest General in the United
States Army, serving as commander of the Alaska Army National
Guard. He was a real "fast burner," as those who are destined for
greatness at an early age come to be known. I felt as though we must be
living charmed lives, everything came easy and life was good. Tom had
survived Vietnam as an infantry officer in the toughest unit fighting on
the front lines. He had come through every sort of training the Army
can throw at a soldier with flying colors and had proven himself
impervious. There was nothing that could stop him professionally or
touch him physically, I was sure of that.

As I saw Tom off for a routine flight in his Army C-12, the designation
for a Beechcraft King Air, on a sunny fall morning, I was absolutely
certain that he would be home in time for dinner, safe and sound. Skies
were clear and weather was exceptionally good. But where they were
going, five hundred miles away, that was not the case. Harsh weather

closed in on the landing field, a small strip wedged between high mountains and a deep bay. The plane was due to land on schedule at 9:04 A.M. and at 9:03 A.M. the co-pilot radioed the tower that they were over the runway and beginning their descent through thick cloud cover. But no plane appeared and no further radio communication ever came.

By 9:15 A.M. the first news bulletins came that "a plane carrying the senior command of the state's National Guard was missing and that a search was in progress." Everyone was busy and hopeful and focused on finding the plane and the eight soldiers on board, and things moved quickly, as they do in a military crisis of any sort. When soldiers train to fight a war, they are ready to handle contingencies like downed aircraft.

At 3:45 that afternoon, the plane was finally located in the mountains, having gone off course in the storm. The fuselage was intact and a flight surgeon was lowered by cable from the Coast Guard helicopter to see if there were survivors. Word was sent back. There were none.

At that moment, with that news, life as I knew it ended. The happiness, the identity, the future, the partnership, all ceased to exist in a news flash. The headlines the next day, ironically Friday, November 13th, read "Eight Die in National Guard Plane Crash." CNN even ran the story since there were two general officers on board, and since it was, after all, another military casualty. Catching glimpses of the news bulletins, I felt detached and surreal. I had seen broadcasts like this so often and had never imagined what it must be like to be a part of that story rather than a casual observer. In the burst of attention that goes with the first ten days following such an incident, I was surrounded by care and competence. The funeral home took over and did everything they could to honor and care for what remained of Tom's body. The military unit he had led now took its turn to lead me through the maze of paperwork that must be done to end a twenty-four-year career of service to one's country. The community wrapped a warm blanket around the families who lost loved ones on that day and did their best to bid farewell.

As the cards stopped arriving and the flowers began dying, it became clear to me that I was very much alone in my loss. My mother-in-law, herself an Army widow, was tremendously supportive and provided incredible insight into a part of her life I had never even thought about before finding myself in her shoes. The teenage children each dealt with the loss in their own way, and together we searched for a new family structure. They too found their lives at a juncture, unsure of their future and fighting the lonely reality that was creeping into our home. My world had stopped turning and I had a hard time understanding that life was continuing for others around me. I did my best to keep a stiff upper lip during the day and collapsed at night in a heap of despair, sinking deeper and deeper into isolation and depression. My professional background included experience that I felt should have prepared me for such a tragedy. I had served as the Executive Assistant for Cabinet Affairs in the White House, working each day on crises that affected millions and presidential initiatives that changed the course of history. I had proven I could handle stress. I should be able to handle this.

After leaving the White House and joining my husband in Alaska, I worked as the Victim Witness Coordinator in the Anchorage District Attorney's Office, helping those impacted by a homicide death cope with the loss of their loved one and prepare for the upcoming trials. I even volunteered my time with a homicide survivors' group called "Victims for Justice" and naively thought I could understand their grief and help them cope. Even in my role as an officer in the Alaska Air National Guard, I volunteered for the additional duty of Critical Incident Stress Debriefer after a KC-135 tanker exploded in 1989 killing three crew members. I knew, or thought I knew, I could handle death and trauma. But I could not help myself. Try as I might, the rational and the logical did not comfort me. All the preparation and all the education in the world did not stop the pain I was feeling. Having seen the power of peer support networks for homicide survivors, I sought out such a group for military families, and made a startling discovery. There was no such organization. No way for the thousands who are affected each year by a death in the armed forces to find each other, to talk through feelings in a safe environment, and to help each other heal. Well, was such a group really necessary? Does aftercare really make a difference? Were my own desperate feelings unique or were they shared?

Six months after the crash came Memorial Day, that day when all Americans pause to pay tribute to our nation's fallen service members. This Memorial Day was my first as a military widow. After a long and lonely winter spent in a desperate struggle to survive, I stood at the cemetery feeling small and frightened and alone. There in the crowd, I saw another wife, another *widow,* from the crash. Her perpetually pained expression mirrored mine, her body weary of the burden borne over a winter alone, but she held her head high as the flag passed by. I was stunned by this irony of pain and pride, the same emotional mix I felt. We talked and found that we shared so much! We had been living parallel lives, experiencing the same feelings of loneliness, pain, grief, fear, yet, on this day, intense pride and patriotism for the nation our husbands died serving. Were we unique? We also found that we had each been searching for support systems. She had attended a support group through Hospice and also sought out a local widow's group. I had tried attending the homicide survivors' support group. Yet none of these programs fit for us. Our husbands did not die of a terminal illness after suffering for months. We were not blaming God. They didn't die of old age in their sleep. They weren't gunned down in a senseless act of violence on an urban street. We weren't awaiting a trial or focusing anger on a criminal behind bars. Our feelings were unique and no one understood them . . . or so we thought.

The more we talked, the more we found we had in common and the more committed I became to seeking the power of aftercare organizations. Was it simply the validation? Letting someone know through simple shared experience and pain, that they were not alone—were not going mad? Validation is the most powerful gift a peer can give; it is that moral authority that comes from having walked the road, lived through the hell, and being able to say "I understand" in a way that is neither trite nor condescending, but purely, sadly, honest.

That began the journey that led to the founding of TAPS, the Tragedy Assistance Program for Survivors, in October of 1994. It would become the first peer support network of its kind, made up of and providing support to *all* those who have been affected by a death in the armed forces. In forming the program, we talked with officials at the Departments of Defense and Veterans' Affairs and found where the voids came in support to survivors. General John Shalikashvili, then Chairman of the Joint Chiefs of Staff, put it best when he said,

> I have been thinking since I heard about TAPS, "Why is it that the military never created something like this?" And then it became patently clear to me that there's no way to organize something like this in the military. What would we do? Have lieutenant so-and-so, or sergeant so-and-so, call you and talk to you? A young man or woman who simply cannot share your experience? It can't be done. It can only be done by people who have walked this very difficult road before you, and who are now willing to devote their energies and their caring and their heart, to take your hand and say, "Walk with me, I can help you."

What tremendous insight for the value of peer support in a specific loss experience.

Then we talked to those involved in other programs like Mothers Against Drunk Driving (MADD), Concerns of Police Survivors (COPS), Hospice, Compassionate Friends, Gold Star Wives and Mothers, Society of Military Widows, Parents of Murdered Children, and other highly successful peer support networks, took the very best of each and brought it into the heart of what TAPS was to become.

In the initial stages, the key elements were organization and funding. First, we created a sound foundation of services that would be provided (peer support, counseling referral, case work assistance, and a system for immediate crisis intervention) for a well-defined target group (all those affected by a death in the armed forces). We worked to identify existing programs and ensure that no services would be duplicated. Gold Star Wives, for example, focuses their efforts on lobbying Congress for government entitlements to widows and Society of Military Widows provides a long-term social structure for widows with regular gatherings. TAPS would rely on these other organizations for their special services, but provide what had been missing, such as the immediate intensive aftercare that follows a sudden, traumatic death and the recognition and inclusion of those who were typically disenfranchised, such as siblings, parents, significant others, and even children.

There are several ways in which those who find themselves on the receiving end of a death notification become aware of TAPS. Thanks to General Shalikashvili, all next of kin (NOK) are informed by their Casualty Assistance Officers of the existence of this support organization and given a brochure describing its services. This brochure contains a tear-off card that the family can send back to receive a complimentary subscription to the quarterly journal, TAPS, and also request a phone call or just to be added to the mailing list for invitations to such events as the National Military Survivor Seminar and Kids' Camp. The families and friends will also learn about TAPS from the following sources: their funeral directors, many of whom keep this very same brochure on hand for military families; Internet research for military casualty assistance; notification by the Red Cross' Armed Forces Emergency Services, whose materials list TAPS as a resource; and information from military chaplains, family support personnel, mortuary affairs officers, and commanders who are aware of the program. While the family may or may not come in contact with the military and Red Cross services, in all cases they will talk with their funeral directors, so that has been the primary resource for information about TAPS.

Today, TAPS is a national non-profit organization with 501c(3) status and relies on donations from private sources. No government funding is sought. The national headquarters is in Washington, D.C., co-located with the Hospice Foundation of America, major supporters of TAPS' work with military survivor families. TAPS is volunteer-based, and not only provides services to, but also is made up of all those who have suffered the loss of a loved one in the Armed Forces. The heart of TAPS has become its national military survivor peer support network called

SurvivorLINK, which brings together the families, friends, and co-workers of those who have died in the military. In 1997, the Department of Veterans' Affairs recognized TAPS as an official Veteran Service Organization, a major step forward in the integration of this aftercare network into the military system. TAPS offers survivors bereavement counseling referrals, provides case worker assistance that carries the work of the casualty assistance officers into the future, hosts the nation's only annual National Military Survivor Seminar and Kids Camp, publishes a quarterly journal mailed at no charge to survivors and caregivers, maintains a comprehensive Web site at http://www.taps.org, and staffs a toll-free crisis and information line available twenty-four hours daily through 1-800-959-TAPS (8277) or on e-mail at info@taps.org. TAPS offers total care and support for the military family experiencing a casualty, and is the first such organization to do this. But it is based on a model that has stood the test of time.

In the day-to-day operations of the program, there is a core staff that ensures the two toll-free numbers are answered twenty-four hours a day, and they then refer those callers appropriately. Those calls fall into one of several categories. They are either a call for emotional support or grief counseling information from a survivor who has experienced the death of a loved one in the armed forces, a call requesting information and assistance from a military care provider such as a casualty officer or military representative, or a call regarding training done by TAPS in coping with casualties or a call dealing with administrative matters of the organization.

First and foremost, aftercare agencies like TAPS provide peer support. Those who have lost a loved one in the military may become part of the TAPS national survivor network, and these family members and friends share their pain and fears in a safe and supportive environment, and help each other heal. They find validation, comfort, and understanding, and there is nothing more powerful. TAPS also provides basic crisis intervention. A network of trained crisis response professionals is now on call in each state twenty-four hours a day through 1-800-368-8277, bringing a wealth of compassion and experience to critical incident stress and trauma, there to help survivors understand the reactions they are having to their sudden loss.

Assistance such as that offered by casualty officers immediately after a death is provided by TAPS long after the official file has been closed. For families, tracking information through an often complicated bureaucracy can be challenging on a good day, and under emotional stress can become overwhelming. TAPS has case workers who can help through their experience, understanding, persistence, and network. Often the anger felt after a death arises out of frustration at administrative problems, and in getting those resolved, healing can take place. This assistance has also been an emotional buffer for military commanders and survivors, providing valuable insight to the armed forces on the reactions of those dealing with a military death.

TAPS is a member of the Association of Death Education and Counseling and the Association of Traumatic Stress Specialists, is listed in the National Directory of Bereavement Support Groups and Services, and offers referrals to the very best bereavement counselors and support groups throughout the nation.

Volunteers come in a variety of forms and are always welcome. The TAPS Advisory Board is fortunate to include a wide range of experts: pathologists, bereavement counselors, military benefits experts, psychiatrists, funeral directors, senior members of the armed services who offer support for this work. There is also a pool of volunteers who are survivors themselves. Over a year past their loss, they may now be ready to turn their pain around to help others learn to cope and heal. This is the heart of TAPS, and it is through these dedicated and caring survivors that TAPS is able to truly offer a unique service of understanding and empathy. Anne McCloud, whose husband, Air Force Lt. General David McCloud, was killed in a plane crash, said of meeting other survivors at the seminar, "I came here treading lightly, thinking, 'Where do I belong?' and 'I don't want to cry,' and all of a sudden, it doesn't matter if I cry, I'm surrounded by people with a contagious desire to keep going." That is the essence of SurvivorLINK, the program that brings peer volunteers together with those who have faced a tragic loss and lets them know they are not alone, and they will survive.

There is a third group of volunteers—the wonderful bereavement counselors and support group leaders who give of their time to take calls and talk with survivors having a particularly difficult time. They speak at the TAPS seminar, answer questions on e-mail, participate in the weekly chat rooms online, and contribute to the newsletter. TAPS has been fortunate to have a strong group of volunteers and counselors who have the heart and compassion necessary to offer hope and provide comfort at critical times. The list of volunteers is rounded out by those who help assemble and mail out materials, do registration at the seminar and events throughout the year, administer and maintain the Web site, assist with fundraising efforts, serve as counselors at the Kids' Camp, and help spread the word about TAPS.

During the spring, the TAPS phone lines are busy with survivors and caregivers registering for and inquiring about the National Military Survivor Seminar and Kids' Camp. This annual event is the focal point for bringing military survivors and caregivers together to learn, to heal, and to grow. There are three aspects to the seminar: workshops that educate the attendee on a variety of subjects, from basic information on bereavement to understanding the spiritual issues surrounding traumatic death to training on helping others cope with a loss; social activities that surround Memorial Day, such as the ceremonies at Arlington National Cemetery and the evening parade at the Marine Corps barracks; and peer support time, when attendees can share with each other in a relaxed, facilitated setting. This four-day seminar is a chance for those who have experienced a tragic loss in the armed forces and are grieving the death of a loved one to come together and find validation, comfort, and information. It is a formula that is in use around the country in local support groups, and is taken to a national level when these military survivors meet in Washington, D.C. each year. The Kids' Camp, conducted in conjunction with the seminar, offers survivor children a chance to meet others, learn how the military honors those who have served and died, and also gives them a chance to have fun in a safe setting. It is often hard for children who find themselves under a microscope as "the kid whose dad's death was headline news on CNN" to just relax in an environment that is both supportive and nonjudgmental.

The Washington Post described the TAPS Kids' Camp this way:

> The children attended a "kids' camp" overseen by counselors. Wearing red T-shirts with the TAPS logo, the children sat on the floor in circles and, at the prompting of the counselors, shared stories about their fathers. They spoke of hunting and camping trips. One child told of how his father had gone off flying in a helicopter. "But it crashed, so he died," the boy said. It's easier for the children to tell the stories to others who have lost parents in similar circumstances. "They don't have to explain so much," said Gina Alzate, a counselor. "J. R. is starting to understand what death means," Darla Reed said. "I wanted him to see all these other children who're going through the same thing." There have been diversions, including the visit by a joint services honor guard. Standing erect in their dress uniforms, the service members showed the children the proper way to fold an American flag and fielded questions about everything from their hats to their haircuts. "You have to reach out to them," said Air Force Senior Airman Chris Houde. "They'll reach out to you" [2].

Another key tool of TAPS is the journal, a magazine of articles by and for survivors. Articles include first person stories of hope and healing that give inspiration to those who know all too well the pain behind the written words. Such an article on the front page of one issue quotes

Karen Hilliard, widow of a Navy pilot who went down in the Mediterranean, as saying,

> I still long to be that happy person Jeff loved so much, and as time goes by, I find myself glad to be alive instead of terrified. I am also no longer feeling guilty about feeling good which was a problem for me at first. The biggest lesson that I learned from TAPS is seeing others who have managed to survive this awful stage of life called death. Hopefully, I can pass the strength that was given to me on to someone else [1].

Does peer support—aftercare—make a difference? You bet! Time and time again, military survivors who find this support group echo that very sentiment in their own experience. The young widow of a Navy pilot who crashed at sea was asked by a local grief support group what had helped her cope. She remembered, "Nothing anyone said would have made me feel better. What I needed was someone who had been there before me. Ironically, that friend came in the widow of the F-18 pilot that my husband had done Search and Rescue for, not six months earlier." A total stranger, yet someone bonded to her because she understood—she spoke the language, had lived the experience, and traveled the road before her!

Aftercare organizations work. In the words of one young widow,

> A weekend to celebrate my thirtieth birthday tragically turned into a permanent change in life. My husband, Marine Corps Captain Mark Robert Nickles, was killed just a couple of weeks before ending his six month deployment in Japan. His FA-18 plane crashed February 9, 1997 in the Yellow Sea off the Korean coast.
>
> During my emotional roller coaster to nowhere, searching for answers, comfort, or even peace, an inner strength took over drawing me to read the Survivors Handbook the Navy had so insightfully prepared. At first, I thought, "survivor of **what?**" Still in shock, only weeks after the devastating news, I found a small excerpt in the casualty manual about the Tragedy Assistance Program for Survivors. Not knowing what this organization was all about, but desperate for answers, I called. Within a half hour, the phone rang and I heard the warm, caring voice of a fellow survivor. This call was filled with empathy, needed advice and, most importantly, information and was one of the most empowering conversations I had ever had. A total stranger relating, sharing and guiding my every thought during this crisis. I was totally amazed there were others like me. People caught in this web of confusion. All of us, desperate for answers, while dealing with the same difficult issues. This complicated grief, as it is termed, reaches new depths

when it involves a sudden loss. Those words from the survivors remain with me today and give me the strength to endure, the power to move on, and the knowledge to succeed in starting my new life [3].

This is the TAPS story, and the story of so many who have been touched by aftercare organizations and their peer support networks. These organizations enable healing, provide comfort, and offer valuable resources both for the bereaved and their caregivers.

REFERENCES

1. K. Hilliard, *TAPS Newsletter,* Spring 1999.
2. S. Vogel, *The Washington Post,* May 31, 1999.
3. K. Nickles, *TAPS Newletter*, Summer 1997.

SECTION 3

General Aftercare Issues

CHAPTER 14

Ritualistic Downsizing and the Need for Aftercare

O. Duane Weeks

The front page of any daily newspaper, on almost any given day, will include at least one article about inhumanity, mutilation, rape, murder, or another act of random violence. The headlines make us aware of an increasing disregard for human life as they report about a chained man who is dragged to death behind a truck, four policemen who killed an unmarried immigrant, or Dr. Jack Kevorkian being found guilty of murder.

Television reports, whether accurate news or exploitive investigative journalism, inform us of increasing disrespect and violence toward both property and persons. Electronic journalists trumpet the news of a young mother who leaves her unborn infant in a trash container or an uncle who sets fire to a house containing his sleeping parents, sister, nephews, and nieces.

Is there a relationship between the increase in social violence and the decrease in social rituals? Can there be a correlation between the lack of respect for the living and lack of respect for the dead?

The more violent, the more disgusting, the more inhumane, the more likely a story is to interest the media and its audience. Violence and death have become our entertainment. It also seems apparent that as our society ages, we become more enamored with the material and less concerned with the intangible or spiritual. We have come to think of life as secondary to possessions, and we often obtain possessions at the expense of life. Confrontations that we once settled by words or fists are now settled by knives or guns. Life has a price, and the price is cheap. Life, like a plastic container, is becoming disposable.

OUR DISPOSABLE SOCIETY

With the introduction of plastic and styrofoam, America has become a society of disposable products. As we approach the twenty-first century, North American society continues its fascination with disposables in many forms. Dating teens, as well as their parents and their grandparents, dine at Burger King or McDonald's or Arby's. They eat from disposable plates and drink from disposable cups. Young parents swath their babies in disposable diapers and attend movies paid for with disposable income. When they begin to argue, disagree, and drift apart, these parents divorce and turn their family into another disposable commodity.

One difficulty with this preference for disposables is that the preference is based on cost and convenience, rather than value. For example, it is the cost of food at fast food restaurants that appeals to most of their customers, rather than the quality of the meal. Another problem with disposition is that it is based on immediate gratification rather than long-term consequences. We enjoy the taste of highly caloric, cholesterol raising, plaque forming fast foods while ignoring the long-term consequences of an improper diet. It is much easier to eat a greasy hamburger from a styrofoam container and toss that container into the trash barrel than it is to use a knife, fork, and plate and have to wash these utensils and put them away. Disposables appear to be by-products of a growing culture that prefers inexpensive and convenient rather than responsible behavior. A third problem with disposables is that they reduce satisfaction. From the mundane chore of doing the dishes to the important responsibility of maintaining a marriage, there can be a sense of accomplishment and a feeling of gratification when the task is completed.

Unfortunately, the American preference for the disposable seems to include attitudes toward the dead. The dead human body, like dirty plates and contaminated cups, soiled diapers, and forsaken marriages, is often seen as no longer of value. As part of the disposition preference, there is a denial of the importance of funerary and death rituals.

Unlike the fast food restaurant, where value is determined solely by cost, the value of death rituals should be determined by the comfort and consolation they provide to the bereaved. This is not to say that funeral service expense is irrelevant, because it certainly is not. Expense, feelings of the most immediately bereaved, the emotions of others, social customs and mores—all must be configured into an abstract equation designed to help the bereaved. Simply put, those who conclude that a certain type of death ritual is of little value because it is too expensive, have miscalculated the equation. They are doing a disservice to the bereaved.

Much inappropriate advice is provided by trusted caregivers of the bereaved like funeral directors, clergy, or hospice workers.

For nearly half a century, funeral directors have been defensive about their chosen profession. Although the cost of death-related merchandise and rituals has been the subject of criticism for centuries [1], only since 1963, with the publication of Mitford's popular exposé about undertakers and our practices [2], has the American funeral director found it necessary to retreat from the negative barrage of media and clergy scorn. One of the defense mechanisms employed by funeral directors has been an attempt to downplay the value of services they provide, thus effectively suggesting that less is cheaper, therefore less is better. Further, funeral directors take the role of surrogate grievers [3] when they make decisions and assumptions on behalf of family members. This is not done consciously or deliberately, since the funeral director is not unlike clergy, hospice workers, or intensive care nurses who find themselves emotionally involved with the dying and their death. It is this emotional involvement that causes the phenomenon to which Fulton refers when he writes that there is a reversal of roles between the caregiver and the survivor.

> The caregiver grieves but is not bereaved, while the bereft survivor may be beyond experiencing his or her grief. Thus, the role of the "surrogate griever" . . . has the capacity for complicating the dying process, . . . casting the muted responses or misunderstood reactions of the immediate survivor into a bad light [3, p. 253].

Even though the role of surrogate griever is not taken deliberately, it can still result in negative consequences for the bereaved. There is a body of solid evidence that indicates the importance of working through mourning [4, 5]. However, in an attempt to legitimize their work and lessen the criticism leveled at them and their industry, funeral directors take the path of least resistance. That is, they simply become order takers instead of helpful funeral directors using their knowledge and experience to assist clients through a difficult period. This order-taking role, combined with the possibility that the funeral director may, in his attempt at helpfulness, become a surrogate griever, deprives family members of their legitimate bereavement.

Hospice workers, well-meaning volunteers who have dedicated themselves to the demanding tasks of companioning the dying and counseling their families, often make the crucial error of equating funeral cost with funeral value. Understanding that their volunteer services are valuable (and they certainly are), hospice workers may mistakenly believe that other death services can only have value if they are volunteered, or very inexpensive, also. During their time with the dying person and his/her family, the hospice worker often becomes attached to, and protective of, that family. The hospice worker sometimes assumes the responsibility of interacting and interceding on behalf of the family with physicians, pharmacists, medical equipment suppliers, and hospitals. The family then becomes dependent on the hospice volunteer for advice and support. It is only natural that the hospice worker would feel responsible to act as a mediator between survivors and the funeral director. This is problematic because it places the hospice worker in the role of a surrogate mourner. It is certainly appropriate for hospice workers, or anyone else, to provide support and companionship for family members as they work with the funeral director. It is quite inappropriate, however, for hospice workers, and others, to make decisions on behalf of the immediate survivors or unduly influence their decisions. They must not, even while trying to be helpful, deny the bereaved the opportunity to participate in grief work that is important.

Clergy, too, sometimes become surrogate mourners. Because they are caring and concerned about their parishioners, they feel a need to be protective of the bereaved parishioner. Thus, they can also inappropriately assume responsibilities of the mourners. In addition, they err when they disparage the importance of death rituals. They need to realize that there is a relationship between funerary rites and other rituals, particularly those that are religious. Those who do not appreciate the importance of ritualizing death will not understand the need to ritualize other of life's events. Baptism, confirmation, Bar Mitzvah, commencement, marriage, and other rituals that are important in most cultures may become old-fashioned and obsolete. Rituals are the threads that bind together the fabric of society and without rituals our social fabric will quickly unravel. Our clergy need to comprehend this importance of social ritual and the relationships between the different rituals, particularly between the religious rituals, including those that venerate the dead. Thomas Lynch has expressed very well the need for clergy to understand death rituals. He explains that all people need to grieve, regardless of their spirituality or faith. And the clergy who are most helpful when death occurs are those who encourage the bereaved to seek comfort in their grief. Further, Lynch writes,

... Those clerics who regard funerals as so much fuss and bother, a waste of time better spent in prayer, a waste of money better spent on stained glass or bell towers, should not wonder for whom the bell tolls. They may have heard the call but they've missed the point [6, p. 81].

Lynch recognizes a shift in social patterns, from traditional to trendy, from religious to secular, and sometimes from sacred to profane. He understands that these social changes are reflected in our funeral practices. For the most part, in the twentieth century we have moved from family structures where death was accepted and experienced as a normal and personal element of life to institutional settings where death is hidden, denied, and impersonal. This social transformation in our responses to death leads to a reduction in the practice of death rituals.

For years men and women have joked about their own deaths, half-heartedly requesting that they be "tossed in the river," or "thrown in a ditch" when they die. Currently, however, those facetious requests are taken more seriously by surviving kin. "This is what Dad said he wanted," or "I don't really want to do this, but Mom said she would haunt me if I didn't follow her wishes" are frequently heard by funeral directors in the 1990s. Comments like these, often made in jest but sometimes meant seriously, have had the effect of discouraging survivors from using funerary rituals to express their feelings of bereavement.

Our fascination with the quickness and ease of disposition, the misconception that value is determined solely by cost, the misleading advice by those whom we trust, and the inaccurate perception that we can help our survivors if we advise them not to be overly concerned about our death, have all led to a trend away from rituals that honor the dead and comfort the survivors. This trend may be seen as "ritualistic downsizing."

Although the manifest intent of ritualistic downsizing is to help survivors by removing them still further from death, the latent result is that the bereaved, both surviving family members and friends, feel somehow cheated and left with a sense of unfinished business. Well-meaning advisors want to spare others the emotional pain of mourning, but they do not realize the importance of grief work and feeling the pain.

WITHOUT DEATH RITUALS

When Jessica Mitford wrote her best-selling critique of the funeral industry in 1963, she struck a responsive cord in many Americans, including some clergy, educators, and other professionals. Many of these in influential positions called for the reduction or abolishment of death rituals. They suggested that the money saved by downsizing rituals could be better spent on more important and practical things, material things.

What these death ritual abolitionists failed to realize is that there is a need for rituals whenever an important event occurs in life. Especially because death is a social event—involving the dying or deceased, immediate family members, extended family, friends, and neighbors—we need rituals to help us understand and mourn the death.

Without death or funerary rituals, we may very well feel that a person never lived. When there are no death or funerary rituals, important links between our past, our present, and our future are broken. When there are no death rituals, we miss the opportunity to say good-bye, the chance to relish someone's life in remembrance, the occasion for emotional closure. Doug Manning has written about the decline in rituals, and he describes absence of ritual surrounding his brother's death:

> My brother was removed and instantly cremated. There was no ritual except a brief memorial service and a cocktail party held several days after he died. We stood around and acted like no one had died and called that a funeral. Someone has said "Those who avoid funeral ritual have their funerals on the psychiatrist's couch." This is the story of my brother's family. Four years later they are still in denial and shock. This experience has turned me from a believer in the value of the funeral to an outright fanatic on the subject [7, pp. 4-5].

IMMEDIATE POST-DEATH RITUALS

Those of us who recall the events beginning November 22, 1963, have an almost innate understanding of the value of immediate post-death rituals. Our President had just been assassinated, we were unsure who or what was responsible, we were overwhelmed with the enormity of the tragedy and apprehensive about the vulnerability of our government.

> From the moment President Kennedy's death was announced, all radio music became funereal and all television networks focused on events following the death of our president. With the exception of one professional football game, the nation stopped to grieve our fallen leader. Through the broadcast media and, to a lesser extent, through the print media, we participated in rituals about our

president, but rituals for us. We heard the pronouncement of his death from Parkland Hospital in Dallas, we saw President Johnson sworn into office aboard Air Force One, a blood-spattered Mrs. Kennedy at his side. We watched as President Kennedy's body was taken from the plane and placed into a hearse in Washington, D.C. We mourned with thousands of others as they passed by the President's coffin, and we ached when John Kennedy, Jr. saluted the caisson carrying his dad's body. Toward the end of the rituals honoring our president, we observed the eternal flame being lighted on the president's grave in Arlington National Cemetery.

These funerary rituals did much to validate the continuity of our political system and provided the American public with a sense of confidence and security. They assuaged our anger, relieved our grief, and prepared us to continue with our lives.

Similarly, the tragic death of Princess Diana in 1997 served to remind the world of the importance of honoring a loved one who has died. We recall Princes Charles, William, and Harry following her casket into Westminster Abbey. We remember seeing floral offerings thrown onto the hearse as it moved slowly toward the burial site. Millions of people, most of whom had never met Princess Diana and were not even citizens of Great Britain, were electronically involved, through television or the Internet, in mourning rituals that were traditional, heartfelt, and consoling.

On the morning of April 19, 1995, our nation's sense of security was forever challenged with the Oklahoma City bombing of the Edward Murtough Federal Building. Condolences from around the world were sent to survivors of the massacre. Help and helpers deluged Oklahoma City with support as the country agonized through the difficult days of digging, searching, and recovering victims. Again, through the medium of television, we grieved as if we were there. Rituals ranged from the simple placing of thank you signs on the barricade fence to the formal memorial service attended by family members and the President. We grieved, and mourned.

These very publicized rituals represent the more personal, but no less important, rituals that we practice when someone we love dies. What, then, is the value of these immediate post-death rituals? Why are they important to the bereaved and the community?

First, death rituals provide us with a sense of purpose. Whether we are involved in planning a death ritual, sending floral offerings or writing a sympathy letter (death rituals in themselves), attending and/or participating in a ritual, we feel we are doing something, and the something we are doing is purposeful.

Second, death rituals discourage our attempts to deny the death. People do not ordinarily come into a funeral establishment to visit, or to browse. They come in to do the business of death. Someone is dying, or has died, and family members and/or close friends are at the funeral establishment to arrange disposition of the body and plan for the accompanying death rituals. Because someone has died, friends, colleagues, and acquaintances come to the funeral establishment to pay their respects, to support survivors, and to express their sorrow. By our presence in the funeral establishment, we acknowledge the death.

Third, death rituals provide the immediate survivors with necessary support at a time when the bottom has dropped out of their lives. When death occurs, especially when the death is unexpected, survivors feel like the world is in disarray, that there is no purpose, no future. Immediate post-death rituals indicate a sense of order, the feeling that someone—God, friends, the clergy, the funeral director—cares and is supportive. More than two decades ago, Clariss Start had her world rocked by the death of her husband. A writer for the *St. Louis Post-Dispatch,* Start eloquently explained the value of immediate post-death rituals to her: "The traditional funeral has had more than its share of criticism. Frankly, I think it is a great device to bridge the shock of death and the awfulness of bereavement which will come later" [8, pp. 23-24].

THE NEED FOR AFTERCARE TODAY

Although traditional funerary rituals still accompany a large majority of deaths in many geographic areas of Canada and the United States, there are strong trends away from traditional funerals and toward downsized rituals, or no rituals at all, both regionally and across both nations. Many of these trends are correlated with the increase in cremation [9].

It has been said that you could buy any color Model T Ford that you wanted, as long as you wanted black. Funerals used to be like those Model T Fords. They were all pretty much the same, at least as far as the rituals were concerned. Until the middle of the twentieth century, nearly everyone who died had a traditional service with what Alan Wolfelt calls "cookie-cutter" rituals [10, p. 45]. Now, thankfully, there are options and changes and the opportunity to personalize rituals. The difficulty for many survivors is trying to understand what rituals will be helpful and valuable to them.

When death occurs, the surviving family members often find themselves distraught and confused. They are unable to make decisions based on careful consideration, but instead make decisions based on what seems to be easiest at the time. Their decisions on death rituals may be based on input like "He always said he didn't want any fuss," "She didn't want anyone to look at her," "He was so old, he hardly has any friends left," "She would come back and haunt us if we had a service for her," "I can't face my friends at a funeral," or "We really would like a service but Dad said 'nothing for him.'" As more and more survivors use these types of misunderstandings to deprive themselves of important immediate post-death rituals, there will be a need for aftercare rituals to fill the unmet need for rites to formalize the process of death separation.

Even when services are held following a death, communities seldom respond as they once did. People perceive themselves as too busy to take time out of their schedules and attend funeral services, they rationalize that they were not close to the deceased or surviving family, they feel that death rituals are too formal or spiritual and uncomfortable to attend. For whatever reason, the sense of community support experienced and savored by survivors of a generation or two ago will probably not be found today or in the next century.

Whether or not immediate post-death rituals are held, close survivors are expected to reconcile themselves to the death in a relatively short period of time. Someone will surely remark that "Life goes on," "You must put that behind you and get on with your life," or "Buck up, it's been three weeks since your wife died." In the fast-paced technological age of the twenty-first century, we are unlikely to be accorded time to mourn those we have loved. Our relationship with that person who has died will be quickly and finally severed by the shears of social correctness. Aftercare can help us retain the relationship with guidance, companionship, and support [5, p. 3].

Not too many years ago, American widows mourned publicly for one year and widowers mourned for six months. The length of time of their mourning could be determined by the clothes they wore and the stationery they used [1]. They were identified as bereaved and they were respectfully allowed time and space to mourn. Today mourners are unidentifiable. Whether or not we have recently experienced a death, social norms require us to act as if nothing had happened or be classified as mentally ill or unusual. Just as we have discarded our respect for life, perhaps symbolically represented in our acceptance of the disposable society, we are discarding our respect for death, and for the feelings of those who are bereaved.

Early in the 1990s, a young woman was drowned when her car careened into a pond. A week after her death, her father returned to work in the office of a large corporation. He placed a photograph of his daughter on his desk. His second day at work, he was approached by his supervisor who asked him to remove his daughter's picture. It was, the supervisor said, making others in the office uncomfortable.

If we cannot grieve and mourn in today's society, we must have a safe place to do so, and that safe place can be provided under the auspices of aftercare. If we do not find comfort and consolation from our friends or colleagues, we must find it from someone else, and that someone can be the aftercare provider. The safety and comfort may come in the form of one-on-one visiting or facilitated support groups. It may be found in libraries, hospital chapels, churches, or funeral homes. It may come from psychologists, psychiatrists, funeral directors, or chaplains. It may be formal or informal and offered in open-ended sessions or in closed time frames. It simply must be offered.

AFTERCARE OFFERINGS

The current need for aftercare cannot simply be described as the culpability of an uncaring society. Even when immediate death rituals are beneficial, valid, and comforting, many people cannot recover from the devastation of death without help. For generations, mourning widows, hapless orphans, and devastated parents have been left to heal their own broken hearts. It is not that we did not care. It may just be that we did not know any better. Now we know better. We know where aftercare is needed and we are learning how to provide it. If, as death care providers, we represent ourselves as both responsible for the complete emotional comforting of the bereaved as well as the care of the dead, then we must assume the obligation and privilege of providing aftercare.

On April 19, 1996, the first anniversary of the Oklahoma City Bombing, our nation observed a moment of silence in memory of those who had died a year earlier. That was an aftercare ritual.

Each Christmas season, many funeral homes across North America hold memorial services to honor those who have died during the past year. These are aftercare rituals.

In the library of a small mountain town, four or five people meet monthly to discuss deaths they have experienced. These are aftercare meetings.

A young man received counseling in a funeral home from a certified counselor for more than a year following the death of his sister and nephew in an airplane crash. That counseling was aftercare.

A hospice organization sponsors an annual seminar to help the bereaved get through the holidays from Thanksgiving through the New Year. The seminars are aftercare.

THE SIGNIFICANCE OF AFTERCARE

So why is aftercare important now? It is important because there is a difference between us and them. Who are they? They are those who are always putting themselves first. They are saying, "I am going to get mine and I don't care about you." They are involved in a success mentality that encourages them to run roughshod over anyone else to reach their goals. They are asking, "Am I my brother's keeper" [10]?

Aftercare is important because it is needed and it is we who recognize and respond to that need. Who are we? We are the ones who respond, "I am my brother's keeper." We believe that our families, social circles, and communities stand together and are only as strong as the weakest link. We are willing to go beyond the convenient and the disposable. We value and respect life, as well as death. We understand how important it is to befriend the bereaved. Our dinner can wait and we can golf another day. We say "We'll help you," and we mean what we say. We are aftercare providers.

REFERENCES

1. R. W. Habenstein and W. M. Lamers, *The History of American Funeral Directing* (3rd Edition), Burton and Mayer, Brookfield, Wisconsin, 1995.
2. J. Mitford, *The American Way of Death,* Fawcett Crest, New York, 1963.
3. R. L. Fulton, The Many Faces of Grief, *Death Studies, 11*:4, pp. 243-256, 1987.
4. W. Worden, *Grief Counseling and Grief Therapy,* Springer, New York, 1982.
5. A. Wolfelt, *Creating Meaningful Funeral Ceremonies,* Companion Press, Fort Collins, Colorado, 1994.
6. T. Lynch, *The Undertaking,* W. W. Norton, New York, 1997.
7. D. Manning, The Clergy Factor, *The Dodge Magazine,* pp. 4-5, January-February 1995.
8. C. Start, *On Becoming a Widow,* Concordia Publishing House, St. Louis, Missouri, 1973.
9. H. C. Raether, Consumers Have Spoken: The Statistics and Projections Released by CANA Show Some Interesting Trends, *The Director, LXXI*:2, pp. 40-42, February 1999.
10. Genesis 4:9, Genesis, *The New American Standard Bible: Red Letter Edition,* Collins World, La Habra, California, 1975.

CHAPTER 15

The Aftercare Worker and Support Group Facilitation

Alice Parsons Zulli

BEING PRESENT TO OTHERS THROUGH THEIR LOSS AND GRIEF IS A CHALLENGE AND A BLESSING!

WHO ARE AFTERCARE WORKERS?

Aftercare workers are a special breed of people. Many have experienced significant losses in their lives and others have not yet embarked on that journey. Those who have worked through the tasks of grief often experience what I call "a deep and personal awakening." Their awakening has left them with a desire to give back to others that which was learned as they moved through the desperate, lonely hours of bereavement. Either through personal experience or a deep desire to help others, aftercare workers are special. They come in many sizes and shapes, male and female, both young and not so young. They all share one common thread and that is the golden thread of compassion.

Having survived their own personal losses, some powerful thing, which refuses to remain quiet, is awakened deep in their souls. It begins as a soft fluttering inside them like the wings of a baby bird yearning to fly. As the weeks and months pass they begin to realize their inner calling. They discover a special mission deep within which brings them to a place of companioning others who face the physical, spiritual, mental, and social challenges of being a bereaved person.

Assisting others through their bereavement is a task not to be taken lightly. It takes time, it requires patience and flexibility, it calls for perseverance and optimism, and most importantly, it demands warmth and compassion. Assisting others through their grief also requires a "state of the art" bereavement education and a deep sense of knowing and understanding boundaries and limits. Those who are struggling and grieving need someone beside them who can understand, someone who can identify with them, someone who can be as human as they are.

Few helping situations are more challenging, or more rewarding, than the opportunity to accompany others who have been impacted by loss. Assisting the bereaved is a demanding interpersonal process that requires energy and focus. To maintain that energy and focus, after-care workers must confront their own losses, fears, hopes, and dreams surrounding both life and death.

Who are aftercare workers? Aftercare workers are you and me. They are people who feel called to support bereaved persons in significant ways. They communicate caring nonverbally through facial gestures and body language. They have an abundance of empathy and, in demonstrating the ability to empathize, they show a willingness to be involved in the emotional suffering that is inherent in the grief work of the bereaved.

Aftercare workers communicate acceptance and a feeling of being understood which helps alleviate fears of rejection by the bereaved. The grieving person who feels understood is more likely to risk sharing deep, personal feelings which subsequently lead to healing. Empathic communication creates conditions that allow thoughts and feelings to become clear, and encourages self-exploration in the mourner. All of this is necessary for self-understanding and eventually closure, or reconciliation of the loss.

Aftercare workers who continually work to develop an understanding of their own experiences with loss are likely to be more effective care-givers to the bereaved. The following questions may elicit an inner search for personal meaning:

How am I being impacted by sharing the grief of the bereaved?
Are my losses being rekindled by working with the bereaved?
Who do I share my feelings with so I can remain intact to support the bereaved?

Aftercare workers meet the mourner's defenses and normal resist-ances with respect, patience, and a desire to understand. Respect is an attitude of trying never to hurt or damage a mourner's self-worth. Patience requires the ability to tolerate emotional outbursts from a gentle and non-judgmental position and to endure the ups and downs of the oftentimes lengthy grief journey of the bereaved. Aftercare workers model what they are teaching and embrace those beliefs that they feel are important to the bereaved.

Aftercare workers search out supportive relationships where they can be listened to and accepted. These relationships should offer opportunities to recharge emotional batteries. It is natural when emotionally wounded and upset to reach out for help and support. The nature of helping others, therefore, is to draw close and simultaneously begin to affect them and be affected by them. Aftercare workers must try to understand what is taking place inside of self, while trying to grasp what is taking place inside others. The double focus on the bereaved and self is essential to being an effective aftercare worker.

And finally, aftercare workers wisely seek out training in how to be effective while helping the bereaved. There is a vast supply of state-of-the-art bereavement education and resources available. Aftercare workers must apply research findings and establish a sound theoretical understanding of grief in order to remain current and updated in a field that is constantly changing. Only then can they support the bereaved with the highest standards of aftercare.

HOW AFTERCARE WORKERS CARE

> Soon after midnight I rose from the tiny cot in my husband's hospital room. He lay terribly sick. As my fears blackened, I pulled on my shoes and fled out into the hospital corridor. Tears trembled on my face . . . a sob crowded my throat. Suddenly I heard a soft ping. The elevator stopped. The doors opened and inside stood an elderly man with thinning white hair and eyes that searched the tears streaming down my face. He pushed a button, then dug into his pocket. As we lurched upward, he handed me a neatly folded handkerchief. I wiped my eyes, staring into his kind, steady gaze. His compassion reached my heart like the first fingers of morning sun dispelling the night . . . [1, p. 88].

Aftercare workers must initially manifest many special and unique qualities. It is through these natural and developed qualities that they show the bereaved how they care.

THEY CARE by helping the bereaved acknowledge what has happened. It is vital that aftercare workers companion the bereaved while they work through the slow and difficult tasks of grief that lie ahead since all bereaved people are unique and their ability to fully comprehend the meaning of their loss will also be unique. Some bereaved persons have had much time to anticipate and prepare for their loss, while others have had no warning. Aftercare workers will encourage the bereaved to talk about their loss until the full reality of primary and secondary loss has been identified, what remains has been appraised, and what lies ahead in possibilities is discovered. Aftercare workers let their genuine caring and concern show.

THEY CARE by conveying the expectation that even though the situation is difficult, the bereaved will be able to tolerate it and at some future time will have less pain and more pleasure. In other words, aftercare workers must continually sow seeds of realistic hope. While the bereaved person is experiencing dark despair, it is common to be unable to grasp any hope in the future. At this point the future may seem uncertain.

THEY CARE by using reflective listening and giving explicit permission to the bereaved to mourn in their own individual way. They support people by encouraging them to express their feelings, legitimizing and normalizing these feelings, and helping them understand the meaning of their loss. Aftercare workers should not rob the bereaved of legitimate sadness by suggesting that other family members need him/her.

THEY CARE by being authentic with the bereaved and supporting them as they struggle to cope with the peaks and valleys of the mourning process. They encourage the bereaved not to try to avoid the pain of grief. They offer their physical and emotional presence to render security and support. The "gift" of presence is very therapeutic and cannot be underestimated, but to be truly effective the aftercare worker must maintain an appropriate distance from the bereaved while preserving professional boundaries.

THEY CARE by accepting the bereaved without judgment. They allow the mourner the opportunity to explore all of their feelings and avoid the urge to quickly explain the person's feelings away. They never attempt to explain the loss in religious or philosophical terms too early. They encourage the bereaved to participate, not to isolate. They tolerate explosive emotional reactions from the bereaved and set reasonable limits.

THEY CARE by offering help to the bereaved and orienting them to the mourning process. They educate the bereaved about grief and healing while encouraging them to do the work of grief in their own time. They also help the mourner grieve the symbolic losses, such as opportunities, beliefs, hopes, and expectations.

THEY CARE by radiating hope to the bereaved and normalizing appropriate emotions, fears, behaviors, experiences, and symptoms. Normalizing can be achieved by allowing the bereaved to tell their story as often as they need to in an atmosphere of caring and emotional safety. As the aftercare worker listens, he or she can then mirror back appropriate responses which begins to normalize the bereaved persons experience. Aftercare workers are sometimes rebuffed by the very people they are attempting to comfort when anger is directed at them. Frequently anger is the outward emotional response to the pain and fear being triggered internally. The aftercare worker knows that this is because the mourner, in accepting help, must acknowledge the pain of the loss that has occurred.

THEY CARE by providing the frequent and regular presence of a stabilizing person during the critical period of bereavement, journeying with the bereaved in their search for meaning through loss, and being alert to the warning signs of depression and/or physical symptoms that may accompany the grief process; they gently encourage the bereaved to seek medical intervention when appropriate as the journey of grief can be very physically rigorous.

WHAT AFTERCARE IS

Expressing the feelings of loss, anger, and sadness that come with the death of a loved one is necessary to reach a reconciliation of the grief. The role of the aftercare worker is to understand the dynamics of grief then assist and encourage the griever to move through these dynamics in a healthy way.

Life brings happiness as well as a series of losses. However, loss is inevitable and it is generally accompanied by grief. People will need varying amounts of support during their period of bereavement to integrate and assimilate the loss and reconstruct a new life.

Death brings separation. For a healthy reconciliation of grief the bereaved must develop a new relationship with the deceased. As the bereaved person begins to reorganize his/her life in the absence of the deceased, a new relationship will be formed. This new relationship will be constructed largely with memories and past experiences. The bereaved must then form a new self-identity. When there has been a strong emotional involvement with another, a part of the bereaved person seems to die also. The bereaved must now seek integration of the new self and the old self. The aftercare worker can participate in the unfolding of this new identity which is separate from the deceased through healthy grief facilitation. Training assists the aftercare worker in ways to offer support and encouragement over a reasonable amount of time which prevents the bereaved from feeling isolated and overwhelmed.

For example, in a hospital-based bereavement support program, support and encouragement may be offered in many ways, often including the following:

- A telephone call to the bereaved soon after the death date lets the bereaved know that you remember what happened and care. It is also a time to mention that support groups are available and that they may soon receive a letter explaining dates and times of the groups. Time limited follow-up letters allow you to keep in touch with the bereaved with a writing plan. The first letter would be issued within the first week following the death and would let them know you remember what happened and care. The subsequent letters would be mailed at reasonable intervals such as one month, three months, six months, and might conclude with a letter sent just prior to the one year anniversary of the death. Each letter includes some statements of encouragement, perhaps poetry, and is a reminder that support groups are available. This is also an excellent opportunity to include educational information on the grief process and what the bereaved may expect to feel and experience during this time.

- A bereavement card may be sent to the family shortly after the death and signed by caregiving staff on the unit. This may or may not preclude a phone call and may or may not be followed by letters during the year offering support and encouragement. The bereavement card is particularly encouraging and thoughtful when the family and the staff have been together over a significant amount of time and some closeness has resulted. Follow-up programs should be tailored to the institution and the type of care extended to the patient and family.

- Newsletters which are tailored to the bereaved should be educational, informative, inclusive (perhaps using poetry or articles written by support group members), and sensitive to the needs of the bereaved. Written articles may suggest the tasks of grief, how the grief process differs with different losses, or perhaps articles that address the issues of holidays and other meaningful milestones a bereaved person may experience during their first year of bereavement. The newsletter should always list types of support groups offered, when and where they meet, and periodically a profile of what each group has to offer. Copies of newsletters could be sent separately or included with the follow-up letter plan.

- Brochures and literature which are especially helpful to specific losses should be made available to the bereaved. Some may be mailed with each letter or racks of brochures can be made available before and after support group meetings.

- Library services can be made available for those who wish to learn about their own grief process or about the experiences of others through text and video. Many wonderful resources gathered in an organized way allows the bereaved to spend time and energy wisely. Resources available in bookstores are often difficult to locate and many bereaved do not have the energy, money, or perhaps transportation available to search them out.

- Community events such as memorial services and/or holiday programs are designed to offer information and support. The holidays are frequently very painful for the bereaved and a gathering tailored to their needs is deeply appreciated by them. This hospital-based bereavement program offers a holiday program including a "Tree of Lights," a "personalized ornament," and/or names of the deceased added to and read from the "Book of Memory." All of the above are offered free of charge and can be a meaningful piece of the healing process.

- Support groups have five basic purposes: 1) to lend emotional support to the bereaved that comes from meeting others who share a similar experience; 2) to provide a place with others present to share and vent feelings that may feel strange or overwhelming alone; 3) to provide a place with a well-trained facilitator who assists in developing coping skills, such as adjustment to financial change, social and family relationships, independence vs. dependence, employment issues, physical adjustments and stamina, and day-to-day living; 4) to provide a place with a well-trained facilitator who can offer information and education about how to proceed and what to expect after a loss, thus making the adjustment easier; and 5) to furnish a place with a well-trained facilitator and co-facilitator who can help the bereaved explore existential issues which assist them in living each day to the fullest by clarifying what is important and meaningful in life.

- Individual grief counseling can be offered as many bereaved persons benefit greatly with individual, one-on-one grief counseling. Grief counseling should be done only by a person who has had specialized training in death education. A grief counselor specializes in orienting the bereaved to the process of grief, then guides and supports them through the weeks and months ahead. The grief counselor should be knowledgeable in family systems as families tend to help the bereaved or complicate the grief process for the bereaved.

• Referrals should be made to other agencies when special needs cannot be met or logistically are inconvenient. Any referrals given must be current.

One important goal of aftercare workers is to encourage the bereaved person to have a medical evaluation and treatment, if there are symptoms and the symptoms warrant. Many side effects of active grieving exacerbate pre-existing medical conditions or bring new and unexpected conditions. Many bereaved persons feel like they are going crazy because they have little ability to focus, or suffer short-term memory impairment. Normal sleeping and eating routines are often interrupted thus causing physical changes which may be alarming. MaryEllen's story is a good example:

> MaryEllen was only thirty-seven when her husband, Tom, was tragically killed as his vehicle was rear ended by a speeding truck. She was informed of his death by two police officers who appeared, unannounced, at her front door about the time she expected Tom home from work. When the officers had delivered the grim news they returned to their duties, leaving MaryEllen alone in the house without support. Aside from the responsibilities of her own job, MaryEllen had two children, eleven and fourteen. MaryEllen needed to prepare herself to deliver the news of their father's death to the children while simultaneously calling friends and relatives. Further complicating the situation was that fact that six weeks prior to Tom's death, MaryEllen had been diagnosed with diabetes.
>
> While she was trying to stabilize from the shock of her young husband's death and all that it would eventually mean to her life, she began having terrorizing high and low blood sugars which caused many physical side effects that were difficult for her to manage. Her doctor gave her information about the bereavement support groups currently being offered at the medical center and gently suggested that she might find much needed emotional support in a group while struggling with health and family issues simultaneously. She accepted her doctor's suggestion.
>
> MaryEllen visited an open, ongoing bereavement support group and found sensitive group facilitators and caring group members who could eventually serve as her linking support system during the first year after Tom's death. One year later, she still maintains some of those friendships and has brought her diabetes back under control.

PROVIDING AFTERCARE SUPPORT GROUPS

The particular setting of aftercare, including support groups, may be done in churches, funeral homes, medical centers or other agencies, and meeting rooms. Bereavement support done within the context of a group is not only very efficient, but can also be an effective way to offer the emotional support the bereaved person is seeking. Before setting up and starting a support group, aftercare providers need to consider the following:

1. *Purpose:* Bereavement support groups usually exist for emotional support, education, or social purposes. I believe that the strongest formula for the above is education and support in a formalized support group setting while encouraging socialization after meetings or at special activities planned and executed by the group participants. The group facilitators may attend certain special activities when appropriate, but must carefully restrain themselves from becoming involved in dual relationships. One of the outcomes of a healthy and viable support group is to allow the group members to develop trust not only in self and other members, but particularly in the facilitators. This can only be done if the facilitator maintains a strictly professional leadership position. Developing friendships with group members can happen after the member completes their grief work and subsequently leaves the group. If a friendship develops between a group member and the facilitator prior to completing the work and leaving the support group, other members may feel hurt, betrayed, or jealous, leading to a faltering of healthy group process.

2. *Structure:* Some groups are closed-ended. People enter and leave the group at the same time and the group is in existence for a specified number of meetings. Closed-ended groups generally try to meet certain goals during each meeting with an overall agenda having been met by the time the group concludes. Other groups are open-ended. People come and go as the group fulfills their individual needs. Open-ended groups may seem more difficult for the facilitator to manage as members are at different points in their grief process. As new members join, a sense of trust must be developed anew among the members. One of the positive outcomes realized in an open-ended group is those who have become established group members can mentor and offer hope to those who are new.

3. *Logistics:* The number of meetings, length of meetings, size of the group, the location, and cost of meetings are all important considerations. Some groups meet weekly and others bi-weekly or once a month. Many professional group leaders concur that the ideal length of a meeting is one-and-one-half hours with eight to twelve members. This limited time period is primarily because the work of grief is difficult and the bereaved are usually experiencing less physical, mental, and emotional energy. Harnessing additional energy for longer meetings may compromise the bereaved person's ability to complete other tasks

such as a normal workday or caring for small children and other family members. Many groups have found that having a social time prior to the start of the meeting with light refreshments helps relieve newcomers' anxiety and all members can benefit from the extra time spent with friends who understand their circumstances.

It is well to remember that ideals are sometimes not easy to achieve in a grief support group. Members come to a group meeting anticipating adequate time to share their stories. This expectation presents an additional task for the group facilitator which is to utilize time wisely, gently limit the long-winded member while encouraging the shy member to share, all within the prescribed time period. Group process should also allow members the opportunity to share suggestions or opinions. This additional input can further stretch the time for the person sharing.

In regards to money, some groups are free, some have a one-time-only charge for participants, while others ask for a donation at every meeting. The location of the meetings should be well thought out regarding lighted parking if the meeting is held at night, and easy access to the meeting room for those who may experience difficulty walking long distances or climbing stairs.

4. *Pre-screening potential members:* Whenever possible it is wise to screen a potential member for the appropriateness of their loss in the group. For example, if most of the group members are grieving the loss of a spouse through illness and have been attending the group for several weeks or months, it may be wise to suggest other resources to a newly bereaved person who lost their spouse to homicide, suicide, or catastrophic loss. The dynamics of the latter person's grief journey will probably bring additional stress to the original group members and it is possible that the needs of the newly bereaved person may not be met in the already existing group.

After the purpose, structure, and logistics have been addressed, it is important to identify leadership. Some groups, such as Compassionate Friends, are run by bereaved individuals and some are run by mental health-care professionals. Other groups are started and run primarily by lay people but with professional supervision.

Leadership styles must also be considered. If the goals are educational, the leader will be more of an informant. If the purpose is emotional support, the leader's role is to facilitate the telling of stories and prompt support and encouragement from the others. Many group leaders incorporate an effective blend of offering information and gently facilitating group interaction.

A co-facilitator is helpful when there are more than five or six group members in attendance. The co-facilitator follows the lead of the facilitator, establishes a relationship of support with the group members, and is available to accompany a group member out of the group setting if a situation arises, leaving the facilitator to keep the group intact and offer reassurance. Facilitators never choose favorites in a group. They understand interpersonal dynamics of group members such as inclusion (Will I or do I fit in?), control (How do I influence the group; am I important?), and affection (Am I cared for?). The facilitator must also handle disruptive behaviors effectively.

Friendships that develop among members of a bereavement support group should be gently encouraged. One of the tasks of mourning is being able to allow new people into one's life and to allow oneself to form new relationships. Friendships that form among members of bereavement support groups and that continue beyond the life of the group are small but important steps in the overall healing that is being facilitated.

WHY SUPPORT GROUPS ARE NEEDED

Aftercare workers come to realize that the emotional and spiritual healing that the bereaved are searching for comes as a result of finding a safe community. In the context of this chapter, community would be the bereavement support group. Healing can manifest itself most forcefully when the members of a support group and the facilitators mobilize themselves to care for each person first as an individual and second as a member of the whole. A group such as this creates a communal effort that encourages direct, supportive, healing relationships. In addition, the members and facilitators create a safe environment where they can listen to the stories and witness the suffering in each other.

In her book *Loss, Grief, and Mourning,* Therese Rando writes,

> The most difficult experiences in life always involve some measure of loss. . . . Caregivers must help individuals undergoing these experiences . . . perceive their reactions as grief and mourning responses. This affords them better understanding, increased meaning, reduced helplessness, and a greater sense of control—all of which improve coping ability [2, p. 26].

Faced with the anguish and suffering of the bereaved, aftercare workers can then choose their response. By answering the call of compassion and choosing loving action, aftercare workers will be nurtured in their work with the bereaved. By providing a stable support group with life-affirming values, they will encourage the development of healthy group process thereby providing members of the group the opportunity to heal their emotional wounds and move forward in their life journey.

A well-trained support group facilitator (aftercare worker) needs extensive knowledge of grief and loss, training in group dynamics, and a working knowledge of family systems and how they can exacerbate existing problems in bereavement. The following is a list of ten guidelines for effective group leaders.

Confidentiality

In an open support group, confidentiality should be stressed but cannot be guaranteed. The facilitator, however, must adhere to strong boundaries of confidentiality.

Coercion and Pressure

Some group members may elicit tendencies to pressure other members to share or accept advice, etc. The facilitator must recognize when this is happening and safeguard the entire group against pressure.

Imposing Leader Values

The facilitator should have values equal to those in the group and should strive to maintain the integrity of the group as a whole. There will be occasions when the leader clearly may not agree with the thoughts or actions of a group member. If this occurs, it is imperative to educate the bereaved about behaviors that may be potentially destructive or harmful, while not imposing personal thoughts and values on the group member.

Equitable Treatment

Grief has the potential to negatively impact one's sense of self-esteem. Therefore, facilitators are trained to value all group members and carefully avoid selecting favorites. When a facilitator does not treat each group member equally, a lowered sense of self-worth in a group member may be exacerbated.

Dual Relationships

Facilitators are trained to avoid dual relationships and maintain clear boundaries of professionalism. Realistically, however, friendships sometimes occur between group members and the facilitator. In the context of this chapter, friendship means a non-sexual, casual relationship. It is important for the facilitator to be clear about crossing over from feelings and fantasies into actions and violations. One also has to be clear about therapeutic touch versus erotic contact. Some group members may have weak boundaries in this area and, therefore, all touch may be susceptible to misperception. Therefore, it is highly suggested that personal relationships between the facilitator and group members not be encouraged until the group member(s) has completed his/her grief work and resigned from the group.

Goal Development

The two primary goals in bereavement facilitation are to resolve the conflicts generated by separation and complete the tasks of grief. The group setting provides the social support system necessary for success-ful grief work to be done and the members offer permission to grieve the loss. A well-trained facilitator will set goals for the entire group and revisit them often. This provides a platform for evaluating alternative courses of group interaction and for considering how each member's behavior may contribute to group accomplishments.

Termination of the Group

Preparation before a group terminates is highly desirable to avoid having members shift into grieving the loss of support which the group setting provided. Additionally, in an open-ended group it is helpful when a group member prepares the group for his/her termination as a group member. This can be done easily if the member confides his/her plan to leave to the group. For example, the first step is for the member to announce during the sharing portion of the group that he/she feels ready to move on but will return the following week to say good-bye. This plan offers individual members the opportunity to emotionally prepare for another separation. It also allows the facilitator or the group to bring refreshments or have everyone sign a card. If the facilitator has a Polaroid camera, he/she can take pictures of the group members to send with the member who is moving on.

Evaluation and Follow-Up

Facilitators are trained to ascertain if a group member who decides to leave the group is ready to leave or if something has occurred within the group and he/she may be leaving prematurely. The facilitator should create an opportunity after the meeting to speak individually with the member who is planning to leave. If the facilitator feels the member is leaving prematurely, he/she may request the member come an additional number of times, such as three or six, in order to receive increased support and prepare the member and the group for this separation. If something upsetting has occurred within the group that cannot be worked through, it becomes appropriate to offer resources for a different group and/or individual grief counseling. Assure the departing member that the door will be open to allow the bereaved to return if they so desire.

Referrals

A well-trained facilitator will know of other resources in his/her area and whenever possible contact the resource before referring any group member. It is appropriate to offer the member the name and phone number of a contact person at this new resource to help smooth the way and reduce anxiety. A follow-up call to the bereaved is also appropriate to ascertain if they contacted the new resource successfully. Group facilitators should always know their limits and stay within them. In the context of this chapter it should be mentioned that the support groups in this hospital-based bereavement support program are clearly for the purposes of bereavement support and education, NOT psychotherapy. Any group member who the facilitator feels needs additional support for reasons not directly related to loss are offered resources and referrals.

Again, the facilitator does this to protect the integrity of the entire group and promote opportunities for the individual to reach out for assistance in other areas.

Professional Development

Bereavement is a very complex issue and individuals experience their grief journey in many different ways. In spite of the fact that people have been grieving on their own for thousands of years, today's reality indicates that people frequently seek assistance in this very difficult process. Over the past twenty years, health care professionals have shown an increased interest in issues relating to grief and bereavement. Therefore, it behooves bereavement facilitators to persevere in seeking continuing education in this field. Many wonderful seminars, workshops, and comprehensive conferences are offered annually in addition to the publication of highly valuable textbooks and informative articles. Even television and movies are being produced that present accurate accounts of grief situations showing the impact of the dynamics of grief on families and individuals. This field grows and changes on a daily basis and continuing education is imperative for facilitators of grief to be effective in their work.

CONCLUSION

Individually and in community, we learn from our losses. In the learning we grow, and in that growth we heal. Today we are fortunate to have compassionate people who listen to our stories, share their stories, and prepare the fertile soil to recover and embrace life again.

These compassionate aftercare workers are people with a deep desire to help others navigate their way through the turbulent emotions of bereavement. They listen authentically and remain present with those who are living through some of the darkest hours of their lives. And aftercare workers strive to be familiar with the literature of death, dying, and bereavement and know how those issues facilitate the grieving process. In formulating thoughtful questions, aftercare workers encourage the real experts, the bereaved, to explore, recognize, honor, and reinforce their own personal strengths.

REFERENCES

1. S. M. Kidd, Compassion, in *Dawnings: Finding God's Light in the Darkness,* P. Hobe (ed.), Guideposts Associates, Inc., Carmel, New York, 1981.
2. T. Rando, *Loss, Grief and Mourning,* Research Press, Champaign, Illinois, 1993.

CHAPTER 16

Visions of Aftercare in the New Millennium: Who Needs It?

Ronald K. Barrett

The concept of aftercare (i.e., caring for the bereaved) is nothing new. The practice of supporting mourners through grief and mourning is a natural social response to loss within most traditional cultures and societies [1]. Family members and significant others routinely gather during times of illness, dying, and death to provide physical, emotional, and spiritual support to the dying and their survivors. Raphel postulates that the provision of comfort and consolation to those who mourn during times of distress reinforces important social rituals and perhaps more importantly serves as a powerful reinforcer of familial and communal bonds [2]. However, a number of factors seem to undermine these traditional support systems causing mourners to be unsupported and more at-risk of not having a healthy course of grief recovery [3]. Families in traditional communities are less likely to be able to support the bereaved due to their own limitations as well as considering the growing dysfunction among families, social and physical distances, alienation, and an erosion of traditional rituals to assist mourners. In addition, the lack of awareness and sensitivity in our society about the critical need for supportive care after the death of a loved one has also minimized the availability of resources to those who mourn [4]. It is the awareness of this need that has facilitated the realization of aftercare within a number of communities of professional care providers.

Traditionally, churches and synagogues have been the providers of aftercare; however, the provision of aftercare by funeral directors is relatively new [5]. While many individuals and cultures are more likely to turn to faith-based communities during times of distress related to loss and grief, many factors tend to minimize the effectiveness of aftercare in these settings. Some of these factors are: 1) the lack of professional training of many clergy to provide grief counseling and related aftercare services that their members may require; 2) a lack of cultural competence of clergy to relate to the needs of a growing culturally diverse membership where rituals and cultural practices and expectations tend to vary [6, 7]; as well as 3) the mere numbers of deaths in a given faith-based community which may overwhelm clergy making it difficult for the needs of many to be addressed, causing them to not receive sensitive and attentive care [8]. In many faith-based communities, the awareness of the limitations of clergy to meet the needs of bereaved members has given rise to the growing trend for lay persons to assist the bereaved via programs for ministry to their bereaved members. In addition, anger at God as a routine aspect of the spiritual crisis many bereaved experience during mourning may limit the effectiveness of the outreach, utilization, and effectiveness of faith-based aftercare programs.

In recent years, hospitals and hospice programs have also offered services to the bereaved members of families for a period of up to one year following a death. While provisions within a hospice serve an important segment of the community, a small percentage of deaths occur in hospices, nursing homes, and similar critical care situations and consequently significant segments of the community have needs that go unattended. Approximately 60 percent of all deaths occur in hospitals or medical centers, while another 16 percent occur in hospices, nursing homes, and similar critical care facilities [9]. In some rare cases aftercare services have been sponsored by offices within local criminal justice systems as well as the offices of the medical examiners. For example, the Baltimore District Attorney's Office has sponsored an aftercare program at no cost to serve community children who are homicide survivors. Similarly, the Philadelphia Medical Examiners Office has sponsored aftercare services at no cost to the community as well.

The practice of aftercare within the professional community of funeral directors (according to the National Funeral Directors Association) is believed to have begun in the 1980s. Accordingly, many funeral homes began providing some form of follow-up services to the families that they served. Initially, the aftercare services targeted widows and widowers, but later were broadened to include all members of the family including the community of significant others following the death of a loved one. Routine direct aftercare provisions might include telephone calls, personal visits, cards, trained counselors for grief support groups, grief counseling, workshops, holding special ceremonies, holiday services, tree planting services, camps for children, and survival workshops for widows and widowers focusing on finances and living alone. Many funeral homes also provide important aftercare via information-oriented services (e.g., grief support handout materials, newsletters, community-based educational outreach, community and professional resource libraries including directories to clergy, trained professionals, and other community referrals and resources, etc.) (see Table 1).

Unlike hospice aftercare, funeral homes tend to organize aftercare programs that go beyond a few days or months after funeralization, but rather make provisions for years. According to the National Funeral Directors Association, a significant portion of those utilizing aftercare services tend to do so typically months to years after the death of a loved one. Aftercare programs that do not extend their provisions over a longer period of time may have limited accessibility for a significant portion of the bereaved who may not utilize services for months or years. Consequently, the aftercare programs that are more prolonged or long-term focused may be more useful and effective in meeting the needs of the bereaved.

BUILDING AN AFTERCARE PROGRAM

Given a most fundamental conceptualization of aftercare as supportive services to assist and support the bereaved [10], a number of thoughtful considerations (e.g., a community needs assessment,

Table 1. Contemporary Aftercare Programs

Information Services:
- Literature on Grief
- Library and Directories of Related Learning Resources and Professional Care Provider Referrals and Resources
- Educational Programs
- Newsletters

Direct Services:
- Self-Help Support Groups
- Professional Grief Counseling and Therapy
- Memorial and Holiday Programs
- Childrens' Camps and Programs
- Widows' and Widowers' Programs
- Personal Outreach (e.g., telephone calls, personal visits, cards, etc.)

program design considerations, selection of culturally relevant and age appropriate materials, personnel selections, training, certification and liability concerns, program evaluation, etc.) should be a part of the planning and implementation of a meaningful and comprehensive aftercare program [3, 11] (see Table 2).

In many communities, there regretably can be professional competition and turf concerns that may limit the accessibility to aftercare services to the bereaved. There is a need for better coordination of the various aftercare resources offered to maximize resources to the bereaved [5]. Given the limitations of other aftercare providers, it is reasonable to conclude that the funeral home is in the most focal position to provide the crucial leadership in organizing aftercare services to the bereaved. Relative to other institutions and professional care providers, funeral homes tend to make contact with a broader, more representative sample of the bereaved public at large and have the greater potential to provide service and outreach to the largest segment of the grief stricken and bereaved.

Currently, most funeral homes provide some form of aftercare service while realizing the benefit for the individuals they serve as well as themselves. Weeks and Johnson argue that it is extremely important to separate one's pre-need sales promotion from one's aftercare program [3]. Irion adds that aftercare is a service, not public relations [5]. Lineberry argues that:

> for a funeral home owner or manager to dismiss responsibility for managing aftercare may be as unethical as a counselor opening up pain in a client and suddenly discontinuing counseling without closure [12, p. 42].

For these and many other reasons, the responsibility for coordinating meaningful aftercare program services should be handled by the funeral service care provider.

Table 2. Components of Aftercare Programs

- Community Survey for a Needs Assessment
- Programmatic Design and Focus
- Culturally Sensitive Materials
- Age Appropriate Materials
- Personnel Selection
- Staff Training
- Staff Certification
- Malpractice Insurance and Liability Concerns
- Program Evaluation

FORECASTING THE NEED OF AFTERCARE— WHO NEEDS IT?

Given the current models of aftercare programs and their inherent limitations, there is much yet to be done to design more effective and comprehensive aftercare services to the bereaved [13-15]. A fundamental priority in this task ought to be a primary goal of reaching more of the under-served bereaved community. As previously discussed, many aspects of the scope and design of current aftercare services within faith-based communities and hospice offerings have limitations—favoring some while excluding others. If aftercare is to be an intentional resource to all who are bereaved and are worthy of comfort and consolation [13, 16-19], future visions of aftercare should be more accessible to all bereaved members of the community. While there is little, if any, empirical data on the scope and nature of needs of the bereaved in America [20], some reasonable inferences can be made from existing data sources to assist in the identification of the scope of the unmet needs among the bereaved.

A sense of social responsibility to care for the bereaved is more than just a humane and "right old fashioned neighborly concern" [3], it is also quite practical. There is an emerging body of empirical evidence and theoretical literature suggesting that the costs associated with the consequences of not attending to matters of loss and grief cannot be ignored. For example, unresolved and complicated grief among the bereaved have been linked to severe mental disorders and alcohol abuse [21] and violence [22-24]. An emerging body of evidence suggests that those bereaved whose grief, pain, and loss is not addressed are more at-risk for a variety of problems in coping and adjusting, which could compromise the quality of their lives and relationships to others. Identifying these groups of under-served and at-risk bereaved is an important challenge in reformulating aftercare outreach efforts.

NON-WHITE ETHNIC MINORITIES

Significant differences in the quality of life, health status, and mortality rates among ethnic minority groups suggest a multitude of losses and associated grief worthy of aftercare consideration and treatment. There is an extensive history and literature on the trend of members of ethnic minority groups to underutilize health services for both physical health and psychological services [25]. Many ethnic minority members do not enjoy the same quality of life, health, and life expectancy as their White counterparts. For 1997, Cose reported higher rates of infant mortality, homicide, poverty, and unemployment and lower rates of high school graduation, coverage by health insurance, prenatal care, and voter turnout for Blacks than Whites [26, pp. 32-33]. Barbara Dixon reported that African Americans die prematurely and at significantly higher rates from the major causes of death in America [27]. This significant higher risk of disease, illness, and death in African Americans (and other non-whites) has been attributed to socioeconomic status, lack of access to health care, as well as cultural and life style situations [28]. In addition to cultural alienation, cultural mistrust serves to delay and promote the underutilization of institutionalized health care among Blacks and other non-whites [25, 29, 30]. Psychiatrist Michelle Clark estimates that among African Americans, nearly eighteen million suffer from clinical depression and 25 percent experience depressive symptoms that are often expressed differently and not recognized and consequently are more likely to be undiagnosed [31]. Although approximately one-fourth of African Americans exhibit symptoms, only 4 to 6 percent are actually diagnosed with clinical depression. Cultural background often plays a large role in how the symptoms are reported and interpreted, and often plays a critical role in how and if clinical depression is recognized and treated appropriately. While women generally experience depression at a rate twice that of men, various studies have shown that the prevalence of depression among African-American females is much greater than that of Caucasian women [31, p. 86]. While any sweeping cultural stereotypes and generalizations can often be misleading, the Barrett Inferential Model suggests that careful consideration of socioeconomic status and spiritual beliefs are two major factors to consider in addition to ethnicity/race in understanding and discerning attitudes toward dying, death, and end of life issues [32]. Consequently, these significant differences in the quality of life, health status, and mortality rates among ethnic minority groups suggest a multitude of losses and associated grief worthy of aftercare consideration and treatment.

A considerable body of evidence suggests many ethnic minority groups are less likely to utilize institutionalized health care resources and more likely to use "natural care providers (e.g., religious leaders, spiritualists, hair dressers, barbers, etc.)." The conventional practice of utilizing certified professional care providers has some constraints given the lack of trust of such agents of aftercare (i.e., "cultural mistrust") as well as the shortage of culturally matched persons to deliver such services. This challenge in cross-cultural counseling and the delivery of professional services in the face of overwhelming need, begs for innovation and creative approaches for the delivery of services to such under-served populations. Exploring some creative ventures of partnering with natural care providers who are an integral part of the cultural tradition and make-up of these under-served ethnic communities may offer some reasonable promise. Partnering possibilities might include establishing referral networks, collaborative partnering for interventions (e.g., community-based self-help groups, buddy programs, widow and widower social groups, holiday memorial ceremonies, etc.), as well as ongoing efforts to conduct research for the development of innovative alternative service delivery systems of aftercare for under-served ethnic communities.

THE MALE SUBCULTURE

A growing literature on the psychology of males reveals evidence that several developmental concerns often are correlated with many behavioral patterns evident over the life cycle. In many ways men are misunderstood—even by other men. A fundamental aspect of the psychology of males is the cultural mandate that males be competent, in control, protectors, and resourceful providers.

The approaches for addressing the concerns for men in aftercare programs may need to be approached differently. An emerging paradigm shift in the grief counseling field suggests some significant differences in patterns of male grief [33]. Accordingly, many of our standing assumptions about grief and the ways people grieve are based on our observations of female grievers. Many of our normative assumptions have come to guide current approaches to grief counseling and aftercare. The under-representation of males utilizing counseling and aftercare services suggests the need for creative innovations that are culturally relevant to better reach and serve the bereaved within the male subculture. Barrett has further cautioned that ethnic and developmental sensitivities should be considered in the design, gender considerations in staffing, and implementation of aftercare programs targeting bereaved males [32]. For example, in attempting to target urban adolescent males the aftercare program, title, design, and staffing play a significant role in the success or failure of such an effort.

CHILDREN AND YOUTH

The nature and course of grief recovery for children and youth is believed to be significantly different from that of adults. There have been some significant strides in recent years in the death education and counseling literature regarding our clarity of understanding the importance of developmental differences among children and youth.

Because the scope and nature of grief with children and youth may be so different, different approaches for clinical interventions and after-care for children and youth seem appropriate [34, 35]. There is considerable work yet to be done in addressing the needs of bereaved children and youth who are also culturally distinguished. In addition, aftercare programs for children and youth should be sensitive to the individual as well as the cultural differences among bereaved children and youth [32, 36]. Presently, too few professional resources and aftercare service options exist to meet the various yet real needs of the many underserved bereaved children and youth.

DISENFRANCHISED SECONDARY VICTIMS

The epidemic of chronic community violence in American society for the past several decades has left behind countless numbers of individuals who witness chronic violence and whose lives have been significantly impacted via their experience [37]. Many of these individuals (children and adults) have become "secondary victims" of such violence, often suffering in silence and seldom having their grief and losses legitimatized or attended to (see Table 3). Most of these individuals cannot qualify for victim services and are often overlooked even among members of the various professional communities. They are likely to go unacknowledged or attended to.

There is little empirical evidence or theory to predict the long-term consequences or outcomes for such untreated victims [22]. Most of these secondary victims experience a variety of losses which go unattended to and are often untreated. While there are too few identified case providers for the growing number of secondary victims, there is a need for more aftercare services and outreach to these untreated victims. Since the bereavement issues for many secondary

---

Table 3. Secondary Victims

Bystanders and witnesses of chronic violence including anyone who witnesses:
- Domestic Violence or Spousal Battery
- Sexual Assault
- Violent Assault
- Homicidal Violence
- Threats of Lethal Violence (e.g., threats with a lethal weapon, etc.)
- Suicide
- Anyone Identifying with the Victim of a Violent Crime
- A Significant Other Dying of AIDS, Cancer, Alzheimer's, etc.

---

victims may involve professional skills beyond those of the conventional counselors, professional collaborations among professional care providers may be most advisable.

CAREGIVERS AS SECONDARY VICTIMS

It is profoundly ironic that those who are professionally called to care for others are often least inclined to take care of themselves. The community of professional care providers (e.g., funeral directors, grief counselors, hospice workers, EMR and ER workers, law enforcement, medical professionals, and clergy, etc.) rarely have the resources or training to recognize and respond to the risks of "caregiver burnout" and its accompanying compassion fatigue (i.e., the resistance and/or inability to empathize with those who are in distress due to one's own emotional limitations) (see Table 4).

Many crisis response institutions lack provisions (e.g., budgets, trained personnel, allowances for staff training and development, etc.) to care for professional staff. For example, in our attempt to provide supportive assistance to others who were dealing with a number of emotionally challenging health crises (e.g., AIDS, SIDS, suicide, Alzheimer's, cancer, homicide, sexual assault, etc.), many staff members are very much at-risk of professional burnout from the intense and consuming demands of their work in caring for others [38]. These professional care providers often contend with the stress of their professional roles, the stress of working with the families in distress, as

Table 4. Bereavement Burnout and Burnout in
Professional Care Providers

Chronic Loss(es)
↓
Bereavement Burnout
The experience of chronic loss(es) so rapidly over time
that prevent normal grief recovery
↓
Compassion Fatigue
The inability and resistance to empathize with another's
distress due to one's own emotional limitations
↓
Professional Burnout
The erosion of professional performance and effectiveness
in serving others

well as contending with their own grief associated with their attachments and subsequent losses associated with each client served. In some cases professional care providers may also be challenged by their own issues as being secondary victims themselves. Attempts to provide services and provisions for professional care providers is a very important challenge for aftercare service of the future.

CONCLUSION

In summary, the primary goal and objective of aftercare services is the provision of meaningful and comprehensive support assistance for the bereaved. The incidence of loss varies among populations, with some experiencing more loss(es) than others. It is also noted that some populations tend to not utilize available resources and appear to be under-served. A growing body of evidence seems to suggest grief that is unattended increases the potential for a number of adjustment problems. A number of under-served at-risk groups have been identified. While aftercare has been a common staple in many traditional communities, a number of professional care providers have begun to develop aftercare services. Many of these professional services have limitations, sometimes are in competition and conflict, and there is also a need for better coordination. The challenge for more creativity and more inclusive outreach are major parts of coordinating meaningful and comprehensive aftercare to the bereaved. Aftercare should not be thought of as a burden, but rather an exciting opportunity for the funeral service industry in the new millennium.

REFERENCES

1. J. Perry and A. Ryan, *A Cross-Cultural Look at Death, Dying and Religion,* Nelson & Hall Publishers, Chicago, 1995.
2. B. Raphel, *The Anatomy of Bereavement,* Basic Books, New York, 1983.
3. D. Weeks and C. Johnson, Developing a Successful Aftercare Program, *The Director,* The National Funeral Directors Association, Milwaukee, pp. 12-18, December 1995.
4. H. Schiff, *Living Through Mourning: Finding Comfort and Hope When a Loved One Has Died,* Penguin Books, New York, 1986.
5. P. Irion, Thoughtful Coordination of Care Essential for Aftercare Programs, *The Director,* The National Funeral Directors Association, Milwaukee, p. 59, December 1995.
6. L. Hazell, Cross-Cultural Funeral Rites, *The Director,* The National Funeral Directors Association, Milwaukee, pp. 53-55, October 1997.

7. L. DeSpelder and R. Barrett, Developing Multicultural Competency, *The Director,* The National Funeral Directors Association, Milwaukee, pp. 66-68, December 1997.

8. P. Moore and A. Marchese-Conboy, Bereavement and African American Churches: A Survey of Pastors, *Black Caucus Journal of the National Association of Black Social Workers, 3*:2, pp. 14-23, 1998.

9. J. Benoliel and L. Degner, Institutional Dying: A Convergence of Cultural Values, Technology, and Social Organizations, in *Dying: Facing the Facts,* H. Wass and R. Neimeyer (eds.), Taylor and Francis, Washington, D.C., 1995.

10. V. Lensing, New Association Strives to Define Aftercare, *The Director,* The National Funeral Directors Association, Milwaukee, p. 24, December 1995.

11. T. Gilligan, The Legal Perils of Aftercare, *The Director,* The National Funeral Directors Association, pp. 10-11, December 1995.

12. S. Lineberry, Is Aftercare a Part of Funeral Service, *The Director,* pp. 41-42, 1997.

13. C. Parkes, Models of Bereavement Care, *Death Studies, 11,* pp. 257-261, 1987.

14. T. Rando, *Grief, Dying, and Death: Clinical Interventions for Caregivers,* Research Press, Champaign, Illinois, 1984.

15. W. Worden, *Grief Counseling and Grief Therapy,* Springer, New York, 1982.

16. R. Deits, *Life After Loss,* Fisher Books, Tucson, Arizona, 1988.

17. D. Kuenning, *Helping People Through Grief,* Bethany House, Minneapolis, Minnesota, 1987.

18. D. Manning, *Comforting Those Who Grieve,* Harper & Row, San Francisco, 1985.

19. E. Price, *Getting Through the Night: Finding Your Way After the Loss of a Loved One,* Walker & Company, New York, 1985.

20. L. Robins and D. Reglier, *Psychiatric Disorders in America: The Epidemiologic Catchment Area Study,* Free Press, New York, 1991.

21. J. Swanson, S. Estoff, M. Swartz, R. Borum, W. Lachicotte, C. Zimmer, and R. Wagner, Violence and Severe Mental Disorder in Clinical and Community Populations: The Effect of Psychotic Symptoms, Comorbidity, and Lack of Treatment, *Psychiatry, 60,* pp. 1-30, Spring 1997.

22. R. K. Barrett, *Trauma, Unresolved Grief, and Adolescent Violence,* full day training conference as a 1998 Kellogg Foundation Expert in Residence at the Kellogg Community College Mawby Center in Battle Creek, Michigan, October 23, 1998.

23. S. Estoff, C. Zimmer, W. Lachicotte, and J. Benoit, The Influence of Social Networks and Social Support on Violence by Persons with Serious Mental Illness, *Hospital and Community Psychiatry, 45,* pp. 669-679, 1994.

24. C. Parkes, Psychiatric Problems Following Bereavement by Murder or Manslaughter, *British Journal of Psychiatry, 162,* pp. 49-54, 1993.

25. R. K. Barrett, Sociocultural Considerations for Working Blacks Experiencing Loss and Grief, in *Living with Grief: How We Are—How We Grieve,* K. Doka (ed.), Taylor & Francis, Washington, D.C., pp. 83-96, 1998.

26. E. Cose, The Good News about Black America (and Why Many Blacks aren't Celebrating), *Newsweek,* pp. 28-40, June 1999.
27. B. Dixon, *Good Health for African Americans,* Crown Publishers, Inc., New York, p. 33, 1994.
28. R. Anderson, K. Kochanek, and S. Murphy, Report of Final Mortality Statistics, 1995, *Monthly Vital Statistics Report, 45*:11(Sup. 2), National Center for Health Statistics, Hyattsville, Maryland, 1997.
29. R. K. Barrett, *Blacks, Death, Dying & Funerals: Things You've Wondered About but Thought It Politically Incorrect To Ask,* Major Plenary presentation at the King's College 15th Annual International Conference on Death and Bereavement at the University of Western Ontario in London, Ontario, May 12, 1997.
30. S. Kent, M. Fogarty, and P. Yellowless, A Review of Studies of Heavy Users of Psychiatric Services, *Psychiatric Services, 46*:12, pp. 1247-1253, 1995.
31. M. Clark, Untreated, Untold: African-Americans and Depression, *Upscale Magazine,* Bronner Brothers Publishers, Atlanta, Georgia, pp. 84-87, May 1999.
32. R. K. Barrett, Contemporary African-American Funeral Rites and Traditions, in *The Path Ahead: Readings in Death and Dying,* L. DeSpelder and A. L. Strickland (eds.), Mayfield, Mountain View, California, pp. 80-92, 1995.
33. T. Martin and K. Doka, Masculine Grief, in *Living with Grief After Sudden Loss,* K. Doka (ed.), Taylor and Francis, Washington, D.C., pp. 161-172, 1996.
34. G. Schneiderman, P. Winders, S. Tallet, and W. Feldman, Do Child and/or Parent Bereavement Programs Work? *Canadian Journal of Psychiatry, 39,* pp. 215-217, 1994.
35. G. Zambelli and A. DeRosa, Bereavement Support Groups for Schoolage Children: Theory, Intervention, and Case Examples, *American Journal of Orthopsychiatry, 62*:4, pp. 484-493, 1992.
36. R. K. Barrett, Bereaved Black Children, in *Readings in Thanatology,* J. Morgan (ed.), Baywood, Amityville, New York, pp. 403-419, 1997.
37. S. Burman and P. Allen-Maers, Neglected Victims of Murder: Children's Witness to Parental Homicide, *Social Work, 39*:1, pp. 28-35, 1994.
38. J. Bodnar and J. Kiecolt-Glaser, Caregiver Depression after Bereavement: Chronic Stress Isn't Over When Its Over, *Psychology and Aging, 9*:3, pp. 372-380, 1994.

REFERENCES NOT CITED IN TEXT

R. Amelio, An AIDS Bereavement Support Group: One Model of Intervention in a Time of Crisis, *Social Work with Groups, 16*:1/2, pp. 43-54, 1993.
R. K. Barrett, Adolescents, Homicidal Violence & Death, in *Handbook of Adolescent Death and Bereavement,* C. Corr and E. Balk (eds.), Springer, New York, pp. 42-84, 1996.

R. K. Barrett, Mourning Lessons: Learning to Cope with Loss can Start at an Early Age, *The Director, LXVII*:4, The National Funeral Directors Association Publications, Inc., Milwaukee, Wisconsin, pp. 24-63, April 1995.

R. K. Barrett, Reclaiming and Reaffirming the Value of Contemporary African American Funeral Rites, *The Director: Trade Journal of the National Funeral Directors Association,* pp. 36-40, 1994.

R. K. Barrett, Psychocultural Influences on African American Attitudes Towards Death, Dying, and Funeral Rites, in *Personal Care in an Impersonal World,* J. Morgan (ed.), Baywood, Amityville, New York, pp. 213-230, 1993.

S. Briggs, Tree Memorial Programs See Growing Popularity, *The Director,* The National Funeral Directors Association, Milwaukee, Wisconsin, pp. 24-25, July 1995.

S. Efron, Japan Shaken by Rise in Juvenile Crime, *Los Angeles Times,* p. A15, October 12, 1997.

J. Gibbs, *Young, Black and Males in America: An Endangered Species,* Auburn House, New York, 1988.

C. Gouvis, *Special Report on Children and Violence,* Maryland Kids Count Partnership, Inc., Baltimore, 1995.

K. Heide, *Young Killers: The Challenge of Juvenile Homicide,* Sage, Thousand Oaks, California, 1999.

D. Irish, K. Lundquist, and V. Nelsen, *Ethnic Variations in Dying, Death and Grief: Diversity in Universality,* Taylor & Francis, Washington, D.C., 1993.

G. Krikorian, Study Ranks Joblessness Top Factor in Gang Toll, *Los Angeles Times,* p. B8, October 27, 1997.

A. Longman, Effectiveness of a Hospice Community Bereavement Program, *Omega, 27*:2, pp. 165-175, 1993.

P. Marzuk, Violence, Crime and Mental Illness: How Strong a Link? *Archives of General Psychiatry, 53,* pp. 481-486, 1996.

J. Monahan, Mental Disorder and Violent Behavior, *American Psychologist, 45,* pp. 511-521, 1992.

E. Mulvey, Assessing the Evidence of a Link between Mental Illness and Violence, *Hospital and Community Psychiatry, 45,* pp. 663-668, 1994.

S. Nazario, Many Teenagers Facing Harder Lives, Study Finds, *Los Angeles Times,* p. A12, April 24, 1994.

G. Nettler, *Killing One Another,* Anderson, Cincinnati, Ohio, 1982.

R. Schilling, N. Koh, R. Abranovitz, and L. Gilbert, Bereavement Groups for Inner City Children, *Research on Social Work Practice, 20*:3, pp. 405-419, 1992.

J. Swanson, Alcohol Abuse, Mental Disorder, and Violent Behavior: An Epidemiologic Inquiry, *Alcohol Health and Research World, 17,* pp. 123-132, 1993.

K. Wagner and L. Calhourn, Perceptions of Social Support by Suicide Survivors and Their Social Network, *Omega, 24*:1, pp. 61-73, 1991.

G. Weaver and L. Gary, *The Role of Life Stress and Psychosocial Resources in the Depressive Symptomatology of Black Men,* presentation for the National Symposium on the Black Male in Crisis: Solutions for Survival, Atlanta, Georgia, September 12-15, 1990.

C. Whitney, Urban Violence, Joblessness, Racial Tension Beset France, *The Dallas Morning News,* p. 21A, January 18, 1998.

CHAPTER 17

How to Care for Yourself While You Care for Bereaved Families

Alan D. Wolfelt

Like you, I'm proud of the work I do with bereaved people. At the same time, I've discovered that good self-care is essential to truly "being present" to those I wish to help. This is the caregiver's conundrum: How do we care well for others while at the same time caring well for ourselves? Perhaps, like me, you are aware that you may be good at meeting the needs of everyone else, but tend to ignore or minimize your own needs for self-care. For aftercare coordinators and other caregivers to the bereaved, good self-care is critical for at least three major reasons. First and most important, we owe it to ourselves and our families to lead joyful, whole lives. While caring for the bereaved is certainly rewarding, we cannot and should not expect our work to fulfill us completely.

Second, our work is draining—physically, emotionally, and spiritually. Assisting bereaved people is a demanding interpersonal process that requires much energy and focus. Whenever we attempt to respond to the needs of those in grief, chances are slim that we can (or should) avoid the stress of emotional involvement. Each day we open ourselves to caring about the bereaved and their personal life journeys. And genuinely caring about people and their families touches the depths of our hearts and souls. We need respite from such draining work.

And third, we owe it to bereaved families themselves. My personal experience and observation suggest that good self-care is an essential foundation of caring for and meaningfully companioning the bereaved. They are sensitive to our ability to "be with" them. Poor self-care results in distraction from the helping relationship, and bereaved people often intuit when we are not physically, emotionally, and spiritually available to them.

Poor self-care can also cause caregivers to distance themselves from people's pain by trying to act like an expert. Because many of us have been trained to remain professionally distant, we may stay aloof from the very people we are supposed to help. Generally, this is a projection of our own need to stay distant from the pain of others, as well as from our own life hurts. The "expert mode" is antithetical to compassionate care and can cause an irreparable rift between you and the families in your care.

So, does this work have to be exhausting? Naturally draining, yes, but exhausting? I don't think so. Good helpers naturally focus outward, resulting in a drain on both head and heart! Of course, you will hear some people say, "If you do this kind of caregiving, you might as well resign yourself to eventually burning out." Again, I don't think so. The key is to practice daily, ongoing, nurturing self-care. To do so, you may need to try on some new ways of thinking and being.

ZEN AND THE ART
OF ERASING WORKTAPES

I'm reminded of the caregiver who goes to visit the wise Zen master. The Zen master instantly sees the caregiver is rather set in his ways and gives to others at all costs to self. He decides to teach the caregiver a vital lesson.

The wise teacher picks up a pitcher of spring water and begins filling the caregiver's cup. He fills the cup and it overflows, spilling out over the edges and onto the floor. "Teacher!" shouts the caregiver in shock. "Can't you see? My cup is already full. There is no room for more water in it!"

"Just the same as your mind," answers the teacher. "If you wish to have room for new ideas, first you must empty your head of the old ideas that are blocking your mind."

This teaching story serves as good counsel for those of you reading this and contemplating your own self-care plan. As caring people, you may have learned some "worktapes" that ultimately become self-destructive.

Caregivers to the bereaved come in many varieties. You may be young or old, female or male, white or Hispanic or African American, Democrat or Republican, Methodist, Baptist, Catholic, or atheist. But there is one thing you all have in common: You work very, very hard and you are very, very busy.

So why do aftercare coordinators seem particularly prone to workaholism? Many have been influenced by what I call "Caregiver Worktapes." These worktapes are mostly unconscious messages about work that are stored away in the recesses of your brain. It is as if your mind plays them over and over again, but at a level so deep that your conscious mind cannot easily articulate them. These messages, which you learn from your parents, from people you have worked for and from colleagues, can program your work behavior in ways you may not even be aware of.

The problem with worktapes is that unless you learn to consciously hear them and to turn down the volume or turn them off completely when they threaten your well-being, they may drive you to exhaustion, frustration, and depression.

Outlined below are four common worktapes for caregivers to the bereaved. If you are honest with yourself, you may see yourself in at least some of them.

Tape #1: Be Available at All Times

"If you really care, you must be available at all times," this worktape insists. True, there are times when being available is important and necessary. However, being always available leads to burnout and is not a good practice to get into.

Why? First, you have limitations, physically and emotionally. No one can sanely work morning, noon, and night AND have a home life. If your "Be Available at All Times" worktape forces you into this type of schedule, you run the risk of having so much energy directed outward that you lose touch with your inner self. Do you ever wonder, "Who is this stranger called 'me'?"

The second reason for turning off this worktape is that it dilutes your effectiveness. Focusing a little bit of yourself on everything means committing a great deal of yourself to nothing. The result can be polyphasic behavior, which means, at bottom, that you have a lot to do but feel like you are not accomplishing much.

This worktape also allows Parkinson's Law to take control of your life: work will expand to fill the time available. Depression, divorce, physical problems, chemical abuse, and premature death are all too common among those who become slaves to this mythic worktape.

Tape #2: If You're Resting, You're Lazy

"What are you doing sitting down? There is always something to do around here." Many people confuse constant activity with productivity. Sometimes managers reinforce this thinking because they find it hard to measure an employee's effectiveness. Therefore, activity replaces results as the measure of performance. The busiest bee is thought to be the best worker and is rewarded accordingly.

Yet, have you ever encountered people who look and act busy but never seem to accomplish much? Effectiveness must take precedence over busy-ness.

To maintain your physical and emotional health, you need to have downtimes where you pull back and recharge. If you don't allow yourself to rest, you will likely not only lose your enthusiasm for your work, you will also become exhausted and depressed.

Tape #3: No Pain, No Gain

"We must go the extra mile." Referred to by some as the "buckets of sweat syndrome," this myth would have you believe that results are directly related to how hard you work.

This worktape can put you in the mode of constantly working hard to the exclusion of restorative times of rest, play, and relaxation. Most successful people work smart, but not always hard. As a savvy someone once said, "When a man tells you he got rich through hard work, ask him, 'Whose'?"

The puritan work ethic may prevent you from faulting this worktape. Many of us believe that hard work is a sign of an upstanding, righteous person. Many of our parents taught us hard work is what won the wars and got us out of the Great Depression. How dare we question this work ethic!

Obviously, hard work has its place. But we sometimes overstate its value and ignore other important criteria for success. Be on the watch for this "No Pain, No Gain" philosophy of life. If, as I mentioned above, your parents modeled this worktape for you in your growing up years, you may have a high need to be in control, to achieve perfection, to do what others want you to do, and to measure your own worth by what others think—all characteristics of the children of workaholics.

Tape #4: If You Really Care, You'll Go Beyond the Call of Duty

"We are here to serve people," this worktape repeats over and over. "You have the opportunity to make a difference. If you are truly concerned, you will stay late and come in early."

Yes, you are working in a service profession and you should be proud of that. However, be careful about becoming a martyr. Caring about and serving others doesn't mean you should have no personal boundaries. If you say no to the requests of others now and then, you are not an uncaring person. You are simply a normal human being who, to remain healthy, needs alone time, family time, "off" time.

Moreover, if you over-dedicate your caring self to work hours, you will have little caring left for your family and for yourself. Working in moderation doesn't mean you don't care, it just means that you care about more things in life than work. Work must be balanced with the rest of your life.

These caregiver worktapes often result in work addiction. An important step toward having more balance in your life is to consciously hear the worktapes that underlie your behavior. Can you think of any others that influence your particular work patterns? Open up your head and heart and see if you are being driven by worktapes. All change begins with insight. You might find it helpful to explore your worktapes with a supportive confidant.

CAREGIVER FATIGUE SYNDROME

What happens when aftercare coordinators repeatedly ignore their own grief needs? Sometimes, influences such as bereavement overload (experiencing overwhelming loss within a short time span or, in this case, being around loss too much), unrealistic expectations about helping all the bereaved people in one's community or discovering that, at times, one cares more about others than they care about themselves results in what I call "caregiver fatigue syndrome." Symptoms of this syndrome often include the following:

- exhaustion and loss of energy
- irritability and impatience
- cynicism and detachment
- physical complaints and depression
- disorientation and confusion
- feelings of omnipotence and indispensability
- minimization and denial of feelings

Let's examine each of these stress-related symptoms and then explore ways in which we as caregivers can strive to take care of ourselves in the face of these symptoms.

Exhaustion and Loss of Energy

Feelings of exhaustion and loss of energy are usually among the first signals of caregiver distress. For many of us, low energy and fatigue can be difficult to acknowledge because they are the opposite of the high energy level required to meet caregiving demands.

Our bodies are powerful instruments and frequently wiser than our minds. Exhaustion and lack of physical and psychic energy are often unconscious "cries for self help." If we could only slow down and listen to the voice within.

Irritability and Impatience

Irritability and impatience are inherent to the experience of caregiver burnout. As effective helpers we typically feel a sense of accomplishment and reward for our efforts. As stress increases, however, our ability to feel reward diminishes while our irritability and impatience become heightened.

Disagreements and tendencies to blame others for interpersonal difficulties may occur as stress takes its toll on our sense of emotional and physical well-being. A real sign to watch for: you have more compassion and sensitivity for the families in your care than you have for your own family.

Cynicism and Detachment

As caregivers experiencing emotional burnout, we may begin to respond to stress in a manner that saves something of ourselves. We may begin to question the value of helping others, of our family life, of friendships, even of life itself. We may work to convince ourselves that "there's no point in getting involved" as we rationalize our need to distance ourselves from the stress of interpersonal encounter.

Detachment serves to help distance ourselves from feelings of pain, helplessness, and hurt. I have also observed that a general sense of impatience with those we care for often goes hand-in-hand with cynicism and detachment.

Physical Complaints and Depression

Physical complaints, real or imagined, are often experienced by aftercare coordinators suffering from fatigue syndrome. Sometimes, physical complaints are easier for us to talk about than emotional concerns. The process of consciously or unconsciously converting emotional conflicts may result in a variety of somatic symptoms like headaches, stomachaches, backaches, and long-lasting colds.

Generalized feelings of depression are also common to the phenomenon of caregiver burnout. Loss of appetite, difficulty sleeping, sudden changes in mood, and lethargy suggest that depression has become a part of the overall stress syndrome. Depression is a constellation of symptoms that together tell us something is wrong, and that we must pay attention and try to understand.

Disorientation and Confusion

Feelings of disorientation and confusion are often experienced as a component of this syndrome. Our minds may shift from one topic to another and focusing on current tasks often becomes difficult. We may experience "poly-phasic behavior," whereby we feel busy, yet not accomplish much at all. Since difficulty focusing results in a lack of a personal sense of competence, confusion only results in more heightened feelings of disorientation.

Thus, a cycle of confusion resulting in disorientation evolves and becomes difficult to break. The ability to think clearly suffers and concentration and memory are impaired. In addition, the ability to make decisions and sound judgments becomes limited. Obviously, our system is overloaded and in need of a break from the continuing cycle of stress.

Omnipotence and Indispensability

Another common symptom of caregiver fatigue syndrome is a sense of omnipotence and indispensability. Statements like, "No one else can provide the kind of care I can," or, "I have got to be the one to help these people" are not simply the expressions of a healthy ego.

Other people can provide care to bereaved families and many do it very well. When we as caregivers begin to feel indispensable, we tend to block not only our own growth, but the growth and healing of others.

Minimization and Denial of Feelings

When stressed to their limits, some aftercare coordinators continue to minimize, if not out-and-out deny, feelings of burnout. The caregiver who minimizes is aware of feeling stressed, but works to minimize these feelings by diluting them through a variety of rationalizations. From a self-perspective, minimizing stress seems to work, particularly because it is commensurate with the self-imposed principle of "being all things to all people." However, internally repressed feelings of stress build within and emotional strain results.

Perhaps the most dangerous characteristic of the caregiver fatigue syndrome is the total denial of feelings of stress. As denial takes over, the caregiver's symptoms of stress become enemies to be fought instead of friends to be understood. Regardless of how loud the mind and body cry out for relief, no one is listening.

AM I EXPERIENCING CAREGIVER FATIGUE SYNDROME?

An aftercare coordinator recently asked me, "How is burnout different from stress?" We might overhear a staff person comment, "I'm really feeling burned out today." All of us may have occasional days when our motivation and energy levels are low. While this fluctuation in energy states is normal, burnout is an end stage that typically develops over time. Once a person is burned out, dramatic changes are necessary to reverse the process.

Psychologist Christina Maslach, a leading authority on burnout, has outlined three major signs of burnout (what I'm calling caregiver fatigue syndrome) [1]:

- Emotional exhaustion—feeling drained, not having anything to give even before the day begins
- Depersonalization—feeling disconnected from other people, feeling resentful and seeing them negatively
- Reduced sense of personal accomplishment—feeling ineffective, that the results achieved are not meaningful.

Step back for a moment and complete the following brief fatigue syndrome survey. As you review your life over the past twelve months, answer the survey questions:

Bereavement Fatigue Syndrome Survey

1. Do you generally feel fatigued and lacking in energy?
2. Are you getting irritable, impatient, and angry with people around you (home and/or work)?
3. Do you feel cynical and detached from the people in your care?
4. Do you suffer from more than your share of physical complaints, such as headaches, stomachaches, backaches, and long-lasting colds?
5. Do you generally feel depressed or notice sudden fluctuations in your moods?

6. Do you feel busy, yet have a sense that you don't accomplish much at all?
7. Do you have difficulty concentrating or remembering?
8. Do you think you have to be the one to help all those people experiencing grief?
9. Do you feel less of a sense of satisfaction about your helping efforts than you have in the past?
10. Do you feel that you just don't have anything more to give to people?

In general, if you answered "yes" to two to four of these questions, you may be in the early phases of caregiver fatigue syndrome. If you answered "yes" to five to seven of these questions, you are quickly moving in the direction of total fatigue. If you answered "yes" to eight to ten of these questions, you are burned out!

EMOTIONAL INVOLVEMENT AND STRESS

The reasons aftercare coordinators feel stress are often multiple and complex. When we care deeply for people in grief, we open ourselves to our own vulnerabilities related to loss issues. Perhaps another person's grief stimulates memories of some old griefs of our own. Perhaps those we wish to help frustrate our efforts to be supportive.

Whatever the reason, the natural way to prevent ourselves from being hurt or disappointed is to deny feelings in general. The denial of feelings is often accompanied by an internal sense of a lack of purpose. After all, the willingness and ability to feel are ultimately what gives meaning to life.

Of all the stresses aftercare coordinators are subject to, emotional involvement appears central to the potential of suffering from this syndrome. Perhaps we should ask ourselves what we lose when we decide to minimize or ignore the significant level of emotional involvement intrinsic to caring for bereaved families. We probably will discover that in the process of minimizing or ignoring, we are, in fact, eliminating our potential to help people move toward a sense of inner peace. As the saying goes, "If you want to help others, the place to start is with yourself."

We probably need to remind ourselves that we are our own most important helping instrument and that what we know about ourselves makes a tremendous difference in our capacity to assist others. While the admirable goal of helping grieving people may alone seem to justify emotional sacrifices, ultimately we are not helping others effectively when we ignore what we are experiencing within ourselves.

Obviously, we cannot draw close to others without beginning to affect and be affected by them. This is the nature of the helping relationship with those confronting death and grief. We cannot help others from a protective position. Helping occurs openly where we are defenseless—if we allow ourselves to be. My experience suggests it takes practice to work toward an understanding of what is taking place inside oneself, while trying to grasp what is taking place inside others. After all, these thoughts and feelings occur simultaneously and are significantly interrelated.

Involving yourself with others, particularly at a time of death and grief, requires taking care of yourself as well as others. Emotional overload, circumstances surrounding death, and caring about the bereaved will unavoidably result in times of caregiver fatigue syndrome. When this occurs, we should feel no sense of inadequacy or stigma if we also need the support and understanding of a caring relationship. As a matter of fact, we should be proud of ourselves if we care enough about "caring for the caregiver" that we seek out just such a relationship!

THE OVERCARING CAREGIVER

Do you care too much about those in your care? Do you care more about helping them than they do themselves? Do you feel it is your duty to worry about all bereaved people and get involved with their problems? On the other hand, do you feel "used" by some bereaved families?

If you've answered yes to some or all of these questions, you may well have issues that need attention.

So what is an overcaring caregiver? I define it this way: someone who continually puts the needs of the bereaved before his or her own, ultimately to the caregiver's detriment.

The overcaring caregiver may appear to feed on providing support and comfort to others; however, self-needs are often minimized, denied, or completely overlooked. They in fact do help those in their care, but usually wonder if they helped enough or "did it right."

CAREGIVING VS. CARETAKING

The overcaring caregiver often confuses caregiving with caretaking. Caretakers (rescuers) often become over-attached to the people they attempt to help.

When we focus all of our energy on people and problems outside of ourselves, little time is left for self-understanding. As a consequence, one of the primary symptoms of the overcaring caregiver is a lack of awareness of the dynamics of caring too much. This lack of awareness may result in feelings of helplessness and frustration, which are in turn sometimes expressed in the form of obsessing and worrying about the families in one's care.

Now a vicious cycle is set in motion. The more the helper ruminates about the bereaved's problems (obviously, worrying doesn't really change anything), the higher the need becomes to rescue. Therefore, more inappropriate over-involvement occurs, with the focus staying outside of oneself.

SIGNS AND SYMPTOMS THAT YOU CARE TOO MUCH

- A tendency to try to please others instead of yourself. A need for approval and a tendency to feel safest when giving.
- A desire to "solve" people's problems rather than create conditions that allow them to move toward reconciliation of their own issues.
- A tendency to over-extend and over-commit.
- A desire to do things for people that they are capable of doing themselves.
- A denial of your own need for support and understanding, resulting in the myth of "super-caregiver" or "being all things to all people."
- A tendency to "feel different" from or "more special" than other people.
- A desire to be and act extremely responsible. You may like to be on twenty-four-hour call and enjoy having a beeper while trying to give the appearance of resenting it.
- A tendency to want to continually "check on" those in your care.
- A desire to be "in control" and a belief that you know how to "make things turn out well" for bereaved people.
- A tendency to need bereaved families as much, if not more, than they need you.
- A tendency to neglect your own intimate relationships in favor of helping "needy families."

WHY CAREGIVERS CARE TOO MUCH

Unreconciled Personal Grief

As my research on this phenomenon progresses, it becomes increasingly obvious that many people enter into grief caregiving as a conscious or unconscious act of healing their own grief. The desire to "fix" someone else's grief is often a projection of a need to "fix" one's own grief. When this occurs, it is a classic form of displacement. The displacer is the person who takes the expression of grief away from personal loss and displaces the feelings in other directions. In this situation, the focus is on the caretaking of other people.

Family of Origin Issues

I've found that many caregivers to the dying and the bereaved were helpers in their families of origin. They may have assumed the responsibility of resolving family conflicts or disciplining other children. In adulthood, they are often those who sponsor family reunions or organize holiday gatherings.

Socially Learned Personality Characteristics

Many caregivers are particularly sensitive to the needs of others. Sometimes this sensitivity goes beyond empathy to over-identification with the suffering of others. It's almost as if they feel most comfortable when they are with people in emotional pain.

CONSEQUENCES OF CARING TOO MUCH

There are a wide variety of fall-out consequences when caregivers care too much:

- A broad constellation of stress-related symptoms, such as exhaustion and loss of energy, irritability and impatience, cynicism and detachment, physical illness (real or imagined), omnipotence and feeling indispensable, minimization, and denial of feelings.
- Deterioration in relationships with family and friends.
- Symptoms of depression, sleeping difficulties, and low self-esteem.
- A displacement of compulsive behavior into other areas of life, such as spending money, overachievement, or drug and alcohol abuse.

PREVENTION AND INTERVENTION STRATEGIES

Perhaps we should remember that just as healing in grief is a process, so is recovering from caring too much for bereaved people. Don't blame yourself if you recognize some parts of yourself herein. Be compassionate with yourself as you acknowledge any potential problems and be hopeful that you might be able to make some positive changes.

The important idea here is that the time has come for us to discuss the need for prevention and intervention strategies:

Create an awareness of over caring and its impact on your life. Once an awareness is present, the process of recovery can begin. This is the important first step of breaking down the denial of self-defeating behaviors.

Work to acknowledge feelings of helplessness over controlling your over caring behavior. In other words, surrender. Begin your work with a new found revelation: You do not have to be all things to all people at all times.

Explore issues of your own unreconciled losses in life. Does your need to help others with death and grief in any way relate to your own unreconciled losses? If so, be certain not to use your aftercare relationships to work on your own issues.

Work on unfinished family of origin issues. Attempt to understand how experiences in your childhood may be impacting your need to take care of other people. Were you an arbitrator, parent, or therapist to your family?

Stop compulsively taking care of bereaved people. Perhaps you need a vacation from caregiving as you explore your own needs.

Develop ways of caring for and nurturing yourself. Explore your own feelings instead of focusing on everybody else's. Play more and make fun a part of your daily life.

Be compassionate with yourself when you occasionally slip back into caretaking and martyrdom. Your tendency to want to be in control will not be overcome quickly or easily. Begin to learn the art of healthy detachment.

Stop seeking your sole source of personal happiness through your helping relationships. You don't need the approval of others to have a sense of well-being. While relationships can help you feel good about yourself, they are not what is inside you. Work to attain self-approval and self-acceptance.

Discover the spiritual part of yourself. Spend alone time focusing on self-understanding and self-love. I have found that nurturing my spirit is critical to my work as a bereavement caregiver. "Spiritual time" helps me combat fatigue, frustration, and life's disappointments. To be present to those I work with and to learn from those I companion, I must appreciate the beauty of life and living.

Spiritual, quiet moments or "downtime" (for me, often spent in nature) recharges my spiritual energy. While you may embrace your spirit differently than I do, I encourage you to ask yourself: How do I renew my spirit?

Some people do this through prayer and meditation. Others might do this by hiking, biking, running, or other forms of physical alone time. Obviously, there is no right way to renew your spirit. But one reality is that to be present to others in healing ways, we must each find a way to massage our spirits.

So, I ask you to ask yourself: How do I keep my spirit alive? How do I listen to my heart? How do I appreciate the good, the beautiful, and the truthful in life?

Helping the bereaved can and should be a healthy activity. We need to counsel, not control. We need to empathize, not over-identify. We need to be responsible to others, not for others. We need to support, not protect. And we need to encourage, not manipulate.

THE AFTERCARE COORDINATOR'S SELF-CARE GUIDELINES

The following self-care guidelines are not intended to be cure-alls, nor will they be appropriate for everyone. Pick and choose those tips that you believe will be of help to you in your efforts to stay physically and emotionally healthy.

Remember, our attitudes about stress and fatigue in general sometimes make it difficult to make changes. However, one important point to remember is that with support and encouragement from others, most of us can learn to make positive changes in our attitudes and behaviors.

You might find it helpful to have a discussion among co-workers about caregiver fatigue syndrome. Identify your own signs and symptoms of burnout. Discuss individual and group approaches to self-care that will help you enjoy both work and play.

THE JOY OF MINI-VACATIONS

What creative ideas can you come up with to renew yourself? Caregivers are notorious for helping others create self-care time while neglecting their own needs. Here are a few ideas to get you started. However, I encourage you to create your own list and pursue them.

- Schedule a massage with a professional massage therapist.
- Have a spiritual growth weekend. Retreat into nature. Plan some alone time.
- Go for a drive with no particular destination in mind. Explore the countryside, slow down and observe what you see.
- Treat yourself to a night in a hotel or bed and breakfast.
- Visit a museum or a zoo.
- Go for a hot air balloon ride.
- Take an afternoon off and go to the movies—maybe even a kid's movie!
- Go to a yard sale or auction.
- Go rollerskating or rollerblading with a friend!
- Enjoy a photographic retreat. Take your camera into nature and shoot away.
- Watch cartoons with a child.
- Visit a farmer's market and shop for fresh produce.
- Drop by a health food store and walk the aisles.
- Go dancing.
- Take a horseback ride.
- Plan a river-rafting trip.

REMEMBER YOUR CHILD-LIKE SELF

Have you ever met overly-serious caregivers who project gloom and doom? Odds are they have forgotten the vitality and enthusiasm of their childhood years. Let's pause and recall some of the characteristics of childhood.

Children:
- are physically connected to the world around them
- take risks
- are open, enthusiastic learners
- imagine and dream
- are naturally curious
- spontaneously laugh and smile a lot
- are passionate and expressive

- try new things when they get bored
- rest when they need rest
- try to have fun whenever they can

So, have you "grown up" and forgotten about the joy of being a child? If so, you may have left behind some of the best self-care strategies ever. Think about the way healthy kids go about their day, then think about how you spend your day. Have you forgotten how vital fun is to life and living?

There is a well-established link between play and energy. Playing often can be a vital part of your self-care plan. Being grown-up doesn't mean always being serious. Most really successful people not only work hard, they also play hard. Childlike behavior generates joy, fun, and enthusiasm. Ask yourself: What can I do to stay in touch with my inner child?

WORK SMART, NOT HARD

Many caregivers never had the opportunity to learn essential time-management skills that result in working smart, not hard. You may find the following helpful:

Create specific goals for personal and professional development. Parse your annual goals into monthly goals. Break up your weekly goals into daily goals. Ask yourself, "What do I want to accomplish this year, this month, this week, this day?" Planning each day can give you a road map to getting to your destination.

Do one thing at a time. Caregivers are notorious for trying to do and be all things to all people and all projects all the time. Quality always suffers when you try to do too many things at once.

End the day by planning for tomorrow's projects whenever possible. That way, you'll not only waste less time getting started the following morning, you'll arrive at work feeling more in control of the day ahead.

Protect yourself from constant interruptions. When you're working on a task, nothing will sabotage you more than interruptions. Block out the necessary time to complete tasks.

Work when you work best. We all have certain natural peak hours of performance. Pay attention to your inner clock. Are you a morning person or a night person? Does a brief nap recharge you?

Focus and reject. This is a reminder to stay focused on the task at hand. Learn to "switch off" those things that prevent you from accomplishing desired tasks. Sometimes this means delaying returning calls and correspondence. If you always "stay available," you won't have time to accomplish what you may really want and need to.

When all else fails, retreat to a hideout. When working on project development, you may need to find a "Skinner Box": a place where you can hole up with no interruptions. Tell only those who truly need to know where you are. You'll be amazed at what you get done.

When you know your energy level is dropping, take a break. After a ten-minute walk or a short nap, you may be able to accomplish much more than you could have otherwise.

Delegate tasks whenever possible. Watch out for "busy work" that might be done more efficiently by someone else.

Throughout the day ask yourself, "What's the best use of my time right now?"

Focus on those tasks that need to be done first. This requires discipline, but will pay many dividends.

BUILD SUPPORT SYSTEMS

Our work requires a natural outward focus: on the needs of those we attempt to help. Such demands can leave us feeling emotionally and spiritually drained. An important aspect of self-care is to allow us to have sounding boards, for this work impacts our lives.

What do support systems provide for us? Ideally, supportive colleagues and friends provide some of the following:

Unconditional acceptance and support. In other words, friendships and the need to be nurtured and understood ourselves.

Help with complicated situations. Assistance in ideas that serve to help us in our efforts to help the bereaved.

Mentoring. Encouragement to continue to develop new tools to assist us in our work. Models that inspire us and remind us of the importance and value of our work.

Challenge. Encouragement to stretch ourselves beyond our current limits.

Referral. To have connection with additional resources for the people in your care. Good caregivers will recognize occasions when it is appropriate to refer those we work with to other, rich sources of support and counsel.

LISTEN TO YOUR INNER VOICE

As an aftercare coordinator, you will at times become grief overloaded (too much death, grief, and loss in your day-to-day life). The natural demands of this kind of work can cause you to have tunnel vision about death and grief. For example, if your own child has a headache, you may immediately think brain tumor. If your partner complains of heartburn, you think heart attack.

I'll never forget the time I returned home from a three-day lecture series on childhood grief to find my office manager had scheduled the following day full of counseling a variety of bereaved persons and two dying children and their families. Sitting there looking at the schedule, my inner voice called out, "I cannot do any more sadness right now. I need and deserve a spirit break." So, I rescheduled all appointments for the day and instead went for a drive through nearby Rocky Mountain National Park. I returned home in the late afternoon and spent the remainder of the day playing with my children and being present to my wife. Caregiving presents you with the gift of an enhanced awareness of the many tragedies that touch people's lives. Just as those you help are changed by death, you are changed by their experiences as well. To embrace our deep appreciation for life and love we must stay grounded—and to do so means caring for ourselves as well as we care for others.

REFERENCE

1. C. Maslach, Understanding Burn-Out: Definitional Issues in Analyzing a Complex Phenomenon, in *Job Stress and Burn-Out,* W. S. Paine (ed.), Sage, Beverly Hills, California, 1982.

Contributors

RONALD BARRETT, Ph.D., is Professor of Psychology at Loyola Marymount University in Los Angeles, California, where he created and teaches a course on the Psychology of Death and Dying. He is an internationally recognized specialist on the study of cross-cultural differences in death, dying, and funeral rites and has published widely on African-American funeral practices and multicultural perspectives. He is also recognized for his expertise on urban homicidal violence and youth. Most recently, Dr. Barrett has begun the study of funeralization and aftercare practices among West African Akan and all Blacks of African descent, including Blacks in the Caribbean.

ROBERT BENDICKSEN, Ph.D., is Professor of Sociology and Director of the Center for Death Education and Bioethics at the University of Wisconsin-LaCrosse. He is editor of *Illness, Crisis, and Loss,* Secretariat of the International Work Group on Death, Dying, and Bereavement, and past President of the Sociological Practice Association. Author of numerous articles and chapters, Dr. Bendicksen has also edited several books on death and dying. In addition, he is an international speaker on issues surrounding end-of-life medical/ethical decisions. He serves on the Institutional Review Board at Gundersen Lutheran Medical Center as well as the IRB at his university.

BONNIE CARROLL is Director of the Tragedy Assistance Program for Survivors, a national organization providing peer support, grief counseling referral, case worker assistance, and crisis intervention for those who are affected by the loss of a loved one in military service. She is the surviving spouse of U.S. Army General Tom Carroll, killed in a 1992 C-12 crash. She is also an officer in the U.S. Air Force Reserve, serving as Chief, Casualty Operations at Randolf Air Force Base.

BEVERLY CHAPPELL, B.A., with a degree in Social Science and an extensive nursing background, began The Dougy Center for Grieving Children in 1982. She was the recipient of the Earl A. Grollman

Lifetime Achievement Award in Bereavement from Children's Hospice International in 1997.

LaVONE HAZELL, M.S., Director of A.L.L., the first all-service bereavement center in the Bronx, New York, is a licensed funeral director, a Certified Funeral Service Practitioner, a Certified Death Educator, a Certified Grief Therapist, and a Certified Family Therapist. She has taught thanatology, psychology, and bereavement counseling at the American Academy McAllister Institute of Funeral Service, as well as death and dying courses for St. Joseph's College. On the Board of Directors for the Association for Death Education and Counseling, she also serves on boards for the National Hospice Foundation, Choice in Dying, the Foundation for Life-Threatening Illness and Loss and the N.Y. Coalition of One Hundred Black Women. Her published articles, book chapters, workshops, and conference presentations emphasize the problems derived from youth violence, cultural diversity, and bereavement issues.

CATHERINE JOHNSON, M.A., is the Bereavement Services Coordinator for Weeks' Funeral Homes in Washington State. With a master's degree in psychology with an emphasis on death, dying, and bereavement, she developed and has facilitated the aftercare program of three funeral homes. In addition, she is certified as a Grief Therapist and Death Educator and serves on the Board of Directors for the Association for Death Education and Counseling. She authored several chapters and articles and is a past chairperson of the Funeral Home Aftercare Special Interest Group within ADEC.

PAUL V. JOHNSON, M.A., served as the Director of Aftercare Services for the Bradshaw Funeral Homes in Minneapolis/St. Paul for over fourteen years. Following ten years as a professor of Sociology at Bethel College in Arden Hills, Minnesota, he left the academic setting to develop and direct a funeral home-based aftercare program. Paul has been a consultant for the Seminary Resources Program sponsored by the National Funeral Directors Association, was editor of *Caregivers Quarterly,* is certified as a Death Educator by the Association for Death Education and Counseling, and has presented many workshops on loss and grief to health care professionals, clergy, volunteers, and grieving individuals in various locations across the country.

VICKI LENSING has been in funeral service in the Iowa City, Iowa area for twenty years. She is co-owner of Lensing Funeral and Cremation Service, where she has overseen the bereavement aftercare program since its beginning in 1986. She is a member of the Association for Death Education and Counseling, on the Board of Directors of Preferred Funeral Directors International, a member of the editorial board of the *Journal of Personal and Interpersonal Loss,* and acting

President of the National Association of Bereavement Support Providers in Funeral Service.

LYN MILETICH, M.P.M., is a trainer and consultant specializing in helping others grow through the various transitions of personal and professional life. She writes from her professional experience as a Bereavement Services Specialist and Staff Development Coordinator at Mountain View Funeral Home and Memorial Park in Tacoma, Washington. Lyn holds a Masters degree in Pastoral Ministry with additional training in grief, loss, chaplaincy, and rituals. She brings eighteen years experience to local and international conferences as a presenter. She is a member of the Association for Death Education and Counseling.

RICHARD PAUL, B. A., a former teacher, is a Licensed Funeral Director and third generation owner of Paul Funeral Home in Powassan, Ontario, Canada. He is a Certified Death Educator and has given many presentations on the subject of grief as well as writing several book chapters. He has served as Director of the North Bay and Area Palliative Care Association and was founding Director of the Near North Palliative Care Network. Currently he is Vice-President of the Bereavement Ontario Network.

STEPHEN R. ROCCO, M.Ed., is an adjunct instructor at the New England Institute of Mortuary Science at Mount Ida College. He has served as a family mediator and legal trainer for the Massachusetts Trial Court, as well as teaching classes in criminal justice. He is a Licensed Funeral Director and part owner of a third generation funeral home, Salvatore Rocco and Sons Funeral Home in Everett, Massachusetts.

DARCIE SIMS, Ph.D., is a Certified Grief Counselor, Certified Pastoral Bereavement Specialist, and a Licensed Psychotherapist and Hypnotherapist. She is the Director of Training and Program Development for Accord Grief Resources in Louisville, Kentucky. She is an internationally recognized speaker and the Coping Editor for *Bereavement Magazine*. Darcie has served on the Boards for the Association for Death Education and Counseling and the Compassionate Friends and co-chaired the World Gatherings on Bereavement in 1991 and 1996. She currently serves on the Board of Trustees for the National Catholic Ministry to the Bereaved.

ROBERT STEVENSON, Ed.D., is an Education Consultant teaching and counseling in a residential rehabilitation facility for recovering addicts. He is also an adjunct professor of counseling at Mercy College, Long Island University. Certified by the Association for Death Education and Counseling as a Death Educator and Grief Counselor, Dr. Stevenson received ADEC's Death Educator Award in 1993. His books, *What Shall We Do? Preparing a School Community to Cope with Crises* and *Death Education in the Schools: A Resource Guide for Educators,* assist educators, parents, and students to cope with crises in the lives of young people. In addition, he has authored over forty articles and book chapters on children and grief.

O. DUANE WEEKS, Ph.D., has been a licensed funeral director and embalmer for thirty-four years and owns four funeral homes in Washington State. He earned a doctorate from the University of Minnesota, where he studied with sociologist and death educator, Robert Fulton. Dr. Weeks is also the author of more than two dozen articles, reviews, and book chapters. He was Director of the New England Institute of Funeral Service Education at Mt. Ida College in Boston until his retirement in the summer of 1999. Certified by the Association for Death Education and Counseling as a Death Educator and Grief Counselor, he is also recognized by the Academy of Professional Funeral Service Practice as a Certified Funeral Practitioner and was honored in 1996 as the Washington State Funeral Director of the Year.

SHERRY WILLIAMS, R.N., B.A., who has spent sixteen years advancing the caring professions, is the President and Co-founder of Accord Aftercare Services, which specializes in grief recovery and bereavement by providing bereavement support materials to funeral homes as well as other organizations and private counselors. Sherry provides enrichment training for caregivers working in a variety of professional fields and has been a featured speaker for numerous organizations.

BEN WOLFE, M.Ed., is a Licensed Independent Clinical Social Worker and founder and Program Director of the Grief Support Program at St. Mary's Medical Center in Duluth, Minnesota. He is a nationally certified Grief Counselor and Death Educator, does individual and family impending death and bereavement counseling, and facilitates various grief support groups for children ages five through seventeen, as well as a grief support group for senior citizens. He has facilitated the medical center's hospice staff support group and has taught a graduate course on death and dying at the University of Minnesota, Duluth, for eighteen years. Ben is a consultant for hospitals, schools, hospices, and organizations throughout the world on loss issues and has published in bereavement books and journals. He is a past Clinical Director of the Northeastern Minnesota Critical Incident Response Team and past President of the Association for Death Education and Counseling.

ALAN WOLFELT, Ph.D., is the Director of the Center for Loss and Life Transition and is on the faculty at the University of Colorado Medical School's Department of Family Medicine. Recipient of the

Death Educator of the Year award from the Association of Death Education and Counseling, Dr. Wolfelt is also an educational consultant to hospices, hospitals, schools, universities, funeral homes, and a variety of community agencies. He is the author of many articles and books, including *The Journey Through Grief, Healing the Bereaved Child, Creating Meaningful Funeral Ceremonies,* and *Understanding Grief: Helping Yourself Heal.*

ALICE ZULLI, a clergy person, is Founder and Director of Beyond Loss, a bereavement ministry in Los Angeles, California. She is a Certified Clinical Thanatologist, Grief Counselor, Bereavement Educator, and Chaplain Associate, as well as Director of Bereavement Support at Glendale Adventist Medical Center. Rev. Zulli, a published author and speaker on topics related to death, dying, and bereavement, is Co-founder and Director of The Southern California Consortium of Bereavement Professionals, a peer support organization.

Index